This book is dedicated to
the loving memory of my father
Jerry P. Dailey

Far better it is to dare mighty

things, to win glorious triumphs

even though checked by failure,

than to take rank with those poor

spirits who neither enjoy much nor

suffer much, but are left in the

grey twilight of neither

victory nor defeat.

Theodore Roosevelt

Contents

*Opportunity rarely knocks on your
door...knock rather on opportunity's
door if you wish to enter.*

The only true measure of success is the ratio between what we might have done and what we might have been on the one hand, and the thing we have made and the thing we have made of ourselves on the other.

H. G. Wells

Preface

Everyone at one time or another fantasizes about going into business and being his or her own boss. Now a growing number of Americans are making that fantasy a reality. In an economic climate that encourages and nurtures entrepreneurship, hundreds of thousands of corporate executives, MBAs, retirees and individuals interested in a career change are striking off on their own. As owners of small businesses, they are creating a dynamic force that is revolutionizing business as we have known it in this country.

According to the U.S. Small Business Administration, small businesses (including the self-employed) account for 58 percent of the U.S. workforce and 40 percent of the gross national product. Moreover, a National Science Foundation analyst reveals that small business has been a more prolific source of innovation per research and development dollar than large business.

And yet studies show that only ten percent of the individuals who want to start their own businesses ever do. Why? The fear of failure has probably killed more potential businesses than all other factors combined. True, starting your own business is risky—statistics show that most new businesses fail. But it doesn't have to be that way. Most failures occur because people don't spend the time up-front to adequately evaluate the venture; their businesses are doomed before they even start. Striking out on your own is certainly an emotional commitment, but don't make an emotional decision—base it on a realistic appraisal of your abilities and a thorough analysis of the proposed business. Success can be yours if you are patient, willing to work hard, and take all the necessary steps.

Abraham Lincoln once said that if he had eight hours to chop down a tree, he would spend the first six sharpening his axe. This book is mostly about those first six hours. The information presented is based on academic and real-life experiences gained day-in and day-out since starting my own business in 1973. I'll share with you what I've read, what I've learned, and what's worked for me. Plain and simple.

An entrepreneur must of necessity be a generalist, knowing something about every aspect of running a business, from accounting and finance to inventory control, marketing and personnel management. Overconcentration on any one aspect of the business to the detriment of everything else is a sure way to fail. As the owner, it is your responsibility to ensure that everything runs smoothly. It is neither expected nor desirable to try to be an *expert* in every area of your business. After assessing your personal abilities and strengths, you will see what skills you should look for when hiring new employees.

Picture yourself as the conductor leading an orchestra. Many of the musicians can play their particular instruments better than you, but you have the unique ability to direct their efforts to create a beautiful symphony. Don't try to be a one-person band—your company will never be any better than your weakest trait. Build a team, recruit the best, and your efforts will be rewarded.

This book particularly addresses individuals starting their first business and presents an overview of what I feel are the most important issues required to "start off on the right foot." You may find that you need more information about a particular subject than what I have presented here. I have included a section at the end of most chapters that contains various options for obtaining further information on the subjects presented. A bibliography located at the back of this book will also assist you in your search.

Several ideas that are of key importance are presented in several chapters. This repetition is intended 'ɔ reinforce the idea. This book should be read from cover to cover before you start your venture. It is also structured to be a reference book. Each chapter is broken into several sub-sections, each listed in the table of contents. For your convenience, an index is also provided for key-word lookup.

Before you start, it is important to distinguish between the urge to *run away from problems* and the urge to *search for something better*. Start your new business because you have the desire to start the business, not just because you are unhappy with your current situation. If you do not have the desire to be your own boss, take risks, and assume total responsibility, then maybe you should simply explore finding a new job.

Starting your own business requires a complete commitment—dig deep and make sure the burning desire is really there. Do you *wish* you were your own boss, *desire* to be your own boss, or *intend* to be your own boss? A wish simply implies a helpless longing of the mind. A desire is stronger than a wish and is usually followed by meager attempts to manifest itself into action. But if you intend to do something, then this indicates a strong commitment expressed through definite action. Fire yourself up and *commit* to do the things necessary to produce your much-craved result. Nothing of value comes easy, but the satisfaction you will gain from having accomplished your dream will be reward beyond compare.

Being an entrepreneur is not for everyone. I personally love it, but don't let my enthusiasm, or anyone else's, sway your decision. This is a decision you, and you alone, must make. Be honest with yourself. There is nothing wrong with working for someone else.

Regardless of your decision, I hope that life is kind to you and I wish you success and happiness beyond your wildest dreams. Always remember that prosperity is more than an economic condition; it is a state of mind.

Gene Dailey

If you hesitate to start something because you fear the consequences of failure, you may find that the consequences of inaction are even worse.

Chapter 1

Choosing and Evaluating Your Venture

There are numerous reasons for wanting to start your own business. Usually the potential for financial independence tops the list. A recent survey by the market-research firm of Phoenix-Hecht, based in Research Triangle Park, North Carolina states that 74% of all millionaires own their own businesses. That means that your chances of becoming truly wealthy are three times greater if you are self employed! The title of Roger Fritz's book *Nobody Gets Rich Working for Someone Else* is a bit extreme but further drives this point home.

Unfortunately a large percentage of new businesses fail. Why? Mostly because of inadequate planning and poor business skills. Start-up entrepreneurs are almost always excellent at whatever job they do (mechanic, gardener, desktop publisher, etc.) but generally are lousy at business. Companies fail not because of a lack of energy, enthusiasm or technical ability, but because the business side of their venture drags them under. I'll show you how to plan for success from the very beginning. If you work smart, your success is almost guaranteed.

Let's start out with a big dose of reality. There is no short-cut to success—it always has, and always will require hard work. Don't think that working for yourself is any easier than working for someone else. Expect to put in long hours, at least for the first few years. If this scares you, then you can probably stop reading right here and forget about starting your own company. However, if this sounds exciting, then you probably have *entrepreneuritis*—that incurable desire for independence.

If you have never worked in a small business, I suggest that before you start your own venture, you take a job with a small company and work there for about a year. This will allow you to experience first-hand what it is like not having a large corporation behind you and may open your eyes to the pitfalls of being an entrepreneur. If you choose a business engaged in the same line of work that you want to start, you may also dispel any illusions you have about that particular industry. Use this time to thoroughly develop the plan for your own company.

There is no place for half-hearted commitment when starting your own business. If you want to do it, then go for it. If you're not sure, maybe this book will give you the confidence to proceed. Starting your own business is a commitment that will require a significant portion of your life from this point forward. Since almost thirty percent of all new businesses in America fail within one year, and 62.2 percent do not survive beyond six years, it is important that you choose a business that will offer you the greatest chance for long-term success. Your first critical step is choosing the correct venture. You are standing at the crossroads of riches and ruin—make your decision wisely.

Business consultants and career advisors agree that choosing the right business can be difficult. You must carefully match your skills, knowledge, experience, preferences, and desires with the requirements of the business you are considering. First, you need to determine if you possess the management skills necessary for working on your own. Second, you must evaluate your preferences and technical skills. And third, it is important that you speak to others who have started similar businesses to gain a real-life understanding of what is required.

Read this book slowly with a pencil, pen, or highlighter in your hand. Highlight key passages and make notes to yourself in the margin. If you think something is particularly important, dog ear the corner of the page or write the page number in the front of the book.

Assessing Your Management Skills

Begin your journey by completing the following management skills survey. This list of traits of successful entrepreneurs has been assembled from several sources including *How to Get Off the Fast Track — and Live a Life Money Can't Buy* by M. Kirsch, *Which Business is Best for You* by Donald R. Teff, *Growing a Business* by Paul Hawken, *Out the Organization* by Madeleine and Robert Swain, and *Do What You Love, The Money Will Follow* by Marsha Sinetar.

Circle the number that best describes the degree to which you possess the trait. To get the maximum benefit from this exercise, you must answer the questions *honestly*. If you are unsure, it is wiser to evaluate yourself too low than too high. In order for this survey to be an accurate appraisal, you must complete it now. If you read on before you answer these questions, you will invalidate the results.

	To a Great Extent					Not At All
1. I am independent	5	4	3	2	1	0
2. I am self-reliant	5	4	3	2	1	0
3. I possess high energy	5	4	3	2	1	0
4. I am flexible	5	4	3	2	1	0
5. I have a keen sense of humor	5	4	3	2	1	0
6. I am tenacious	5	4	3	2	1	0
7. I am optimistic	5	4	3	2	1	0
8. I need to be in charge	5	4	3	2	1	0
9. I question the status quo	5	4	3	2	1	0
10. I am organized	5	4	3	2	1	0
11. I am persuasive	5	4	3	2	1	0

12.	I am a hard worker	5	4	3	2	1	0
13.	I am creative	5	4	3	2	1	0
14.	I am self-motivated	5	4	3	2	1	0
15.	I am a problem solver	5	4	3	2	1	0
16.	I am people oriented	5	4	3	2	1	0
17.	I have a strong desire to win	5	4	3	2	1	0
18.	I am profit oriented	5	4	3	2	1	0
19.	I am decisive	5	4	3	2	1	0
20.	I am honest	5	4	3	2	1	0
21.	I am persistent	5	4	3	2	1	0
22.	I have high self esteem	5	4	3	2	1	0
23.	I am goal oriented	5	4	3	2	1	0
24.	I am patient	5	4	3	2	1	0
25.	I am a risk taker	5	4	3	2	1	0
26.	I am inquisitive	5	4	3	2	1	0
27.	I easily accept criticism	5	4	3	2	1	0
28.	I am innovative	5	4	3	2	1	0
29.	I am willing to sacrifice	5	4	3	2	1	0
30.	I am accountable	5	4	3	2	1	0
31.	I have good judgement	5	4	3	2	1	0
32.	I spend time doing things I enjoy most	5	4	3	2	1	0
33.	I am happy	5	4	3	2	1	0
34.	I have a strong marriage	5	4	3	2	1	0
35.	I have family support	5	4	3	2	1	0

Although all the items in the list have been identified as important, psychologists, consultants, and business owners generally agree that the even numbered items are the most crucial self-management skills and traits for entrepreneurs, and that the areas of being organized, self-motivated and tenacious are the critical "make or break" skills required.

If you rated yourself 3 or lower on any *even* numbered skill, you should carefully consider how important it is to the business you are planning to start. Verify your feelings with others in the industry.

Now add up your score for all questions.

If you scored between 140 and 175, you will probably do well as an entrepreneur.

If you scored between 115 and 140, you will probably be successful but you may want to improve your skills in your weaker areas. This can be accomplished by either improving yourself in these areas or by hiring someone with these skills.

If you scored between 90 and 115, you probably should not attempt to start a business on your own. Look for a business partner who can compliment you in the areas where you are weak.

If you scored below 90, you will probably be happier and more successful working for someone else.

Look at items 32 through 35. Nothing undermines personal relationships as much as tension. If you are generally happy and spend time doing things you enjoy, you will better be able to cope with the ups and downs of your new business. Your marriage may be strained as the business requires more and more of your time. It is not unusual to work long hours, skip a vacation, or not get paid when times are rough. Make sure your family understands this and you have their support.

An interesting, and often informative exercise is to have your spouse or best friend also assess your management skills and compare their scores and individual answers with yours.

Ten Businesses Most Likely to Fail

A column by L.M. Boyd in the *San Francisco Examiner* recently stated that according to researchers, the ten small businesses most likely to fail are: laundries and dry cleaners, florists, used car dealers, gas stations, trucking firms, restaurants, infants' clothing stores, bakeries, grocery and meat stores, and computer stores.

Top Ten Businesses for the 90's

According to *Entrepreneur Magazine*, the top ten are child-care services, medical claims processing, utility bill auditing, printer maintenance services, property tax auditing, in-home health care, food delivery service, gift baskets, financial aid services and mobile automotive window service.

Which Business is Best For You?

Too many entrepreneurs start with a product or technology and try to impose it on a market. In the process, they ignore their customers' real needs and do their clients a disservice. Forget about your products. Find a group of people who have a set of common problems. Once you have identified this group, define the products and services which can address their problems. Determine if you have the ability and are willing to solve these problems. If not, look for another market. There are more potential opportunities to choose from than you could possibly deal with in a lifetime.

In defining your venture, try to select an emerging market with emerging needs instead of a mature market. Where would you rather be in the life cycle of a product—at the beginning phases or at its peak? Positioning yourself at the beginning of a life cycle allows you to grow with the increasing demand. Entering at the peak leaves the market nowhere to go but down. The peak of the life cycle is characterized by heavy competition, price cutting, and commodity type marketing. If you position yourself correctly with an emerging market, you can often be carried by its sheer momentum. "When the wind is strong enough, even a turkey can fly."

Consider areas that take advantage of your special talents, interests, hobbies, and work experience. See Appendix D for several suggestions.

- What types of activities do you really like to do? If you could do anything in the world, what would it be?

_____

_____

_____

_____

_____

- What occupations or businesses fascinate you?

_____

_____

_____

_____

_____

- How do you like to spend your free time?

_____

_____

_____

_____

_____

- What are you good at?

_____

_____

_____

_____

_____

- What do you know a lot about?

  _____

  _____

  _____

  _____

  _____

- On the last day of your life, when you look back at your accomplishments, what specifically would you like to see? What will you need to have accomplished to say you are really satisfied?

  _____

  _____

  _____

  _____

  _____

You should begin to see opportunities. Your chances for success will be greatest if you consider a business you *like* and one that you know something about.

Trying to learn a business as you go can be difficult and frustrating. Neither your clients nor your competition will make allowances for your lack of experience. Don't make the mistake of gambling your fortune and reputation in an area where the odds are against you. Beware of "get rich quick" schemes. If it seems too good to be true, it probably is.

Home-based Businesses

Many people find working at home to be the ideal work arrangement and decide to set up businesses in their homes. The Small Business Administration estimates that there are now three million home-based businesses operating throughout the country. With today's rising demand for service-oriented businesses and recent technological advances, the opportunities seem to be endless.

Working at home certainly has some financial benefits. Not only do you eliminate the cost of an office, but if set up correctly, you can actually write off part of your house payment, your utilities, and home maintenance costs. The guidelines are very specific in this area so check with your accountant for the latest requirements.

Working under the same roof with your family may not prove to be as easy as it seems. It is important that you work in a professional environment. One suggestion is to set up your office in an area that is only used for business. Running your business from the kitchen table doesn't work as well as setting it up in the spare bedroom. Try to isolate yourself even if it means working in the garage or basement.

Working at home requires some additional skills. Do you have the self-discipline to actually *work* at home? Can you deal with the isolation of working from your home? Are you easily distracted by home activities?

A home-based business is subject to many of the same laws and regulations affecting other businesses. Here are some general areas to watch out for, but be sure to consult an attorney and the state department of labor to find out which laws and regulations will affect your business.

- Be aware of your city's zoning regulations. If you violate them, you could be fined and/or shut down.

- Certain products cannot be produced in the home. Most states outlaw the home production of fireworks, drugs, poisons, explosives, sanitary or medical products, and toys. Home-based businesses in some states are also prohibited from making food, drink, or clothing.

- You may need to obtain a work certificate or license from the state.

- You will still need to register your business name and obtain a sales tax number.

- A separate business telephone and bank account are normally required.

- If you have employees working with you, you must comply with employee health and safety laws.

Eleven Common Causes of Failure

1. *Choosing a business that isn't very profitable.* Even though you generate lots of activity, the profits never materialize to the extent necessary to sustain an on-going company.

2. *Inadequate cash reserves.* If you don't have enough cash to carry you through the first six months or so before the business starts making money, your prospects for success are not good. Consider both business and personal living expenses when determining how much cash you will need.

3. *Failure to clearly define and understand your market, your customers, and your customers' buying habits.* Is your product or service seasonal? What will you do in the off-season? How loyal are your potential customers to their current supplier? Do customers keep coming back or do they just purchase from you one time? Does it take a long time to close a sale or are your customers more driven by impulse buying?

4. *Failure to price your product or service correctly.* You must clearly define your pricing strategy. You can be the cheapest or you can be the best, but if you try to do both, you'll fail.

5. *Failure to adequately anticipate cash flow.* When you are just starting out, suppliers require quick payment for inventory (sometimes even COD). If you sell your products on credit, the time between making the sale and getting paid can be months. This two-way tug at your cash can pull you down if you fail to plan for it.

6. *Failure to anticipate or react to competition, technology, or other changes in the marketplace.* It is dangerous to assume that what you have done in the past will always work. Challenge the factors that led to your success. Do you still do things the same way despite new market demands and changing times? What is your competition doing differently? What new technology is available? Be open to new ideas. Experiment. Those who fail to do this end up becoming pawns to those who do.

7. *Overgeneralization.* Trying to do everything for everyone is a sure road to ruin. Spreading yourself too thin diminishes quality. The market pays excellent rewards for excellent results, average rewards for average results, and below average rewards for below average results. Which category you fall into is up to you.

8. *Overdependence on a single customer.* At first it looks great. But then you realize you are at their mercy. Whenever you have one customer so big that losing them would mean closing up shop, watch out. Having a large base of small customers is much preferred.

9. *Uncontrolled growth.* Slow and steady wins every time. Dependable, predictable growth is vastly superior to spurts and jumps in volume. It's hard to believe that too much business can destroy you, but the textbooks are full of case studies. Going after all the business you can get drains your cash and actually reduces overall profitability. You may incur significant up-front costs to finance large inventories to meet new customer demand. Don't leverage yourself so far that if the economy stumbles you'll be unable to pay back your loans. When you go after it all, you usually become less selective about customers and products, both of which drain profits from your company.

10. *Believing you can do everything yourself.* One of the biggest challenges for entrepreneurs is to let go. Let go of the attitude that you must have hands-on control of all aspects of your business. Let go of the belief that only you can make decisions. Concentrate on the most important problems or issues facing your company. Let others help you out. Give your people responsibility and authority.

11. *Putting up with inadequate management.* A common problem faced by successful companies is growing beyond management resources or skills. As the company grows, you may surpass certain individuals' ability to manage and plan. If a change becomes necessary, don't lower your standards just to fill vacant positions or to accommodate someone within your organization. Decide on the skills necessary for the position and insist that the individual has them.

Eleven Rules For Success

1. Work smarter, not harder. It's not how much you do, but what you do and how well you do it. There are better ways to run your business than by brute force.

2. Strive for accuracy first, then build momentum. You don't have a second chance to make a good first impression.

3. Build a good reputation on the quality of your products and support services.

4. Find a niche. Become an expert in your field. Stick to what you do best.

5. Always better your best. Constantly strive to improve your products and services.

6. Be creative. Adapt and apply innovative techniques from outside your specific field.

7. Be market driven, not product driven. Listen and react to your customer's needs.

8. Plan for success; know where you are going and how you are going to get there.

9. Capitalize on change. Use change as a springboard to improve your products, procedures, and reputation. Never allow yourself, your products, or service to become obsolete.

10. Think before you act. There is nothing so useless as doing efficiently that which should not be done at all.

11. Always promise a lot...and then deliver even more.

Soliciting Advice From the Experts

Go out and talk to individuals engaged in the same type of business you are considering. You may find local companies a bit hesitant to share this information with you since you may be perceived as a competitive threat. But if you travel outside your immediate geographic area, people in the same line of business will usually provide you with a wealth of information and insight. Take the time to talk with seven to ten business owners. Ask questions such as:

- How long have they been in business?
- Why did they start their business?
- Would they start the same kind of business again?
- What would they do differently if they could do it over?
- What special skills are necessary for this type of business?
- What special knowledge is needed?
- What is the most difficult thing about this type of business?
- What do they feel are the important skills required for success?
- What do they like most about their business?
- What do they like least?
- How much should I expect to make my first year?
- How much can I expect to make after five years?
- How much money should I set aside to start my business?
- How many months passed before your business showed a profit?
- How seasonal is the business? Do the revenues vary from month to month?
- What does the future look like for the business?
- Is there any proposed local, state, or federal legislation that may have an impact on the business—positive or negative?
- What advice can they give you?
- Can they recommend anyone else you should talk to?

_____

_____

_____

_____

_____

Put Your Choice in Writing

Now make an honest comparison of your skills and traits to those needed for success.

Describe in detail the venture you would like to start.

_____

_____

_____

_____

_____

_____

_____

_____

_____

Do you feel you have the skills required for this type of business? List them below.

_____

_____

_____

_____

_____

_____

_____

_____

_____

Did you learn anything that surprised you during the interviews? How will you adjust your plans?

_____

_____

_____

_____

_____

_____

Does the proposed venture meet your profit and growth expectations for one and five years? What are they?

One year: _____

_____

_____

_____

_____

_____

Five years: _____

_____

_____

_____

_____

_____

_____

How much money do you feel you will have to invest in your new venture before it turns a profit? How did you arrive at this figure? A 1990 survey of 1,650 owners of businesses with revenues ranging from $2 million to $100 million shows that 29% started with less than $10,000, 19% with between $10,000 and $25,000 and 26% with between $25,000 and $100,000.

_____

_____

_____

_____

_____

_____

To be on the safe side you should plan for 25% more money than you feel you will actually need. List all the sources you currently have available to raise this money and how much you feel you can get from each source.   Don't be discouraged if you aren't sure where to get all the money—Chapter 3 is devoted entirely to this subject.

_____   _____

_____   _____

_____   _____

_____   _____

_____   _____

_____   _____

If the business isn't going as planned, when will you call it quits? It's not wise to risk your entire savings on any one venture, so you need a *pre-defined* bail-out point. It is much easier (and safer) to choose this point now. If the business ever goes into a downward spiral, you may be too emotionally tied to it to make the best business decision at that time. It's too easy to rationalize "just one more month" and pretty soon you've lost everything.

This doesn't mean that you should enter the new business with your focus on failure—quite the contrary. By having a well-defined jumping-off point, your whole effort and energy from this point forward can go into making the venture a success, and you won't need to spend any more time on this issue.

_____

_____

_____

_____

_____

_____

_____

_____

Evaluating Your Proposed Venture

Now you will evaluate your proposed venture to make sure it has a good chance of succeeding.

This process will take from 25 to 50 hours (including research time). This may sound like a lot of time but it is far better to evaluate your idea on paper, at a relatively minor cost, than to blindly begin a venture that is ultimately doomed to failure. This early analysis will save you considerable time and money by allowing you to experiment with various scenarios before actually starting your business.

When answering the following questions, you will be required to make several creative assumptions about your proposed venture. Try to be as realistic and accurate as possible.

It is very important that you *write down the answers* to the following questions.

You may have to do some research to find all the information requested. Again, I would like to stress that research time is time well spent. Good sources of information include potential customers, trade associations, libraries, your accountant, consultants, the Small Business Administration, any regulatory agencies involved with your type of business, and the Better Business Bureau.

If you are planning to go into business with others (partnership) it is very important that all parties *independently* answer the following questions. When you have all finished, get together and discuss your answers to make sure you all have the same expectations, desires, and commitment.

How Committed are You?

Being self-employed usually requires more time, effort, and energy than working for someone else. Make sure you are willing to commit to whatever it takes to make your venture a success. As a general rule of thumb, figure the amount of time you think you'll spend running the business and double it.

You might want to adjust your business aims to meet your lifestyle goals. How hard do you want to work? Do you want to hustle sales all day? If you always want your weekends free, you should eliminate retail sales, real estate, and many service businesses. Don't get discouraged, there are businesses to match every lifestyle—you just have to find the one that's right for you.

Involve your family in the decision. Make sure you have their support. Their input may really help you focus your search. With their support behind you, there's no mountain you can't climb.

Do You Know Who Your Customers Are?

You must know precisely who your customers are and what they really want, and need, if you are to excel (or even survive) in these competitive times. Being out of touch with your customers is a mistake that can kill your business. Identify your customers, talk to them, find out what they want now and what they want next, then satisfy those needs and your business will thrive.

Who will your potential customers be? Describe them as precisely as possible. (Examples: All automobile, pickup, and RV owners within 25 miles; all homeowners within 50 miles with household incomes of at least $30,000; all homeowners and commercial painters within 40 miles)

_____

_____

_____

_____

_____

_____

_____

_____

Will you be selling directly to the consumer (retail) or to others who will in turn resell your product (wholesale) or both? If you have selected "both," what percentage of your business do you expect to obtain from each?

Percentage of Business that will be Retail   _____

Percentage of Business that will be Wholesale   _____

How many potential customers does this represent? The number you enter here should be a fairly accurate, "educated" guess. Retail customer counts might be obtained from the city planning department, police or fire departments, better business bureau, census information, or the library. Wholesale customer counts might be obtained from the phone book, trade associations, city business department (business licenses issued), Better Business Bureau, or the Chamber of Commerce.

Number of Potential Retail Customers   _____

Number of Potential Wholesale Customers   _____

How Will You Market Your Product or Services?

Describe all the ways you initially intend to let potential customers know about your business. Some suggestions might be yellow page advertising, mailing or hand delivering flyers, newspaper advertising, radio, television, billboards, face-to-face sales calls, telemarketing, and trade journals. If you are relying heavily on the yellow pages of your local phone book, remember that the phone directories only come out once per year. Find out when the next one will be printed and the cutoff date for you to submit advertising copy. What will you do until the new phone book comes out?

Estimate the *initial* amount you will spend in each area of your marketing plan. If you are unsure about the costs, make some phone calls to find out the rates.

Description	Estimated Cost

Now estimate how much you will spend in each area on an on-going monthly basis for the first year. You must advertise to get business, but don't go overboard on fancy brochures or other expensive advertising right away. Save those for later when your company is making a profit and can justify the expense.

Description   Cost per Month

_____   _____

_____   _____

_____   _____

_____   _____

_____   _____

_____   _____

_____   _____

Various Ways to Structure Your Business

Now that you have identified your potential customers, let's examine various ways of setting up your business that will satisfy their needs.

Try to come up with as many alternatives as possible. Reserve making judgments on the ideas until you have finished brainstorming. Examples of alternative opportunities might be:

Type of business
- Retail (selling directly to the consumers)
- Wholesale (selling to contractors or distributors)
- Mail order (selling through catalogs or advertisements)
- Telemarketing (telephone selling)

Business location
- Work out of your home (low overhead, but possible family distractions and zoning restrictions)
- Shopping mall location (expensive but lots of exposure to new customers and walk-by traffic)
- Warehouse location (lower cost but with minimal walk-by or drop-in traffic)

Selling options

- Inside sales only (sales clerks all working inside your store)
- Outside sales force (sales force made up of employees that work for you who call on customers at their location)
- Independent distributors (non-employee sales reps who buy products from you and then resell them)
- Telemarketers (employee or non-employee telephone solicitors)
- Catalog sales (direct mail marketing)

Inventory options

- Maintain large inventory for maximum customer convenience (this will cost you a lot of money for product and warehouse space so you'll have to charge more for your items)
- Maintain minimal inventory and offer lowest possible price (you keep only the most common items in stock; everything else must be special ordered — not nearly as convenient for your customers)
- Drop ship orders directly from your suppliers (you maintain little or no inventory — possibly selling from only a catalog, samples, or a showroom — customers place orders with you, and you have the product shipped directly from the factory to them (lowest cost — least convenience).

Pricing options

- Full retail pricing
- Full retail but offer lots of sales
- Everything priced at a discount
- Variable discount schedules based on annual or projected purchase volume of each customer
- Special discounts for contractors, professionals, teachers, senior citizens, students, etc.

Narrowing Down the Alternatives

Now pick the two or three alternatives you feel offer you the greatest likelihood of success—the ones that best satisfy *the customers' needs*. For example you love to fish and consider yourself somewhat of an expert in this area. You want to start a business around this life-long hobby. You have decided to evaluate three options:

1.   Open a retail store in an outdoor mall. You would sell a full line of fishing products priced slightly below the prevailing retail price.
2.   Open the same store described in your first option, but add light-weight fishing boats, kayaks, canoes, outboard motors, carriers, etc.
3.   Open the same store described in your first choice but add local and exotic fishing trips, clinics, private lessons, and a casting pond.

For another example, you may want to evaluate five entirely different types of businesses.

1.   A gourmet coffee store
2.   A utility bill auditing company
3.   A travel agency
4.   A cooking school
5.   A golf store

Using a separate piece of paper for each alternative, list all the benefits and drawbacks you can think of. Consider such issues as:

●   How much competition exists for each alternative?

    If there is no competition, verify that the need exists — that there are sufficient customers to support your venture. If there is a lot of competition, are there enough customers to support *your* business also?

●   Who are your competitors?

    To successfully compete, you must know who the competition is. Where are they located? What products do they handle? What are their prices?

●   What are the competitor's strengths and weaknesses?

    If you don't know, do some research—call people who use this product or service. Find out where they purchase it, if they happy with their current supplier, what they like

23

most about their current supplier, what they like least, and what would make them change to a new supplier.

- What makes your product or service unique?

  If you are not unique, why would anyone want to buy from you as compared to the other suppliers? Items you may want to consider include product, service, and price.

- Compare the amount of time, effort, and money required to start each of the alternative ventures.

  How much will each alternative cost? Can you obtain the necessary capital for each alternative? Are you knowledgeable about each alternative or will you have to spend some time learning about a new aspect of the business?

- What are the risks associated with each venture alternative you are considering?

  How much do you know about this alternative? Do you have experience in this area? How much risk are you willing to take? Do not risk *everything* on a new venture — reconfirm your fallback position.

- Is this a business that you really like?

  People tend to work harder, be happier, and do better when working in a business they like. It is surprising how many people seriously consider starting a business that they know little or nothing about. Don't be swayed by others who make statements like "You should buy a video store because you can make a lot of money renting movies" or advertisements like "Be your own boss, earn $60,000 or more per year working part time at home." Do some research first and make sure you are embarking on something *you* really want to do.

Business Location and Leasing Options

For each alternative, answer the following questions about the business location:

- Where will you locate your business? Have you chosen this location because its convenient for you or because its the best location for the business?
- How much space do you need and how much will it cost?
- Is there space currently available?
- Check with the planning department for any special requirements for hazardous materials, fire codes, building requirements, etc.
- Is the landlord willing to make the modifications necessary to meet these requirements?
- How much will all this cost you?
- Can you run this business out of your home or do you absolutely have to rent office space?
- Are there any zoning or licensing restrictions on home-based businesses in your area?
- Will you be able to draw or find employees in this area?
- Is the area safe and secure? Check with the local police department to determine frequency of break-ins, and other crime in the immediate area. Ask them for their recommendations on alternative areas.
- Check with your insurance agent for insurance costs. Rates sometimes vary based upon type and age of the building, location, suitability for your type of business, etc.

Choosing the Best Alternative

Now it's time to review your alternatives and choose the one that feels best to you. Consider your lifestyle again. Realize that once you start your business, you may own it for a long, long time. Choose a line of work that you really enjoy. If you don't like the business, it doesn't matter how much money you make.

Use the tally sheet below to help you with your evaluation. Assign a 3 to the alternative you feel is the best, a 2 for the second best, and a 1 for the remaining alternative.

	Venture Alternative		
	1	2	3
Amount of Money Needed	____	____	____
Greatest Customer Need	____	____	____
Least Competition	____	____	____
Knowledge of the Venture	____	____	____
Most Experience	____	____	____
Like the Most	____	____	____
TOTAL	____	____	____

Using the above evaluation process as a guideline, you should now have a fairly good feel for the type of business that seems right for you.

Sole Proprietor, Partnership, or Corporation?

Every new business must decide whether it will start as a sole proprietorship, a partnership, or a corporation. Most one-person and husband and wife businesses start as sole proprietorships, simply because a sole proprietorship is the quickest, easiest, and least expensive form of business to start. If you don't incorporate and you don't have a partner, you automatically become a sole proprietorship.

If you have one or more partners, other than your spouse, and have not incorporated, you have legally started a partnership. A husband and wife who start an unincorporated business can be either a sole proprietorship or a partnership.

If you decide to incorporate, you must file incorporation papers with your state's Department of Corporations, prepare articles of incorporation and corporate bylaws, issue state-approved stock certificates, and pay filing and registration fees as well as prepaid franchise taxes, which are minimum corporate income taxes. Either your accountant or attorney can help you with this paperwork.

In a sole proprietorship, the owner of the business and the business are one and the same. There is no legal separation. If your business cannot pay its bills or gets sued, your personal non-business assets are at stake. All profits are treated as personal income and you pay taxes at your individual rate. Some personal benefits such a health insurance are not deductible as a business expense. These laws change from time to time, so check with your accountant for the most current rules.

Similarly, the partners in a partnership are personally liable for all business debts and lawsuits. Additionally, each partner can be held personally liable for the acts of any other partner in the business. If your partner, representing the business, borrows money from the bank, you can be personally responsible for the debt, even if you didn't sign the papers yourself—*even if you didn't know about the loan*. You must file partnership tax returns and all profits are treated as personal income. You pay taxes at your individual rates. Business deduction allowances are similar to those of a sole proprietorship. There is a big advantage to partnerships, however. With more than one founder you have more capital, you tend to generate more sales earlier, and work longer hours.

A corporation is a legal entity separate from the owner or owners. Generally the owner or stockholders of a corporation are not personally liable for the debts and obligations of the business; only the corporate assets are at stake, but there are many exceptions!   The amount of personal liability of the owner in a corporation is a complicated issue. So if you are considering starting a corporation merely to protect yourself from creditors or lawsuits, you should first contact your attorney or accountant for professional advice.

A corporation may hire its owner as an employee and pay that person a wage and offer company-paid benefits, such as health insurance. The wages and insurance are tax-deductible expenses of the corporation.

The owner-employee pays income taxes on the wages received, but not on any profits the corporation makes. The corporation, of course, must pay a corporate tax on its profits. If the profits are or become excessive, the corporation must pay dividends to the stockholders which are first taxed at the corporate level and then taxed again as personal income to the stockholders. Tax reporting for corporations is more complicated than for either a sole proprietorship or partnership; therefore, you can expect your accountant to charge you more for corporate returns.

A hybrid between a corporation and a partnership is the S corporation. The S corporation offers limited liability protection to the stockholders and pays no corporate income tax. All the profits (or losses) of the S corporation are passed on to the owners, who are taxed at their individual rates. Benefits are treated as corporate expenses just like in a standard corporation. There are numerous restrictions on S corporations, so many, in fact, that many companies find it difficult to comply.

A new alternative is the Limited Liability Company (LLC). This is a business structure that is currently available in 17 states: Arizona, Colorado, Delaware, Florida, Iowa, Kansas, Louisiana, Maryland, Minnesota, Nevada, Oklahoma, Rhode Island, Texas, Utah, Virginia, West Virginia and Wyoming. Legislation is pending in Illinois, Michigan, Mississippi, Missouri, New Jersey, New York, Pennsylvania and South Carolina. The move to LLCs is spreading rapidly, so if your state isn't listed above, ask your accountant if it now offers this option.

LLCs are like the S corporation, with the tax benefits of sole proprietorships and partnerships, but with the protection from liability of a normal corporation. However, they offer much more organizational flexibility.

A business may start as a sole proprietorship or partnership and incorporate at a later date. In fact, this is what most businesses do.

Guidelines for Partnerships

Breaking up a partnership can be just as emotional as a divorce. Many partnerships consist of friends, relatives, and former business colleagues. When you combine these relationships with the strains of running a small business, you can see why a failing partnership creates bruised egos, bitterness, hurt feelings, and anger. Following these simple guidelines will improve your chances for success.

1. **Share everything equally.** Partners may have different opinions on what risk is justifiable, how money should be managed, and what the work ethic really means.

Will all partners initially contribute an equal amount of money? If not, how will this be handled? Where will the money come from and how quickly can each partner get it? Can all the partners survive without pay during rough times? Because of varying financial situations, some partners may not be able to do so. This will place the psychological strain of "unequal sacrifice" on the relationship. Discuss the personal ability of each partner to persevere through periods of reduced income. Agree on what will be expected of each partner if the worst case occurs—ideally it should be the same for each.

Agree on the amount of time to be dedicated to the partnership. Is everyone willing to do an equal share of the overtime? One of the secrets of success is hard work—make sure you agree on what hard work means. All partners should also be willing to do all jobs which include such tasks as emptying the trash cans, making coffee, running to the post office, etc. In young, small businesses everyone has to do a little of everything. To avoid potential problems down the road, make sure you agree on these items before you sign your partnership agreement.

2. **Have a Written Agreement.** Have your attorney draw up a formal partnership agreement. Include as an attachment everything agreed upon above. Putting the agreement in writing forces each partner to take the rules seriously.

Attach your plans for the overall operation of the company including each partner's unique responsibilities.

Doing this before you start your business will allow you to focus on, and solve, problem areas before they destroy your company and ruin your friendship.

3. **Don't Lie.** Be completely open and honest with each other. Generally people don't tell big lies, but even those little white lies can be devastating to a partnership. Confide in each other. Trust each other.

Not sharing bad news is lying through omission. Share all bad news with your partners. Bad news is not necessarily a sign of personal failure. Treat it as information that must be addressed in the context of your business plans. You must be open and honest with all matters if you want your relationship to work.

Don't lie to yourselves. If your employees are not producing, don't make excuses—find out why and face the consequences. If you spot problem areas, discuss them with your partner. If things aren't going well, talk about it. Don't make your partner handle all the problems; do your fair share of the dirty work.

Don't lie to your customers or vendors. Don't oversell. Don't promise what you can't deliver.

It is important that you agree on all these issues. Too many partnerships fail simply because of misaligned views or differing expectations of the partners.

Ten Rules for Family Businesses

Rule 1. Deal objectively with each person's qualifications. Don't assume that age brings wisdom. Consider each individual's unique talents, education, and experience, and place people in your organization based on their abilities, not just their age.

Rule 2. Relatives should preferably acquire practical experience somewhere else. This allows the person to grow and mature away from home and will give him or her a different perspective of the company. This is especially true for a son's or daughter's first job.

Rule 3. Clearly define responsibilities. Just because you are working with family, don't assume they can read your mind. Define goals, tasks, and responsibilities as clearly as you would with someone you don't know.

Rule 4. Divide responsibilities. To avoid power struggles, assign each family member a job that he or she does best.

Rule 5. Establish working hours in advance. In general, individuals going into a family business should expect to work longer hours and much harder than they have ever worked before. If you don't sense this level of commitment, be careful.

Rule 6. Make sure it is clear who reports to whom. Make sure this is understood and completely agreed upon up front. Individuals in positions of responsibility should be there because of ability, period.

Rule 7. Discuss salary and benefits in advance. This includes your policy on raises, bonuses, vacation time, health insurance, sick time, etc.

Rule 8. Fight issues, not emotions. Don't let family issues spill over to the work environment. Run the business like a business.

Rule 9. Establish a family council. This is an excellent way to communicate and to air any problems or differences that might otherwise be overlooked or ignored if they had to be discussed during the normal course of business.

Rule 10. Consider each relative carefully before hiring him or her. Firing a relative puts strains on the entire family. Not firing a relative that deserves to be fired just because he or she is a relative creates just as much strain—both on you and the rest of your employees.

One organization that specializes in the unique challenges and problems of family businesses is the Sons of Bosses (SOB), originally founded in 1969. In 1976, the national organization and several chapters were renamed the National Family Business Council. Those chapters which still go by SOB now have no affiliation with the national organization. More information may be obtained from the NFBC at 1000 Vermont Ave. NW, Washington, DC 20005; Phone (202) 347-2048.

Family Business Forums are another source of information and workshops for family-based businesses. To locate a group near you, contact Craig Aronoff, director of the Family Business Forum, at Kennesaw State College, in Marietta, GA (404) 423-6045.

Buying an Existing Business

Buying an existing company will reduce risk and save time. If you buy smart, your company's operational practices, supplier relationships, and distribution channels will already be established. Key employees and managers will already be there. Since you're buying an existing cash flow, you can easily project how much you'll make.

With reduced risk comes reduced reward. Available cash flow will be burdened by the debt you incur to buy the business. You won't be able to reap the investment leverage enjoyed by individuals starting a business from scratch. You may also inherit some problems.

Why is the seller selling?

- According to *Inc.* magazine, fifty-four percent of all owners list burnout and/or boredom as the primary reason they want to sell their businesses.

- Another school of thought suggests the most common reason for selling is that the business isn't making any money or there is a trend toward making less and less. I don't feel this contradicts *Inc.*'s findings in any way. The question is: Which came first, the boredom or the declining revenue? An analysis of the financial statements and tax returns for the last few years will highlight any decline. If this is the case, you will need to uncover the cause of this decline and determine if you have the ability to reverse the trend.

- Personal reasons such as poor health, divorce settlement, recent death in the family or the desire to retire are the next most common reasons for selling.

- The fourth group consists of owners who know that bad times are coming and want to get out before the market crumbles. This could be caused by pending legislation (check with your attorney), a major new competitor moving into the area (check with the city planning commission or business office) or technology changes rendering their product obsolete.

- The last group is rare but should still be mentioned. It involves businesses that were having problems, were sold, and were turned around by the new owner. That individual now wants to re-sell the business at a profit.

Your first task is to determine into which category your seller belongs.

You may want to solicit the help of a *Business Broker*. Be aware that this is largely an unregulated industry. In 19 states and Washington D.C., brokers must have a real estate license. Elsewhere they need no permits or credentials. Some are good, especially those who are CPA's or attorneys. Others are not so good. In virtually all cases, the broker works for the seller. With commissions running as high as 12%, the broker is looking to get top dollar for the seller.

You don't have to limit your search to companies that are for sale. If there is a company you like, call the owner and ask if they're interested in selling. Surprisingly, statistics show that three of every ten such cold calls attract some interest.

Below is a checklist to follow if you are seriously considering buying a existing business.

A.   Before you begin your negotiations.

1.   Establish a friendly relationship with the potential seller, especially if he or she is retiring out of the business. Most business owners think of their company as more than just a business. They often look for someone who will love and nurture their enterprise the same way they have for "all these years." Often in this case, a seller's decision on a buyer comes as much or more from feelings than from the actual dollar amount.

2.   Have your attorney prepare a non-binding "letter of intent" that both you and the seller must sign. This document should give you an exclusive right (but no obligation) to buy the business for a certain period of time (say four months). This protects you from spending a lot of time analyzing the business only to have it sold out from underneath you. It also protects you from having the seller play two potential buyers against each other and forcing you to make a decision before you have completed your investigation. This document should also state reasonable time frames for the production of documents and other information you need to assist you in your analysis, exactly what (stock or assets) is being sold, confidentiality for the seller, and what must be accomplished before the sale is consummated.

B.   After you have signed this initial document.

1.   Assemble your advisory team. You need an accountant who understands how small businesses keep their books. You also need a lawyer to examine all papers and to check on any litigation or tax problems.

2.   Obtain an appraisal of the business assets and determine if there are any existing liens on the assets. Do this by contacting the Secretary of State and searching the public records of the county where the assets have been used for any Financing Statements which may have been recorded under the Uniform Commercial Code.

3.   Examine certified financial statements and federal income tax returns of the business for at least the last three years. If certified (or audited) financial statements are not available, have your accountant do an audit. Just because information is printed on an internal financial statement, doesn't mean that it is necessarily accurate. Has the company ever been audited by the IRS? Be aggressive on the tax side, as it can really come back to bite you. Compare the business ratios with industry norms. These can be found in the book *Industry Norms and Key Business Ratios* published by Dun & Bradstreet. Also compare the financials with the *Annual Statement Studies,* a book published by Robert Morris Associates. Your library probably has both of these books.

4. Prepare cash flow projections for the next 12 months *with the seller's assistance.* It is important to include the seller in this step. Attached these worksheets to your Bill of Sale. If the seller makes any untrue representations or projections, you will have documentation of these claims.

5. Closely examine the outstanding accounts receivable. Are they factored? If so, they are not an asset. Discount their value by the age of the debt. If an invoice is 90 days old, assign it a value of only 90% of its face amount. Assume that all receivables which are six months or older are uncollectable—give them a value of zero.

6. Examine any notes receivable. Are they just old accounts receivable? If so, they have no practical value unless they are guaranteed by some collateral.

7. Check all outstanding loan agreements to ensure they will not be accelerated upon the sale of the business. If they contain an acceleration clause, this means that they become immediately due and payable *in full* upon the finalization of the sale. If you find this wording in any loan document, go to the lender and see if the provision can be removed or the loan renegotiated. Get it in writing.

8. Review all contracts to make sure they are transferrable or assignable. If they are not, go to the party and negotiate this clause out of the existing contract or establish new contracts, contingent on your ultimate purchase of the business. Get the seller to assist you if necessary. Again, get all agreements in writing.

9. If there is any chance of environmental liability, have an expert conduct an audit.

10. Obtain a complete list of the seller's suppliers. Check how long each has been supplying products to this firm and what the current selling terms are—COD, net 10 days, net 30, etc. See if there are any commitments to purchase materials and supplies from each vendor.

11. Check the relationships with all major customers. Are there any requirements to sell merchandise at prices other than current market price?

12. Study the seller's business operation, plant location, available labor markets, services, key personnel, and qualifications to do business in various states.

13. Investigate the laws and regulations applicable to the business and determine the company's compliance with them. Determine whether existing business licenses are in order and assignable.

14. Have a title search done on all real estate to be purchased.

15. Examine any and all leases on premises occupied by the seller to determine terms and conditions of tenancy and assignability. If required, obtain the approval of the lessor to the assignment of the lease to you by the lessee.

16. Examine collective bargaining agreements, employment contracts, and pension or profit sharing agreements. Do any employees have stock options? Have any employees been promised, or are expecting, raises or bonuses?

17. Assess the employees. Are they bright and competent? What are they paid, and what exactly do they do? Do they seem honest? Do they seem to get along well together? Meet individually with each employee (without the seller). They can tell you things the seller would never tell you. If their true allegiance is to the old owner, will they stay? They will be naturally concerned about their jobs. Discuss this openly with them.

18. Examine inventory to determine that you aren't buying old or obsolete material or products. If the inventory is more than six months old, reduce its value to zero—just because something is carried on the books with a value doesn't mean that you have to pay that amount for it. Make sure that part of the inventory isn't located somewhere else. Perform a physical inventory to verify the "book" inventory.

19. Examine machinery and equipment to determine its condition. How old is it? How well does it work? Ask to see repair logs. Is it obsolete? Call the manufacturer if you aren't sure. How expensive is it to repair? How much was spent on repairs during the last 24 months? Does it meet safety

standards? Call OSHA if your aren't sure. Is it leased or owned? If it is leased, what are the terms of the lease? Review all depreciation schedules. If you aren't sure what you're looking at, get an expert to assist you.

20. Examine all patents, trademarks, and copyrights that relate to the business. Make sure they belong to the company and not the owner or employees personally.

21. Investigate any subsidiary companies, if applicable.

22. Request estoppel letters from all lien holders and request, in writing, their permission to assume the obligations of the seller along with any conditions and instructions for assumption. Have your attorney help you draft your letter.

23. When negotiating the value of goodwill, refer to the IRS Guidelines. Your accountant will help you in this area.

24. When negotiating the final price, never make the opening bid. Don't show how eager you are to buy the business. Don't make any offer or agree on a final price until you have completed your evaluation. The fair market value of a business is based on more than just the book value. Also consider the maturity, reputation, history, economic outlook, and earning capacity of the business. (You should get at least 8-10% return on your investment). IRS guideline 68-609 may assist you in this area.

Make sure the final price reflects the real value. If you are overburdened with debt which the cash flow cannot service, both you and the seller lose. If you default, the seller never receives the price agreed upon. According to David Bishop, president of American Business Appraisers, based in Sunriver, Oregon, "One of the main reasons businesses fail once they are bought is that their real value has never been identified."

If you can't agree on a price, offer to base the price on the continued performance of the business. The better the business does, the more the seller gets. If the seller really believes the business is going to perform, he or she will probably agree. If the seller is unsure about the future, this may be the catalyst required to agree on a fixed price.

37

25. After establishing the selling price, structure the sale for your best tax advantages. Even though you buy the business as a whole, for tax purposes, the purchase of an unincorporated business is viewed as a purchase of the assets. The total purchase price is allocated over all the assets. You get your greatest tax advantage by negotiating with the seller to allocate the purchase price to those assets that give you the greatest tax deductions during operations and the largest capital gain on disposal. Be sure to involve your accountant in this process.

Value the following items at a *high* price:

- **Merchandise inventory.** A high cost in this area reduces taxable profit.

- **Supplies and similar items not used in the manufacture of your product.** These supplies are fully deductible as expenses.

- **Accounts receivable.** If any of these don't pay, the loss is fully deductible.

- **Patents, copyrights, franchises, and amortizable intangibles.** Do this if the remaining life is short.

- **Machinery, equipment, and buildings.**The costs of these assets is recovered under accelerated rates and periods that are set by law.

- **Covenant of seller not to compete.** To get this deduction, the sales contract must include the covenant and allocate a specific amount to it. Further, the contract should state that the agreement not to compete is not part of the transfer of goodwill.

Value the following items at a *low* price:

- **Land.** You get no depreciation deduction to recover the cost.

- **Stocks, bonds, and securities.** You get no annual depreciation for these.

- **Goodwill.** You get no annual deduction for depreciation of this. The cost would be recovered only through the sale of the business.

26. Don't pay all cash for the business. Insist the seller carry back a note so you have some recourse if the seller misled or lied to you. Also structure part of your payment as a "covenant not to compete."

C.   Executing the paperwork

1.   Have your attorney prepare the following documents and any others he/she feels you may need. They will become part of the purchase paperwork:

a. Bill of Sale or Purchase Agreement. This is the most important document. It is to your benefit to make it as specific as possible.

b. Promissory Note, if required.

c. Security Agreement, if required.

d. Real Estate Sublease or Assignment of Lease, if required.

e. Notice Under Fictitious Name Statute.

f. Standard RAMCO Form UCC-1/Financing Statement.

g. Covenant Not to Compete.

h. Business Closing Statement.

2.   Both you and the seller should review all the documents prior to the "closing ceremony." Make sure there is agreement on every last item before you get together to sign the final papers.

3.   Sign all the appropriate closing documents. This should just be a formal ceremony, since everything has already been reviewed and agreed on. Don't make any public announcements until *all* the paperwork has been signed.

4.   Record UCC-1's with the Secretary of State UCC Bureau, and also in the public records of the county where equipment is located.

5.   Publish the Notice Under Fictitious Name Statute with local newspaper once a week for four consecutive weeks or as required in your area.

Franchises

Buying a franchise may be appealing if you want to be your own boss, but have limited capital and business experience. However, without carefully investigating a business before you purchase, you may make a serious mistake. It is important to find out if a particular business is right for you and if it has the potential to yield the financial return you expect. Also, if you are starting your own business because you can't stand working for someone else, think twice before buying a franchise. With a franchise you have to play by the franchisor's rules. This may include how you run the business, dress codes, hours, products you must or are allowed to carry, reporting procedures, etc.

But if you can live with the above restrictions, franchising may be the best answer for you. The initial assistance and support provided certainly give you a head start over normal start-ups. A common saying in the industry states that with a franchise you're in business *for* yourself, but not *by* yourself. The franchisor is sincerely interested in helping you succeed. After all, they have a vested interest in your success.

Franchises offer a system that includes assistance with business setup, personnel training, site selection, lease negotiations, collective buying power, and advertising that has been proven over many years. Most importantly, franchises offer instant name recognition which can be an extremely important factor in your success. However, you pay a price for all this. Besides the initial franchise fee, you are usually required to pay a percentage of your monthly gross sales back to the parent company. Many franchises also require you to buy your products directly from the parent company (which means that you may not always get the best prices).

When selecting a franchise you should keep several things in mind.

- Pick a franchise that you will still enjoy working at in five to ten years. Don't pick a franchise solely on its profit-making potential; make absolutely sure you will enjoy doing it.

- Look at how much local competition you have. Visit their locations and see how busy they are. Can your community support another business like this?

- Don't assume the profit projections presented to you by the franchisor are accurate—after all, franchisors want to sell you a franchise. Do your own homework and come up with your own figures. In particular, make sure you create all your projections using the forms in Appendix A.

- See if the franchisor offers financing. There are over 250 franchises that do.

- Federal law requires franchisors to provide prospective buyers with a detailed disclosure document called the Uniform Franchise Offering Circular. This document must be given to you at the earlier of either (1) your first personal meeting with the franchisor, or (2) ten business days prior to you paying any money or legally committing yourself to a purchase. This document will assist you in evaluating the overall strength of the franchisor.

The packet gives the following 20 important items of information about the business:

1. Identifying information about the franchisor.

2. Business experience of the franchisor's directors and key executives.

3. The franchisor's business experience.

4. Litigation history of the franchisor and its directors and key executives.

5. Bankruptcy history of the franchisor and its directors and key executives.

6. Description of the franchise.

7. Money required to be paid by the franchisee to obtain or commence the franchise operation.

8. Continuing expenses to the franchisee in operating the franchise business that are payable in whole or in part to the franchisor.

9. A list of persons with whom the franchisee is required to advised to do business, and any business relationship these individuals or companies may have directly with the franchisor.

10. Any items which the franchisee is required to purchase, lease, or rent, and a list of any persons from whom such transactions must be made.

11. Descriptions of royalties or commissions paid by third parties to the franchisor or any of its affiliates as a result of a franchisee's purchase from these third parties.

12. Description of any franchisor assistance in financing the purchase of a franchise.

13. Restrictions placed on a franchisee's conduct of its business.

14. Required personal participation by the franchisee.

15. Termination, cancellation and renewal of the franchise.

16. Statistical information about the number of franchises and their rate of termination.

17. Franchisor's right to select or approve a site for the franchise.

18. Training programs for the franchisee.

19. Celebrity involvement with the franchise.

20. Financial information about the franchisor.

The disclosure must be made to you in a single document and the document may not include information other than that required by the FTC Rule or by state law. However, the franchisor may furnish you other information "which is not inconsistent with the material set forth in the disclosure document."

In addition to the disclosure document, you must receive a copy of all agreements which you will be asked to sign.

The information presented to you must be current as of the completion of the franchisor's most recent fiscal year.

If you are not given a disclosure document, ask why. Some franchise sellers may not be required to give it to you. If any franchise says that it is not covered by the rule, you may want to verify this with the FTC, an attorney, or a business advisor. Even if the business is not legally required to give the document, you should still ask for the data to help you make an informed decision.

The FTC Rule prohibits earnings representations about the actual or potential sales, income, or profits of existing or prospective franchisees unless (1) reasonable proof exists to support the accuracy of the claim, (2) the franchisor has in its possession, at the time the claim is made, information sufficient to substantiate the accuracy of the claim, (3) the claim is geographically relevant to the prospective franchise proposed location (except for media claims) and (4) an earnings claim disclosure document is given to the prospective franchisee at the same time that the other disclosures are given. The earnings claim document must contain six items:

1.   A cover sheet in the form specified in the Rule.

2.   The earnings claim.

3.   A statement of the basis and assumptions upon which the earnings claim is made.

4.   Information concerning the number and percentage of outlets tat have earned at least the amount set forth in the claim, or a statement of lack of experience, as well as the beginning and ending dates of the time period covered by the claim.

5.   A mandatory caution statement, whose text is set forth in the Rule, concerning the likelihood of duplicating the earnings claim.

6.   A statement that information sufficient to substantiate the accuracy of the claim is available for inspection by you.

You must be notified of any material changes in the information contained in the earnings claim document prior to your becoming a franchisee.

Be aware, however, that no government agency has checked the accuracy of the information outlined in these documents. It is your responsibility to verify the information and determine if the investment is right for you. Have an attorney familiar with franchise law review all the documents and explain them to you before you sign anything.

- Get all the facts.

    1. *Study the disclosure document* and proposed contracts carefully.

    2. Ask the franchisor these questions:
        - Will you have an exclusive territory? If so, how big is it? How long are you guaranteed this territory? If the exclusivity is tied to performance on your part, is the requirement reasonable? How many past franchisees have lost their exclusive territories? Ask to talk to one of them.
        - Can your franchise be revoked? How? Do you get any of your franchise fee back?
        - How long is the franchise agreement for? Does it automatically renew? Are there any additional fees upon renewal? Under what circumstances would they refuse to renew your franchise?
        - Can you sell your franchise? Do they receive part of the money? Does the new buyer have to pay the parent company anything to take over the franchise. (This will dilute the value of your company should you decide to sell it)
        - Can you terminate your franchise if it is not working out for you? Is there a penalty for early termination?
        - What training is included in the franchise fee? Is there other training available, and if so, how much does it cost?
        - Can you have more than one location? What is the fee for additional locations?

3. *Check the company's credit rating.* Call Dun & Bradstreet at (800) 362-2255 to get a D&B report on the franchisor—have your credit card handy before you call since there is a charge for this information.

4. *Talk to current owners.* The disclosure document must list the names and addresses of other people who currently own and operate the franchise. Call a number of owners to find out about the company. Ask them how the information presented in the disclosure document compares to their actual experience with the company. Ask if they are happy with the company, the training they received, and the financial arrangements? If they had it to do over, would they buy this franchise again? How long did it take them to break even? How much are they making now? What do they like most about the company? What one area do they feel could stand improvement?

5. *Investigate earnings claims.* Earnings claims are only estimates. Make sure you understand the basis for a seller's earnings claims. Remember that broad sales claims about a successful area of business — such as, "Be a part of our four billion dollar industry" — may have no bearing on the likelihood of your own success.

6. *Shop around: compare franchises with other available business opportunities.* Talk to some competing franchise owners and ask them why they went with the company they did and not the company you are considering. You may discover that other companies offer benefits not available from the first company you considered.

7. *Listen carefully to the sales presentation.* Some sales tactics should signal caution. For example, if you are pressured to sign immediately "because prices will go up tomorrow," or "another

buyer wants this deal," you should slow down, not speed up, your purchase decision. A seller with a good offer doesn't have to use this sort of pressure.

8. ***Get the seller's promises in writing.*** Any important promises you get from a salesperson should be written into the contract you sign. If the salesperson says one thing and the contract says nothing about it or says something different, your contract is what counts. Request that all documents, advertisements, literature, projections, videos, spreadsheets, etc. that have been given or shown to you by the franchisor be incorporated in the contract as attachments. This ensures that any promises made in these documents become part of the franchisor's legal obligations. Quite often more is said in sales literature than the franchisor is comfortable including in the contract. Whatever the reasons, if the seller balks at putting verbal promises in writing, you should be alert to potential problems. You might want to look for another business.

9. ***Consider getting professional advise.*** Unless you have had considerable business experience, you may want to get your lawyer, your accountant, or a business advisor to read the disclosure document and proposed contract to counsel you and help you get the best deal. Remember the initial money and time you spend on getting professional assistance and verifying facts, such as making phone calls to owners, could save you from a major loss or bad investment.

The following phone numbers are for the state agencies administering franchise disclosure laws. Call them for specific state regulations and to assist you with any problems.

California .... (213) 620-6515
Hawaii .... (808) 548-2021

Illinois	(217) 782-1279
Indiana	(317) 232-6681
Maryland	(301) 576-6360
Michigan	(517) 373-7117
Minnesota	(612) 296-6328
New York	(212) 341-2211
North Dakota	(701) 224-4712
Oregon	(503) 378-4387
Rhode Island	(401) 277-3048
South Dakota	(605) 733-4013
Virginia	(804) 786-7751
Washington	(206) 753-6928
Wisconsin	(608) 266-8559

The International Franchise Association at (800) 543-1038 sells a *Franchise Opportunities Guide* for $15 and a pamphlet of basic information called *Investigate Before Investing* for $5.

Business Opportunity Companies

Business opportunities are much like franchises. They allow you to use their name and distribute their product or they sell you some specific equipment and materials. You receive less training and much less (if any) on-going support. They exert no control over the way you run your business—you are entirely on your own. The initial fee is less than what you would pay for a franchise and you usually do not pay any royalties. Often, a business opportunity buyer can operate a profitable business, either full or part-time, from home, out of a van, or even from the trunk of a car.

These organizations are regulated and monitored in much the same way as franchises. They are bound by the same disclosure laws as a franchise. See the last section for the details.

Unfortunately, this industry has the reputation of being a group of quick-hit artists who promise a lot, sell you their product, and then quickly move on to the next investor. Not all of them fall into this category, but do be extra careful. Don't buy on the spur of the moment;

if the offer is legitimate, it will be around next week. Be sure to call several others who have already purchased this business opportunity. Also check with the Better Business Bureau, the state attorney general and the state consumer affairs office of the secretary of state to see if any complaints have been filed against them. As always, have your attorney review and explain all documents to you before signing anything.

Below are the phone numbers for those states with specific business opportunity laws. Call them for current regulations.

California .... (619) 237-6553
Colorado .... (303) 566-4560
Florida .... (800) 435-7352
Georgia .... (404) 651-8600
Indiana .... (317) 232-6331
Iowa .... (515) 281-4441
Kentucky .... (502) 564-2200
Louisiana .... (504) 342-7373
Maine .... (207) 582-8760
Maryland .... (301) 576-6360
Michigan .... (517) 373-7117
Nebraska .... (402) 471-2171
New Hampshire .... (603) 271-3641
North Carolina .... (919) 733-3924
Ohio .... (800) 282-0515
Oklahoma .... (405) 521-2451
South Carolina .... (803) 734-2168
South Dakota .... (605) 773-4823
Texas .... (512) 475-1769
Utah .... (801) 533-6601
Virginia .... (800) 451-1525
Washington .... (206) 753-6938

Multi-Level Marketing Companies

In this business scenario, also known as MLM, you not only sell products yourself, but you recruit others to also sell as well. You receive a commission on everything you purchase and everything they purchase. Your agreement will dictate how far down the line you earn your commissions.   If it specifies three levels, you receive commission on everything purchased by you, by everyone you recruit and by everyone they recruit. The MLM shows you how you can make large sums of money by selling the product yourself and recruiting several individuals to do the same. The truth is that 90% of everyone who has ever sold for this type of company is no longer doing it. Examples of companies that use multi-level compensation techniques are Amway, Shaklee, and the Fuller Brush Company.

You really have two businesses when you get involved with a MLM. You have a retail selling business and you also have a recruiting business. Your primary emphasis has to be on selling the product and not on recruiting, or the business turns into an illegal pyramid. However, you only make lots of money if you recruit lots of people. Catch 22.

If you decide to pursue this type of venture, look for a sponsor who is enthusiastic about the company and its products and is successful in selling the product. You want a sponsor who will take the time necessary to help you succeed. The better your sponsor does indirectly affects how well you will do. Your sponsor's enthusiasm and positive attitude will keep you charged with energy. When you recruit others, you must take the same thorough approach to nurturing them that your sponsor takes with you. You must continually *motivate, manage,* and *train* your down-line staff.

When looking for a MLM company, find one that has a quality product or service that you enjoy using and selling. Also pick one that has been around long enough to have a track record. Don't be sold by high-pressure, hype, or emotionalism. Talk to other recruits and see if they get paid on time, receive product on time, and are making as much as they thought they would. Make sure the product is reasonably priced and that *you* can sell enough to make a living even if all your recruits quit (since many people quit within just a few months of signing up).

Ask how many levels down you will be paid and the commission rate for each level. Be suspicious if the company requires you to buy over $500 worth of start-up inventory or if the company won't buy back unsold inventory. Also beware of any MLM that is being sold as a "get rich quick" scheme.

The good news is that MLMs offer a relatively risk-free way to start a business; the bad news is that you don't get paid until you sell product. But then again, tens of thousands of individuals supplement their income or even make a living working for MLMs. If you would like more information and a listing of MLMs, call Down-Line News/Books at (212) 355-1071 and ask for *The Multi-Level/Network Marketing Resource Directory*. It sells for $28.00.

How to Check Out Business Scams

If you are even the least bit suspicious of an opportunity being presented to you, call the state Business Opportunity Office and State Attorney General's Office in your own state and in the state where the business is located, if different. Twenty-two states have Business Opportunity Laws and have special offices that will assist you in checking out salesman's or company claims. Their phone numbers are listed a few pages back in the Business Opportunity Companies section.

Financial Projections

This is absolutely the most important step in your pre-planning evaluation. Even if you ignore every other suggestion in this book, prepare these projections. Skip this section and your chances for success drop dramatically.

You will be preparing some likely scenarios in this section. These are known as *proforma financial statements* (meaning that you are projecting figures based on your best estimates). Don't worry if you don't have any formal financial background. All you need to do is enter some assumptions and I will walk you through the calculations. You will be preparing proforma income statements (sometimes called profit & loss statements), and proforma cash flow statements.

The Income Statement shows **Revenues** (sales), **Expenses** (costs), and **Net Income** (profit or loss) for a specific period of time based on when you *make* the sales and when you *incur* the costs. The Cash Flow Statement shows **Cash Receipts** (money *received*), **Cash Disburse-**

ments (money *paid*) and **Monthly Cash Surplus or Deficit** (how much money you have left) at a specified point in time based on when you *receive* the cash and when you *pay* your bills.

Running out of cash (cash flow) is one of the mistakes that can kill your business. You can be consistently making a profit and still run out of cash. In the excitement of starting your own company, it is easy to overlook the time span between making a sale and getting paid. Often this wait is long, and without proper planning you can simply run out of money. This exercise will assist you in avoiding this pitfall.

Since the information and format of these reports vary slightly by industry type, I have included instructions for completing the worksheets for several industries:

- **Retail**

  Any business where you sell products directly to the consumers. Examples would be a shoe store, a candy shop, a hardware store, etc.

- **Wholesale Distribution**

  Any business where you sell products to other businesses who in turn sell to the end-users. Examples are distributors or jobbers who sell to retailers. A distributor might sell tires to service stations who in turn resell them to their customers.

- **Manufacturing**

  Any business that actually makes the products it sells. Examples are cabinet makers, sheet metal fabricators, bakeries, etc.

- **Contract Services**

  Any business engaged in doing specific jobs for customers where purchased materials are used. Examples are plumbers, painters, roofing companies, etc.

- **Professional Services**

    Any business that primarily provides a service. Typically professional services require little or materials. Examples are accountants, attorneys, programming services, court reporters, and graphic artists. Professional services usually bill by the hour rather than by the job.

- **General**

    Any business that does not fall into one of the above categories.

The worksheets and more detailed instructions for completing them are located in Appendix A in the back of this book.

Create one projection for each month for one full year. The figures will change month by month as your sales increase, you purchase additional inventory, you hire additional personnel, etc. Try to be as accurate as possible. This will give you a realistic view of your income and cash flow for the first 12 months. Make twelve (12) copies each of the Projected Income Statement and Cash Flow Statement and begin filling in your projections at this point. Do them in pencil.

Other Important Sources of Information

Appraisers. To locate qualified business appraisers, contact the Institute of Business Appraisers, PO Box 1447, Boynton Beach, FL 33435, (407) 732-3202 or the American Society of Appraisers, PO Box 17265, Washington, DC 20041 (800) 272-8258. Both groups conduct certification programs.

Brokers. To find reputable business brokers, contact the International Business Brokers' Association, 118 Silver Hill Road, Concord, MA 01742, (508) 369-5254. The IBBA bestows a designation called "certified business intermediary "(CBI). To earn it, brokers must take classes and pass examinations.

Creating Effective Boards for Private Enterprise. Once you've got your business up and running, buy this book by John Ward (Jossey-

Bass, 1992, $25.95). It offers concrete suggestions on how and when to select board members, how to put them to use, and more.

Organizational Documents: A Guide for Partnerships and Professional Corporations. This book by Mark F. Murray is a good introduction to the rules and reasoning behind standard partnership and incorporation documents. Buy-sell agreements, employment contracts, and partnership agreements are among the documents discussed. Published by the American Institute of Certified Public Accountants, this 124 page book costs $25.00. The book is also available on diskette for $40. To order call AICPA at (800) 334-6961.

Professional/Venture Groups. One of the best sources of outside advice. Groups range from local networking clubs to branch offices of national organizations like the National Federation of Independent Business (202-554-9000) based in Washington, D.C. Consider only groups that allow you to "sample" a meeting for free.

Service Corps of Retired Executives (SCORE). This Small Business Administration program provides free individual sessions with seasoned business veterans who will advise you about your venture. Call the SBA at (800) 827-5722 for more information.

Small Business Development Center. Programs are operated in 47 states and are partially funded by the Small Business Administration. Individual business consulting and seminars on special topics important to small businesses are free or very inexpensive. Call the SBA at (800) 827-5722 for more information.

The Whole Work Catalog. This free publication covers books and periodicals on alternative workstyles and careers. It is available from The New Careers Center, 1515 23rd Street, P.O. Box 297-CT, Boulder, CO 80306 or call (303) 447-1087.

101 Best Businesses to Start. If you are having trouble thinking of that perfect business, browse through this book by Sharon Kahn and The Philip Lief Group (Doubleday, 1988) for some good ideas.

All glory comes from daring to begin.

Eugene Ware

Chapter 2

Developing an Action Plan

Having a good plan of action gives you the best chance of both survival and prosperity. In fact, if you rely purely on instinct to guide your business, instead of a written plan, my experience indicates that you're headed for trouble. Spend the time necessary to develop a *thorough* plan. I firmly believe that you severely limit your chances for success if you start your venture with only vague and ill-defined goals. You will end up with a lot of activity and only minimal results. There are better and smarter ways to run a business than by brute force.

Despite the critical nature of a plan, many owners drag their feet when it comes to preparing a written document. They argue that their marketplace changes too fast or that they just don't have enough time. But just as a builder won't begin construction without a blueprint, eager business owners shouldn't rush into a new venture without a plan. Without a plan you just end up working day-to-day with no long term goal or focus, drifting from here to there, wherever the currents of life lead you. Most failures don't plan to fail, they just fail to plan.

Before you can commit your plan to writing you must determine why you are starting your business. What is the most important reason for your company's existence? Are you primarily in business to make the most money you can, regardless of the quality of your product or service? Or do you want to produce the best product or provide the best service, regardless of the cost? Or maybe you want to treat your employees the best, regardless of the cost? Do you want to grow the company as big as you can and are you willing to pump 100% of the profits back into growth at the expense of raises, bonuses, and profit sharing? More than likely, it's a mixture of all the above and maybe more. Collectively these are known as your business objectives.

Business Objectives

The achievements of an organization are the result of the combined efforts of each individual in the organization working toward common objectives. These should be realistic, clearly understood by everyone in the organization, and reflect the organization's basic character and personality.

If the organization is to fulfill its objectives, it should strive to meet certain other fundamental requirements.

1. There should be highly capable, innovative people throughout the organization. These people should continually strive to upgrade their skills and capabilities. Techniques that are good today will be outdated in the future, and people should always be looking for new and better ways to do their work.

2. The organization should have objectives and leadership which generates enthusiasm at all levels. People in important management positions should not only be enthusiastic themselves, they should be selected for their ability to engender enthusiasm among associates. There can be no place, especially among the people charged with management responsibility, for half-hearted interest or half-hearted effort.

3. The organization should conduct its affairs with uncompromising honesty and integrity. People at every level should be expected to adhere to the highest standard of business ethics and understand that anything less is totally unacceptable. As a practical matter, ethical conduct cannot be assured by written policies or codes; it must be an integral part of the organization, a deeply ingrained tradition that is passed from one generation of employees to another.

4. Even though an organization is made up of people fully meeting the first three requirements, all levels should work in unison toward common objectives, recognizing that it is only through effective, cooperative effort that the ultimate in efficiency and achievement can be obtained.

Below is an example of one company's business objectives. I hope that it provides some insight and helps focus your ideas.

Objective Number One— PROFIT.

To achieve sufficient profit to finance our company growth and to provide the resources we need to achieve our other corporate objectives.

In our economic system, the profit we generate from our operations is the ultimate source of the funds we need to prosper and grow. It is the one absolutely essential measure of our corporate performance over the long term. Only if we continue to meet our profit objectives can we achieve our other corporate objectives.

Our long standing policy has been to reinvest substantial portions of our profits back into two primary areas. First, back into the company to finance growth, and second, back into our people through our profit sharing plan. We have come to depend on this reinvestment of profits to finance these areas.

Profits vary from year to year, of course, reflecting the changing economic conditions and varying demands for our products. Our needs for capital also vary, and we depend on cash short-term loans to meet those needs when profits or other cash sources are inadequate. However, loans are costly and must be repaid; thus, our objective is to rely on reinvested profits as our main source of capital.

Meeting our profit objectives requires that we design and develop each and every product so that it is considered a good value by our customers, yet is priced to include an adequate profit. Maintaining this competitiveness in the marketplace also requires that we perform all our functions as economically as possible.

Profit is not something that can be put off until tomorrow; it must be achieved today. It means that all our jobs must be done correctly and efficiently. The day-to-day performance of each individual adds to—or subtracts from—our profit. Profit is the responsibility of all.

Objective Number Two— COMMITMENT TO EXCELLENCE.

To provide products and services of the highest quality and the greatest possible value to our customers, thereby gaining and holding their respect and loyalty.

The continued growth and success of our company will be assured only if we offer our customers innovative products that fill real needs and provide lasting value, and that are supported by a wide variety of useful services after the sale.

Satisfying customer needs requires the active participation of everyone in the company. It demands a total commitment to excellence, a commitment that begins with the person answering the phone and extends to every phase of our organization. Products must be designed to provide superior performance and features, and be developed and marketed at a reasonable cost.

Careful attention to quality not only enables us to meet or exceed customer expectations, but it also has a direct and substantial effect on our operating costs and profitability. Doing a job right the first time, and doing it consistently, sharply reduces costs and contributes significantly to higher productivity and profits.

Once a quality product is delivered to the customer, it must be supported with prompt, efficient services of the same high quality. This means striving always to achieve excellence in every aspect of our business. In the final analysis, it will be our history of performance and our reputation for quality service that will allow us to realize our full potential.

Good communications are essential to an effective sales effort. Our customers must feel we have a clear understanding of their needs and a genuine interest in providing proper, effective solutions to their problems.

We want all our people, regardless of whatever role they play on our team, to make a commitment to excellence in the performance of their contribution to the products and services our company provides.

Objective Number Three— GROWTH.

To let our growth be limited only by our profits and our ability to develop and produce innovative products that satisfy real customer needs.

How large should a company become? Some feel that when a company reaches a certain size there is no point in letting it grow further. Others feel that bigness is an objective in itself. We do not believe that bigger is better

59

for its own sake; however, for at least two basic reasons, continuous growth in sales and profits is essential for us to achieve our other objectives.

In the first place, by the very nature of our business, we serve a dynamic and rapidly growing segment of our society. To remain static would be to lose ground. We cannot maintain a position of strength and leadership in our fields without sustained and profitable growth.

In the second place, growth is important in order to attract and hold high caliber people. These individuals will align their future only with a company that offers them considerable opportunity for personal progress. Opportunities are greater and more challenging in a growing company.

Objective Number Four— OUR PEOPLE.

To help our people share in the company's success which they make possible; to provide job security based on their performance; to insure them a pleasant work environment; to recognize their achievements; and to help them gain a sense of satisfaction and accomplishment from their work.

We are proud of the people in our organization, their performance, their attitude toward their jobs and toward the company. The company has been built around the individual, the personal dignity of each, and the recognition of personal achievements. We believe in our people. We want all our people to believe in each other.

Relationships within the company depend upon a spirit of cooperation among individuals and groups, and an attitude of trust and understanding on everyone's part. These relationships will be good only if employees have faith in the motives and integrity of their peers, supervisors, and the company itself. We want to create an atmosphere of camaraderie and cohesiveness that generates the kind of enthusiasm and energy that propels a winning organization.

Job security is an important company objective. Over the years, the company has achieved a steady growth in employment by consistently developing good new products. The company wants our people to have stable, long-term careers—dependent, of course, upon satisfactory job performance.

We want to instill in all employees an awareness that their best efforts are essential and that they will share in the company's success. This is reflected in our profit sharing plan.

Advancement is based solely upon individual initiative, ability, and demonstrated accomplishment. Since we promote from within whenever possible, all employees should continually broaden their capabilities and prepare themselves for more responsible jobs.

We want people to enjoy their work and to be proud of their accomplishments. This means we must make sure that each person receives the recognition he or she needs and deserves. In the final analysis, people at all levels determine the character and strength of our company.

Objective Number Five— CONSISTENT MANAGEMENT STYLE.

To foster initiative and creativity by supporting and encouraging the individual and facilitating involvement in problem solving and decision making.

Is there a best management style? Democratic managers are accused of being too soft and easy, while their autocratic counterparts are often called too tough and domineering. We believe in empathic, people-oriented management utilizing a mixture of directive and supportive styles. We feel that providing direction is not enough, we must also provide encouragement in a supportive atmosphere where individuals are treated as competent, contributing members of the team. It is management's responsibility to provide the resources and working conditions needed for the accomplishment of our goals.

The successful practice of this management technique is a two way street. Management must be sure that each individual understands the immediate objectives, as well as corporate goals and policies. Thus another primary management responsibility is communication and mutual understanding. Conversely, employees must take interest in their own problems and be willing to stick their necks out when they have something to contribute. This management style offers opportunity for individual freedom and contribution; it also imposes an obligation for everyone to exercise initiative and enthusiasm.

It is important to recognize that cooperation between individuals and between departments is essential to our growth and success. We are a single company whose overall strength is derived from mutually helpful relationships and frequent interaction among departments.

It is important, as well, for everyone to recognize there are some policies which must be established and maintained on a company-wide basis. We welcome recommendations on these company-wide policies from all levels, but we expect adherence to them at all times.

Levi Strauss & Co.'s values are outlined in their Aspirations Statement:

> We all want a company that our people are proud of and committed to, where all employees have an opportunity to contribute, learn, grow, and advance based on merit, not politics or background. We want our people to feel respected, treated fairly, listened to, and involved. Above all, we want satisfaction from accomplishments and friendships, balanced personal and professional lives, and to have fun in our endeavors.
>
> When we describe the kind of company we want to be in the future, what we are talking about is building on the foundation we have inherited: affirming the best of our company's traditions, closing gaps that may exist between principles and practices, and updating some of our values to reflect contemporary circumstances.
>
> What type of leadership is necessary to make our aspirations a reality?
>
> **New Behaviors:** Leadership that exemplifies directness, openness to influence, commitment to the success of others, willingness to acknowledge our own contributions to problems, personal accountability, teamwork, and trust. Not only must we model these behaviors but we must coach others to adopt them.
>
> **Diversity:** Leadership that values a diverse work force (age, sex, ethnic group, etc.) at all levels of the organization, diversity in experience, and diversity in perspectives. We have committed to taking full advantage of the rich backgrounds and abilities of all our people and to promoting a greater diversity in positions of influence. Differing points of view will be sought; diversity will be valued and honestly rewarded, not suppressed.
>
> **Recognition:** Leadership that provides greater recognition—both financial and psychic—for individuals and

teams that contribute to our success. Recognition must be given to all who contribute: those who create and innovate and also those who continually support the day-to-day business requirements.

Ethical Management Practices: Leadership that epitomizes the stated standards of ethical behavior. We must provide clarity about our expectations and must enforce these standards through the corporation.

Communications: Leadership that is clear about company, unit and individual goals and performance. People must know what is expected of them and receive timely, honest feedback on their performance and career aspirations.

Empowerment: Leadership that increases the authority and responsibility of those closest to our products and customers. By actively pushing responsibility, trust, and recognition into the organization, we can harness and release the capabilities of all our people.

As a third example, another company's credo states that permanent success is possible only when modern industry realizes that:

1. Service to its customers comes first;

2. Service to its employees and management comes second;

3. Service to the community comes third; and

4. Service to the stockholders comes last.

Such statements might seem like motherhood and apple pie to those who have not seen the way a clear sense of purpose and values can affect key business decisions. In the 1980s, a well-known company faced a disaster when some of its products were tampered with, resulting in several deaths. The company immediately responded by pulling all of this particular product off the shelves of retail outlets. Substantial amounts of this product were destroyed even though they were tested and found to be safe. Although the immediate cost was significant, this organization had no alternatives given its credo.

Purpose Statement

This first exercise will assist you in developing a purpose statement which will provide the focal point for your plan. It lets everyone know where the company is going and how it's going to get there. A purpose statement expresses business goals, values, and practices intended to win commitment and support for an organization over the long term.

A well-developed purpose statement provides direction and definition to the business. It establishes what the organization wants to succeed in, and what it does. It will help you keep focused when you are presented with new business opportunities. A typical purpose statement might read "We are in the business of developing, manufacturing, and marketing sealing coatings, adhesives and other bonding agents for use under extreme pressure or temperature." This defines exactly what your company does, is, and why you are in business.

With the above purpose statement in mind, suppose a prospective customer walks into your office and wants you to develop an adhesive that will easily dissolve in water for gluing paper labels on plastic bottles. Do you do it or not? Before saying "Sure, hey business is business, right?", look at your purpose statement—does this product fit in with your long term goals? Do you have expertise in this area? Will this project divert your attention from your real business? Being too fragmented and losing your focus can destroy your company. *Specialization wins.* Find a market, learn everything about it, and be the best company doing it. It's tough turning down business. But it can be fatal trying to support too many products.

But what if the opportunity looks *really good*—maybe even better than your original "core" business? Analyze it again, carefully and objectively. If it still looks good and seems to have long-term potential, do it. The "rule" is intended to stop you from trying to be everything to everybody. If you feel there is real potential, then be an opportunist. But make your decisions based on fact and not emotion.

Here are eight good reasons to say "no" to a potential customer.

1. **The job is outside your expertise.** Say no if you are asked to do something that you don't know how to do.

2. **The job is outside your business focus.** Maybe you know how to do it but it falls outside your primary purpose. Don't feel that you must offer a "complete range" of products. Unless an activity contributes 15 to 20 percent return on investment, you shouldn't do it.

3. **The timing is bad.** Say no if you don't feel you can meet the schedule.

4. **There's not enough profit in the job.** If you can't agree on a price that is acceptable to you, don't take the job.

5. **The project is poorly defined.** How can you possibly quote a price when you don't know what you are bidding on?

6. **Taking on the project will interfere with your overall business.** It does you no good to get a new customer at the expense of losing an old one. Your business will end up like a revolving door with customers leaving as fast as you can get new ones—this creates lots of activity but little profit.

7. **You won't or can't do a good job.** Doing less than your best is bad for business in general. It's better to turn down work than to get a bad reputation.

8. **The job is too risky.** Say no if you feel the customer or the job is a bad risk in any way.

A purpose statement also helps you distinguish your organization from others by identifying your company's unique qualities. It tells your people how and where to channel their efforts to sustain company strength and your competitive advantage. When your purpose is clearly communicated, employees know what to work on and, as competitive pressure increases, where to put their emphasis.

A purpose statement can be simple, such as IBM's cornerstone of "Customer service, excellence, and respect for the individual" or J.C. Penney's "To serve the public, as nearly as we can, to its complete satisfaction" or Honda's "Quality in all jobs — learn, think, analyze, and improve." These messages have provided meaning and a sense of purpose to employees for many years.

A purpose statement can be several sentences long such as this one from a Midwestern company of 2000 employees.

> Be the quality leader and the most cost-effective supplier in each of our markets. Create the opportunity for each employee to grow, participate, and be recognized as a valuable contributing member. Increasing after-tax earnings by an average of 18% per year and working toward revenue growth of 14% per year.

Mastercare, the autoservice subsidiary of Bridgestone/Firestone, says in part, that their company's goal is "to provide their service-buying public with a superior buying experience that will encourage them to return willingly and to share their experiences with others" (word of mouth selling).

Your purpose statement should express the values of your organization—how your company wants to be seen both internally and externally. It defines what is acceptable and what is not. A well thought out purpose statement can simplify some decision making by defining what is OK and what's not. Now take a moment and write your purpose statement.

_____

_____

_____

_____

_____

_____

_____

_____

67

Start-up Checklist

The first phase of your plan is quite simple. It just involves listing the items necessary to get your business started. List as many items as you can think of.

Keep track of all the money you spend relating to your new business, even the money spent prior to officially starting your business, as many of these expenses will be considered business related and therefore deductible for tax purposes.

Here is a partial list to help you get started:

❑ Read the rest of this book. Many of the items on this list are covered in detail later in this book.

❑ Choose a name for your business. See *On Choosing a Name* in Chapter 9.

❑ Draw up a partnership agreement if you are setting up your business with one or more partners. Include a Buy-Sell Agreement. It is best to have an attorney help you with this. It is important to do this before you start so that all parties agree on the key issues and you have pre-defined procedures to follow should the partnership not work out. Review the *Guidelines for Partnerships* in Chapter 1.

❑ Raise the necessary capital. See Chapter 3.

❑ Pick a location for your business.

❑ Sign the lease papers for your office or store — it is recommended that your lease contract be contingent upon the approval of all your permits and licenses.

❑ Locate an accountant and set up your books.

❑ Obtain a business license from your city's business office.

❑ File for any other special licenses you may need.

❑ If your business will be known by anything other than your full real name, you must file a Fictitious Business Name Statement with your county clerk.

❑ File for a Federal Tax ID Number (or Federal Employer Identification Number - EIN). Request form SS-4 from the IRS. You may be able to use your social security number if you are operating as a sole proprietor and have no employees (you, as owner, do not count as an employee). Check with your accountant. You'll need this number before you can open a business bank account.

A new IRS procedure allows you to receive your EIN over the phone. You must first get a copy of form SS4, available from most Social Security Administration or IRS offices, or you may order one by calling (800) 829-3676. After filling out this form, you may either mail it in, in which case you will receive your EIN in 4-6 weeks, or call the special Tele-TINS number on the back of the form. If you phone the information in, you will receive your EIN instantly over the phone.

❑ File for a State Employer Identification Number from your state employment department.

❑ File for a Sellers Permit (also known as a resale number or resale permit) from your state board of equalization. Every business that sells goods must have one.

❑ File the necessary paperwork with the state for collecting and reporting sales tax.

❑ If you will have employees, fill out the necessary paperwork for collecting and reporting payroll taxes with both the state and federal tax boards.

❑ Contact your insurance agent about a workman's compensation insurance policy if it is required in your state.

❑ It may be necessary for you to register with your State Department of Consumer Affairs. Check with your accountant to see if this is required in your area.

❑ If you will be handling food, you may need to obtain a permit from your county health department.

❑ Get medical insurance.

❑ Order a business phone.

❑ Order utility hookups for gas, water, and electricity.

❑ Open business checking and savings accounts.

❑ Set up a retirement account with the help of your accountant. See Chapter 8.

❑ Establish a line of credit with your bank if necessary.

❑ Set up credit card processing with your bank. See chapter 8.

❑ Contact local credit agencies for doing credit checks. See Chapter 8.

❑ Order business cards, letterhead, envelopes, labels, and any special business forms you need such as employment and credit applications, installment contracts, workorders, invoices, billing statements, gift certificates, etc.

❑ Order office furniture and supplies.

❑ Contact your suppliers and order your initial inventory.

❑ Order display fixtures and a cash register.

❑ Decide how many employees you need and draft job descriptions for each position.

❑ Interview and hire employees.

❑ Develop marketing materials.

❑ Coordinate the painting or construction of business signs.

❑ Coordinate "grand opening" advertising.

❑ Train your employees.

Setting Goals

Your goals don't start in the brain, they start in your heart.

What is a goal? A goal defines a desired result. It must be specific, measurable, and have a clear deadline. It should be both realistic and challenging. Setting a goal too low encourages mediocre performance; even a dead fish can float downstream. But don't set your goals too high either; people won't buy into unrealistic goals. Make your goals as challenging as possible but still believable and attainable.

Goals are a great opportunity to challenge yourself. Never be satisfied with past performance; you can always better your best. Asked which of his works he would select as his masterpiece, architect Frank Lloyd Wright, at the age of 83, replied "My next one."

Make sure that your goals address the most important issues facing you and your new company. Don't spend precious time doing the wrong things. Work smart.

> **Businesses do not usually fail because of a lack of effort or enthusiasm, but because of errors in strategy, planning, or execution.**

Goals define the big picture. As you begin your execution, you will break each goal into several projects (planned undertakings to reach your goal) and each project will be further broken into several tasks (single, well-defined parts of a project).

A goal stated as "I want to focus my activities on getting sales my first year" is a poor goal. It is too vague to be of any real value and it lacks commitment. "I want" is merely desire, "I will" is real commitment. "I will generate sales of $50,000 per month by March, $55,000 by June, $60,000 by September, and $65,000 by December while maintaining a 10% pre-tax profit." That's a goal.

The process of goal creation can be broken into seven steps.
1. Identify the goal.
2. Set a deadline for accomplishing it.
3. List all the obstacles to be overcome.
4. List the people and organizations you will need to work with to accomplish the goal.
5. List the skills and knowledge you will need.
6. Develop an action plan.
7. List the benefits of achieving the goal (to make sure it is really important).

When thinking about your goals, consider your vision (what do you want your company to become), your purpose (why are you starting your company), your objectives (what do you want to accomplish), your resources (what do you have available and what will you need), your strategy (how are you going to accomplish your desires), and your policies (what are your acceptable rules of conduct).

Your first year goals might center around dollar sales volume, dollar profit, number of customers, building of staff (number of employees), production capacity, market penetration, cost containment, etc.

Here is an example:

Goal: "I will generate $800,000 in sales by December 31st."

After you have identified your goal, break it into projects.

Projects: Generate $25,000 in gross sales in January.
Generate $30,000 in gross sales in February.
Generate $40,000 in gross sales in March.
etc.

Now break each project into several tasks. Before writing down a task, ask yourself:

What is the purpose of doing this task?
What am I trying to accomplish?
Is this the most efficient way of accomplishing it?
How much will this activity cost?
Who is going to do it?
Is this the most important thing this person or your money could be doing?

Project: Generate $25,000 in gross sales in January.

Tasks:

- Develop direct mail marketing piece announcing Grand Opening by Dec. 1st.

- Have printer print 10,000 copies of marketing flyer by December 10th.

- Obtain a mailing list of all the homeowners within 35 miles of my location by Dec. 15th.

- Mail 8,000 Grand Opening flyers by Dec. 20th.

- Distribute 2,000 Grand Opening flyers by hand to the following neighborhoods ...... on Dec. 27th.

- Contact newspaper by Dec 15th and place "Grand Opening Special" advertisement to run every other day from Dec. 20th through Jan. 31st.

If you don't have clear goals, no amount of fact gathering or the trying out of different tactics will work for you. You will continue to dissipate your energy, and inevitably end up as a pawn of those who do have goals, or of the forces of nature and the economy.

You must have some pretty strong personal reasons for wanting to start your own business. These personal goals are probably the driving force behind your business goals. Before you write down your business goals, take a few minutes to examine these personal goals. Your business and personal goals must be consistent with each other. If your personal goal is to take a six week vacation next year, then your business goals must ensure that your business is correctly structured to allow you to take the time off.

First list five personal goals for the next year, ranked from most to least important. Make sure they are reasonable, attainable, and they have specific deadlines. Make sure they don't create insurmountable conflicts with each other, given the fact that you have limited time and resources available to accomplish them.

1. _____

_____

_____

_____

_____

_____

_____

2. _____

_____

_____

_____

_____

_____

3. _____

_____

_____

_____

_____

_____

_____

_____

_____

4. _____

_____

_____

_____

_____

_____

_____

_____

_____

5. _____

_____

_____

_____

_____

_____

_____

_____

75

Now do the same thing with your business goals.

1. _____

_____

_____

_____

_____

_____

_____

_____

2. _____

_____

_____

_____

_____

_____

_____

_____

3. _____

_____

_____

_____

_____

_____

_____

4. _____

_____

_____

_____

_____

_____

_____

_____

5. _____

_____

_____

_____

_____

_____

_____

_____

Now on a separate piece of paper, break each goal into several projects. Each project must also have a specific deadline and someone responsible for either doing it or seeing to it that it is done. Repeat this process breaking projects into individual tasks, again with due dates and specific responsibilities. The combined tasks from all your goals will become the basis for your first year's action plan.

Next organize your resources to achieve these goals. Roughly calculate the costs of implementing your plans. Make sure your goals, projects, and tasks are realistic based on your resources. If you find your goals are a bit too aggressive or not aggressive enough, now is the time to alter them.

Most organizations go through fairly predictable growth cycles, which look something like a staircase. At each growth phase there is substantial risk of failure as the organization attempts to climb to the next step.

In the heat of growth, many companies do not realize that there are inherent limits to growth. These limits are determined by the infrastructure which is in place, and by the limitations imposed by financial and human resources. Growth really cannot be pushed beyond the capabilities of your people and the organization to absorb it. An organization with no slack, in which human and financial resources are taxed to the limit, is extremely vulnerable to an unexpected or unplanned external or internal event. These events can be a lawsuit, a downturn in the economy, the loss of a key employee, development cost overruns, or any number of similar events.

If you do not build enough slack into your plans to deal with these developments, the impact of these unexpected events can be fatal.

Once you've finalized your goals, type them up and tape them to the wall in your office. Look at them every day. Explain them to your employees and make sure everyone understands them. It's easier to hit a target when everyone knows what the target is. Success is much more likely if you generate the feeling that the achievement of the goal is imperative, not merely desirable.

Most employees respond well to goals. They like a challenge. Hitting goals not only means success for the company, it also means satisfaction for the individuals.

It requires discipline to stick to your plan. Do not allow yourself to get sidetracked into wasting time on tension-relieving activities. Focus your efforts and energies on accomplishing your goals. Before you start a task, ask yourself if it is the most important thing you could be doing with your time. If it isn't, don't do it. Staying focused on your goals will be the most important element in attaining the success you desire.

**Focus your efforts and energies on
results not on activities.**

One secret of making sure your plan is implemented is to tie a substantial portion of your employee's compensation to it. This is known as rewarding the behavior you want to encourage.

Company Policy Manual

It's important to have a company policy manual, but they are very time consuming to write from scratch. For that very reason, I have included a complete sample manual in Appendix B at the end of this book. Feel free to copy any sections you want when making your own.

A good company policy manual ensures that everyone knows the rules up front. It can eliminate arguments and hurt feelings down the road.

Other Important Sources of Information

SBA's Business Plan Outlines. These outlines are industry specific and cost around $1.00 each. The series includes separate 15 to 20 page guides for retailers, service businesses, manufacturers, construction companies, and home-based businesses. Available at your local Small Business Administration office. Call (800) 827-5722.

Do-It-Yourself Market Research. By George E. Breen and Albert B. Blankenship (McGraw-Hill, 1989, $16.95), will introduce you to the fundamentals of market research. You'll find step-by-step instructions for conducting a research study, including many sample questionnaires.

The Entrepreneur's Guide to Venture Formation. This 40 page workbook is available from Ball State University for $12.95. It features extensive checklists to be used before and after writing your plan. Call (317) 285-1588.

Rent-A-Researcher, a program offered by some public libraries, is a reasonably priced research option. Researchers at the Cleveland Public Library's fee based service agency, the Cleveland Research Center, (216) 623-2999, consult more than 2,000 on-line databases for around $60.00 an hour.

No matter what business you are in, if you try to see how much you can give for a dollar, instead of how little, you're bound to succeed.

Chapter 3

Raising Money to Finance Your Venture

Going after the ideal amount of financing, rather than the smallest practical amount, is probably the most common mistake start-up entrepreneurs make. The next most common mistake is thinking that raising money for their company will be relatively easy.

Figure out how you can start your company with the least amount of cash. According to figures from the U.S. Small Business Administration, 89 percent of all businesses are started with $100,000 or less. Of these, more than 17 percent start with less than $5000! Entrepreneurs are famous for starting on a shoestring.

Attracting funds is easier if you are organized and have specific plans for the use of the money. Having a written **loan proposal** when approaching potential investors simplifies the process of obtaining funds; it shows that you are a savvy business person, and it provides the potential investor with a look at the current value of your business and how the loan will improve the worth of your company.

When writing a loan proposal, start with the summary. This single page should include the company name and address, your name and title, the line of business you are in, the amount sought, what the money is going to be used for, and where you are going to get the funds to pay it back.

On the next page you need to sell yourself, your partners, or top executives to the potential lender. Write a paragraph or two about each of you, stressing background, education, experience in the industry, business experience, and accomplishments.

Now start another page and describe your company. If you are just starting your business, write a one page summary explaining your plans and attach a copy of your action plan for the first year. If you are an established business, tell when your company was started; whether it is a sole proprietorship, a partnership or corporation; how many employees you have; your annual gross and net sales; your major products and customers; and who your major competition is. (Knowledge of your competition shows the potential investor that you are a good business person and understand your marketplace—this is important in building their confidence in you.)

Continue by describing your inventory in terms of size and rate of turnover. Explain the status of your receivables. How much money is owed you and how old are these debts? (for example, "Our total accounts receivable is $100,000 of which 91% is current, 6% is 30-60 days old and 3% is 60-90 days old.") Is the total amount spread over several customers or concentrated in a few? Next report on the status of your payables. How much do you owe? How long do you typically keep invoices before paying them?

Now talk about your projections for the future. Explain what makes you unique in your market and project your growth over the next year and five years.

Next assemble year-end balance sheets and income statements for the last three years, along with your current month's financial statements. You will also need a personal financial statement and copies of your last three years' tax returns. If you are just starting your business, insert your proforma financial and cash flow statements in place of actual financial statements.

On a new page, explain in detail exactly what the money will be used for. The more specific you are, the better. Next list the amount you are requesting, backed up by whatever documents you used to arrive at this figure. If you have worksheets that you used to calculate the amount needed, include them here.

The last section deals with your ability to repay the loan. If you are going to use the money to buy equipment, the term of the loan should not exceed its useful life. And the new piece of equipment should generate the funds necessary to pay off the note by increasing efficiency, reducing costs or increasing production. Explain how you arrived at your figures. Lending institutions also like to see an alternative method (alternative source of funds) for paying off the loan. This is their insurance if your first source of repayment funds doesn't materialize. Including this information in your initial proposal makes you look more sophisticated and increases your chances of getting funding.

If the money is being used for something other than equipment, you will still need to show how your return on the amount borrowed will be greater than the amount needed to repay the loan. If you have problems with your justifications, maybe you should reconsider your decision to borrow the money in the first place. Remember, this is not a game of big buildings, new equipment, fancy office space or impressing people, but rather a game of making money.

You have several options for obtaining the financing you need. Below is a short discussion of each.

Friendly Funds

Your own personal savings accounts, your family and your friends are the most likely sources of start-up capital. Make a list of individuals who might be gratified to be a part of your success. Draw up an agreement that states how much you are borrowing, when it will be paid back (monthly payments, quarterly payments, annual payments, or a balloon payment in say two to five years) and the interest rate. Both parties should date and sign this agreement. Have two witnesses who are not relatives also sign the document. The person lending you the money keeps the original agreement and you keep a copy.

Life Insurance Policies

Consider borrowing against the cash value of your life insurance policy. This is a source of funding that most forget about. Call your insurance agent for the amount you can borrow and any restrictions.

Pension Plans

Your 401(k), 403(b) or company profit sharing program can be tapped for start-up capital. Even when you include the taxes and penalties you must pay for early withdrawal, this may still be cheaper than a loan.

Refinance Your Home

You can tap the equity in your home by either taking out a new *first mortgage* or by adding a *second mortgage* on your property. If you have a low interest first mortgage and the rates are higher now, you would probably want to get a second mortgage. If the current rates are more that one percent lower than the rate on your first mortgage, it may be to your advantage to take out a new first, depending on the size of your current mortgage and the amount you want to borrow. Check with your accountant to see which is your best option.

Another type of "second" loan that may be available to you if you're in a less solid financial position is a *wrap-around loan*. The holder of the wrap-around note receives all your mortgage payments, keeps its portion, and forwards the amount due to the first mortgage company.

Personal Loan

A personal loan may be easier to negotiate than a business loan — especially when you are just starting out. Most banks will loan you money with your personal assets as collateral. This collateral can consist of any personal asset including marketable securities, bank accounts, certificates of deposit, real estate, IRA accounts, etc.

Line of Credit

A line of credit is a form of short-term financing (the period may run anywhere from 30 days to 2 years) available from your bank. It consists of a specific amount of money that you can draw upon for any business purpose. You only pay interest on the amount borrowed. For example, you may have a $50,000 credit line but if you have only used $15,000 of it, you will only be charged interest on $15,000. Often there is an annual commitment fee of anywhere from 1/2 to 1% of the total credit line amount since the bank reserves these funds specifically for your use.

Revolving Loan Funds

Depending on where you are and what you need money for, you may be eligible for a loan from a revolving loan fund. More than 30 states have such funds to support the working-capital and fixed-asset requirements of businesses that are expanding in targeted communities or hiring low-skill workers. Other revolving funds are sometimes sponsored by non-profit groups. Loans from revolving loan funds are usually granted at favorable rates and terms, and those loans may make it easier for your bank to come in with more money as a senior lender.

Even if there are no locally sponsored sources, there may still be loan funds that are capitalized by grants from the Economic Development Administration (EDA), an arm of the U.S. Department of Commerce, or from the Department of Housing and Urban Development (HUD). Typically, such funds are managed by local government, nonprofit development corporations, or rural planning districts. See the "State by State Sources of Funding" section later in this chapter for phone numbers.

Floor Planning Loans

A floor planning loan is a kind of inventory loan where the bank uses specific inventory items (usually big-ticket items) as collateral for the loan. Funds are made available just like with a line of credit; they are borrowed as needed and repaid in installments as inventory is sold and receivables are satisfied. Check with your bank.

Commercial Loans

Commercial loans are loans that have no installment payments. They have one single payment due at the end of the loan period. Banks typically write these loans for three to six months. Contact your local banker or accountant for more details.

Term Loans

A term loan is a loan granted for the purchase of a specific item. It is usually written for a term of five years. Your bank will only loan you 80 to 90% of the cost of the item. You make either monthly or quarterly payments consisting of principal and interest. The principal payments remain constant through the life of the loan, but the interest portion, which is computed on the outstanding balance, declines over the term of the note. Therefore, the payments are the largest in the beginning and gradually get smaller as time go on.

Federally Guaranteed Loans

The advantage of a loan guarantee is that it can prod a bank to lend more money and provide it for a longer period, often at a lower interest rate. The best known program is the **Small Business Administration's 7(a) loan-guarantee program**. These loans are guaranteed up to 90% by the SBA. For information, call your SBA regional office. Their number can be found in your telephone directory under U.S. Government or call the Small Business Answer Desk at (800) 827-5722 (for the hearing impaired, call (202) 205-7333) and ask for the names of certified (CLP) and preferred (PLP) lenders in your area. When working with one of these lenders, you can be confident that the lender knows the program and the paperwork will get processed quickly. These loans typically have a term of 12 years, which is longer than most banks would carry the paper on their own. Twenty-seven percent of all 7(a) loans go to start-ups.

It is also worth your while to investigate the loan guarantee program administered by the Department of Housing and Urban Development (HUD). This program operates through cities and towns (using **Com-**

munity Development Block Grant funds). Several states, among them California, Maine, and Mississippi, also have guarantee programs of their own.

The Farmers Home Administration's **Business and Industrial Loan Program** has a loan guarantee program that will guarantee up to 90% of loans being used to improve or establish businesses that preserve or create jobs for rural people. (Rural being defined as countryside or towns of up to 50,000) They can be contacted at FmHA, Department of Agriculture, 14th & Independence Avenue SW, Washington, DC 20250. Their phone number is (202) 447-4323.

Loan guarantees are available from the **Commercial Fisheries Financial Assistance Program** for the purchase of commercial fishing vessels and facilities. Contact the National Oceanic and Atmospheric Administration, National Marine Fisheries Service, Department of Commerce, Financial Services Division, F/TWI, 1825 Connecticut Avenue NW, Washington, DC 20235 or phone (206) 673-5424.

See also the Nonfarm Enterprise Loan program in the next section.

Direct Federal Loan Programs

The **Small Business Administration** can directly make loans up to $150,000. However, in order to qualify, you must have applied for an SBA guaranteed loan and have been turned down. Direct loan funds are very limited and sometimes only available to certain types of borrowers, such as those operating in high-unemployment areas, individuals with low incomes who own businesses, handicapped persons, Vietnam-era or disabled Veterans. Contact your local SBA Office or call (800) 827-5722.

Youngsters from ages 10 to 20 may qualify for **Youth Project Loans** from the Farmers Home Administration if they live in rural communities. These loans can be used for almost any kind of income-producing project. For more information write to Youth Project Loans, Farmers Home Administration, 14th and Independence Avenue SW, Washington, DC 20250 or phone (202) 382-1632.

Nonfarm Enterprise Loans are available to individuals who are owner-operators of family-sized farms or tenants on such a farm. These loans are for up to $200,000 (or guarantees of up to $400,000). The money can be used to finance ventures such as welding shops, grocery stores, barber shops, riding stables, restaurants, service stations, etc. Contact the Farmers Home Administration at (202) 447-4323 and ask for the Nonfarm Enterprise Loan pamphlet.

The **Department of Energy** sponsors a direct loan program to assist minority businesses in securing contracts with the DOE. The loans allow financing up to 75% of your costs involved in preparing a proposal or bid for a DOE contract. The maximum amount that can be borrowed is $50,000. Contact the Minority Economic Impact Office, Department of Energy, 1000 Independence Ave. SW, Room 5B-110, Washington, DC 20585 or phone (202) 585-1594.

Equity Loans

Equity investments and long term financing are also available from **Small Business Investment Companies** (SBICs). These organizations are privately-owned businesses licensed by the SBA and partially funded by the Federal Government. They typically loan money for growth purposes and in the financing of high-technology start-ups. You can get assistance in preparing a loan proposal from your local SCORE office (Service Corps of Retired Executives), a Small Business Administration program providing free individual sessions with seasoned business veterans. To locate the office nearest you, call your local SBA office or (800) 827-5722.

There is a group of SBICs chartered under section 301(d) that specialize in socially or economically disadvantaged small businesses.

For more information on this program, contact the Small Business Administration, Office of SBIC Operations, Room 810, 1441 L Street NW, Washington DC 20416 or phone (202) 653-6584.

Certified Development Company Loans

The SBA 504 program establishes Certified Development Companies whose notes of indebtedness are guaranteed by the Small Business Administration. Loan amounts can be arranged for up to $750,000. To qualify, you must personally contribute at least 10 percent and private financing must contribute at least 50 percent. The Certified Development Company will then provide up to the remaining 40 percent. Example: You want to borrow $250,000 — you must personally come up with $25,000 (10%), get bank or other financing for $125,000 (50%), and the Certified Development Company will provide the remaining $100,000 (40%). Phone numbers for these programs are found in the State by State Sources of Funding section later in this chapter.

Grants

A grant is money that is given to you for a specific purpose. Grant money does not typically have to be repaid.

If you are an inventor with an idea involving non-nuclear energy technology, you may qualify for a cash grant from the **Energy-Related Inventions Office** of the Department of Commerce. Contact them at Energy-Related Inventions Office, National Institute of Standards and Technology, Department of Commerce, Building 202 - Room 209, Gaithersburg, MD 20899 or phone (301) 975-5500.

The **National Endowment of the Arts** awards grants for architecture, landscaping, interior decorating, and urban design. For more information contact the Director, Design Arts Program, National Endowment for the Arts, 100 Pennsylvania Ave. NW, Washington, DC 20506 or phone (202) 682-5437 and ask for the *National Endowment for the Arts, Guide to Programs* and *Design Arts Guidelines* booklets.

Federal Income Tax Deferment

The **Capital Construction Fund Program** allows for the deferment of federal income taxes for owners of commercial fishing operations. The funds must be used for the acquisition of commercial fishing vessels or reconstruction projects. For more information contact the National Oceanic and Atmospheric Administration, National Marine Fisheries Service, Department of Commerce, Financial Services Division, F/TWI, 1825 Connecticut Avenue NW, Washington, DC 20235 or call them at (206) 673-5424.

Interest Subsidies

If you had a choice between a loan at 11% and an otherwise identical one at 9.5%, which would you choose? Depending on where you are, below-market-rate money may be available. Several states, including Ohio, Iowa, and Oklahoma, have interest-rate subsidy or **"linked-deposit" programs**, which permit qualifying small businesses to get favorable loans from local banks.

In Oklahoma, for instance, participating banks can qualify for low-cost funds from the state, provided they agree to pass along the savings to customers. To qualify, companies must have revenues of less than $4 million and employ fewer than 200 people. To find out about such programs in your area, contact your state economic development agency. Also call local business groups such as the Chamber of Commerce in your community.

Seed Capital Funds

In recent years a number of seed funds have been created by state and local governments eager to generate jobs and growth in certain technology-based areas. The National Business Incubation Association at 1 President Street, Athens, OH 45701 publishes the *Survey of State Sponsored Seed Capital Funds* which was originally prepared by the Advanced Technology Development Center in Atlanta. Another publication, the *Survey of Seed Capital,* is available from Richard T. Meyer, Emory University Business School, 1602 Mizell Drive, Atlanta, GA 30322. Check your library for these books before you purchase them.

Business Consortium Fund

If you are a minority vendor working on a contract with a major company, there is a good chance that you can qualify for a special loan

90

under a program of the **National Minority Suppliers Development Council, Inc.** (NMSDC), based in New York City. This program provides money to ethnic-minority-owned companies having problems obtaining money. NMSDC may be reached at (212) 944-2430.

Special Loans For Women Only

The National Association for Female Executives (NAFE) will invest up to $50,000 in companies where all the owners are women. This is an investment and not a loan. If the company should fail, you are under no obligation to pay the amount back. If, however, the company is successful, you give NAFE back a percentage of your profits. You may obtain more information from NAFE, 127 West 24th Street, New York, NY 10011 or call (212) 645-0770.

The Woman's Initiative for Self-Employmnet (WISE) helps women by providing them with the training, information, and financing they need to start their own business. You may receive as much as $10,000 to start up or expand a business. Contact WISE, 450 Mission Street, Suite 402, San Francisco, CA 94105 or telephone (415) 247-9473.

The SBA's office of Women's Business Ownership has compiled a list of alternative financing sources available. To obtain a free copy of this list, write to the Office of Women's Business Ownership, U.S. Small Business Administration, 409 Third Street, Washington, DC 20416.

Classified Ads

Run an ad in your local newspaper's want ad section under the category of Business Opportunities or Capital Wanted. State that you are a new business looking for financing.

Credit Cards

This potentially risky way to get quick cash should be used only after you have exhausted all other sources. The obvious drawback is the high interest rate charged on bank cards. If you are considering doing this, first locate a card with low interest rates. Shop around by calling the banks in your area.

State by State Sources of Funding

Below is a partial list of federal, state, and state-sponsored programs available to you. In addition to financial support, many of these organizations provide informational brochures, seminars, and consulting specifically targeted at small businesses. Several states offer financial incentives to lure your company into their state. If your location is not important, you should check out some of these programs.

Alabama

The Southern Development Council has loans for all businesses in the state. Contact their Montgomery office at (205) 264-5441.

The Alabama Development Office provides financing for land, buildings and equipment. The Industrial Development Program sponsored by this office also offers additional technical services for small businesses and acts as a one-stop-shop for state business licenses. Their phone number is (205) 263-0048.

The Alabama Economic Development Administration offers direct loans to any small business in the state. Their number is (205) 832-7008.

The Alabama State Treasurer offers agricultural loans to anyone engaged in the production of agricultural products in the state. Contact this office at (205) 261-7500.

Three Minority Business Development Centers provide assistance to minority-owned businesses. In Birmingham call (205) 930-9254, in Mobile call (205) 344-9650, and in Montgomery call (205) 263-0818.

Alaska

The Alaska Business Development Center operates small business support centers in Anchorage (907) 274-7232 and Juneau (807) 789-3660.

Alaska's Department of Community and Regional Affairs provided technical and financial assistance. Call the Block Grant Administrator, Rural Development Division, Department of Community and Regional Affairs at (907) 465-4708.

The Umbrella Bond Program provides long term financing for companies to obtain buildings, plants, property, and equipment. Call the Alaska Industrial Development and Export Authority at (907) 274-1651.

The Alaska Department of Natural Resources provides loans for farm development, general farm operations, and land clearing. Contact their office at (907) 745-7200.

Minority business assistance is provided through the Alaska Minority Business Development Center. Their phone number is (907) 562-2322.

Arizona

The Arizona Department of Commerce administers small business financing programs. Call the Community Development and Finance Division at (602) 255-4967 for more information.

The Arizona Enterprise Development Corporation is certified by the SBA and offers financing to independently owned businesses. Contact them at (602) 255-5705.

Arizona minority business assistance programs are available from the American Indian Consultants, (602) 945-2635; the Navajo Minority Business Development Center at (602) 871-6486; and the Phoenix Minority Business Development Center at (602) 277-7707.

Arkansas

The Arkansas Capital Corporation (a non-profit organization funded by the state) provides financing for fixed assets, land, and working capital. They may be reached at (501) 374-9247.

The Seed Capital Investment Program supports organizations that will stimulate the economy of Arkansas. They may be reached at (501) 371-3544 for program details.

The Small Business Innovation Research Grants Assistance Program helps small businesses obtain Federal R&D funds. Call (501) 371-3554.

Arkansas minority assistance programs are available from the Arkansas Industrial Development Commission at (501) 682-1060 and the Little Rock Minority Business Development Center at (501) 372-7312.

California

The Alternative Energy Source Financing Authority provides financial assistance to companies using new energy products developed by private businesses. Call (916) 445-9597.

The State Assistance Fund for Energy (SAFE) makes loans in conjunction with the SBA for energy-related projects, firms that export California products, and firms owned by minorities or women. (916) 442-3321.

Business and Industrial Development Corporations provide financial assistance pursuant to the SBA 7(a) loan program. For more information, contact the California Department of Commerce's Office of Small Business at (916) 445-6545.

The California Pollution Control Financing Authority provides tax-exempt project financing to companies that must comply with pollution or waste disposal regulations. Their number is (916) 445-9597.

The Small Business Loan Guarantee Program, the New Product Development Program, Energy Reduction Loans, the Hazardous Waste Reduction Loan Program, and the Farm Loan Program are all administered by the Office of Small Business. They can be reached at (916) 445-6545.

The California Export Finance Office provides both working capital and accounts receivable guarantees to companies exporting California products. You can reach them at (415) 557-8912.

The California Pollution Control Financing Authority provides tax-exempt financing for companies that have waste disposal projects or that fully comply with air and water quality regulations. They may be reached at (916) 445-9597.

The Office of Local Development administers the Enterprise Zone Loan Program, the Community Development Block Grant-Nonentitlement Program, the Small Business Revitalization Program, and the Sudden and Severe Economic Dislocation Program. Call (916) 322-1398.

The State Assistance Fund for Energy, Business and Industrial Development Corporation also makes loans in conjunction with the SBA's guarantee program. They may be reached at (800) 343-7233.

California minority assistance programs are available from the California Office of Small and Minority Business at (916) 322-5060 and the Minority

Business Development Centers in Fresno (209) 252-7551, Oxnard (805) 483-1123, Salinas (408) 754-1061, San Francisco (415) 989-2920, and Stockton (209) 477-2098.

Colorado

The Colorado Agriculture Development Authority offers financing for Colorado agricultural producers. Their number is (303) 866-2811.

The Colorado Housing and Finance Authority offers three programs. The Quality Investment Capital program and the bank participation ACCESS program both provide fixed rate financing for SBA guaranteed loans. The Colorado Export Credit Insurance program offers commercial and political risk insurance to exporters. You can get information about all three programs by calling (303) 861-8962.

The Office of Business Development provides loans to new or expanding businesses for up to 40% of the total financed amount.   They can be reached at (303) 861-8962.

SBA 503/504 Certified Development Companies offer financing up to $750,000. However, you must create one new job for every $15,000 you receive. Call the Community Economic Development Company of Colorado at (303) 893-8989 for more information. Also call, in Denver County (303) 575-5540, in El Paso County (303) 578-6962, in southern Colorado (303) 545-8680, and in Pueblo County (303) 544-7133.

Connecticut

The Connecticut Development Authority offers the Umbrella Bond Program, the Mortgage Insurance program, the Naugatuck Valley Revolving Loan Program, the Connecticut Growth Fund and the Comprehensive Business Assistance Fund. They may be contacted at (203) 522-3730 for more detailed information about each program.

The Connecticut Product Development Corporation offers dollar for dollar matching of funds from the private sector that are used for the market introduction of new products. Call (203) 566-2920.

The Exporters Revolving Loan Fund encourages businesses to locate or invest in Connecticut and provides incentives to small businesses who export from within the state. Their phone number is (203) 566-3842.

Delaware

The Delaware Economic Development Authority provides statewide financial assistance to new or growing companies. They may be reached at (302) 736-4271.

The Delaware Development Corporation provides loans through the SBA 504 program. They may also be reached at (302) 736-4271.

District of Columbia

The Economic Development Finance Corp. provides loans to directly stimulate business in the District's neighborhood commercial corridors. Their phone number is (202) 775-8815.

The D.C. Local Development Corporation offers a wide range of financing options from SBA 503/504 fixed asset financing to direct revolving loan funds to facade improvement loans. Contact them at (202) 727-6600.

Minority assistance programs are available through the D.C. Minority Business Opportunity Commission (202) 939-8780, the Native American Indian Consultants (202) 547-0576, and the Washington D.C. Minority Business Development Center (202) 785-2886.

Florida

The Finance Section of the Florida Department of Commerce helps businesses locate SBA and other financing alternatives. They can be reached at (904) 488-9357.

The Florida First Capital Finance Corporation offers financial assistance to small and growing businesses in conjunction with the SBA loan program. Their phone number is (904) 487-0463.

The Florida High Technology Innovation Research and Development Fund is a venture capital pool offering equity financing to new and existing high-tech businesses for research and development activities. Contact them at (904) 487-3136.

Minority assistance programs are available from the Florida Black Business Investment Board (904) 487-4850, The Florida Department of General Services Minority Business Assistance Office (904) 487-0915, the Florida Regional Minority Purchasing Council, Inc. (305) 653-6164, the

Florida West Coast Minority Purchasing Council (813) 875-2686, the Greater Florida Minority Development Council (305) 828-3586, the Minority Business Development Centers in Jacksonville (904) 353-3826, Miami (305) 591-7355, Orlando (407) 422-6234, Tampa (813) 289-8824, and West Palm Beach (407) 863-0895.

Georgia

The Rural Development Initiative encourages economic development in south central Georgia by financing start-ups and expansions. They may be reached at (912) 529-3367.

The Georgia Department of Community Affairs provides information on federal and state funding sources. Call them at either (404) 656-3836 or (404) 656-5526.

Minority assistance programs are available from the Office of Special Assistance for Minority Affairs (404) 656-1794 and the Minority Business Development Centers in Atlanta (404) 586-0973, Augusta (404) 722-0994, Columbus (404) 324-4253, and Savannah (912) 236-6708.

Hawaii

The Agricultural Loan Division provides loans to qualified farmers through a number of different programs. Call (808) 548-7126 for the details.

The Hawaii Department of Agriculture administers the New Farmer Loan Program, the Emergency Loan Program, and the Aquaculture Loan Program. Their phone number is (808) 548-7106.

The Financial Assistance Branch offers two financing programs, the Hawaii Capital Loan Program and the Innovation Development Loan Program. The first offers financing to small businesses who have been turned down by conventional sources and the second provides financing for new products or inventions. Information is available on both programs by calling (808) 548-4616.

While the Small Business Information Service does not directly provide financing, it does assist with locating alternative financing. Their number is (808) 548-4608.

The Honolulu Minority Business Development Center provides minority assistance programs. Call them at (808) 531-6232.

Idaho

The Idaho Department of Commerce offers Community Development Block Grants, Industrial Revenue Bonds, and Idaho Travel Council Grants. They also assist in obtaining venture capital through the Economic Development Division and the Division of Science and Technology. Contact them at (208) 334-2470.

Illinois

The Business Finance and Energy Assistance Division of the Department of Commerce offers financial assistance through several programs which include the Build Illinois Small Business Development Loan Program, the Micro Loan Program, the Equity Investment Fund Program, the Business Innovation Fund Program, the Minority and Women Business Loan Program, and the Energy Conservation Interest Write-Down Program. Contact them at (217) 785-2708.

The Small Business Innovation Research Program awards money to small innovative firms encouraging them to participate in government research. They also assist in converting the results into commercial applications. Their phone number is (217) 785-6160.

The Illinois Export Development Authority provides pre- and post-shipment export financing. Their number is (312) 917-3401.

The Illinois Department of Commerce Small Business Development Program provides direct financing in cooperation with private sector lenders. Call them at (217) 782-3891.

The Illinois Department of Commerce's Small Business Investment Companies provide direct loans to small businesses. You can contact them by calling (217) 782-6861.

Illinois minority assistance is provided through Chicago North Minority Business Development Center at (312) 856-0200.

Indiana

Contact the Business and Financial Services Division of the Indiana Department of Commerce at (317) 232-8782. They administer grant and loan programs for the state.

The Indiana Community Business Credit Corporation offers private financing for small businesses who have been turned down by conventional sources. Contact them at (317) 255-9704.

The Corporation for Innovation Development is a private, state-sponsored, venture capital firm that invests in small businesses. You can contact them at (317) 237-2350.

The Indiana Corporation for Science and Technology is a non-profit company that has a capital base of state funds which it invests in research development activities. Contact them at (317) 635-3058.

The Indiana Institute for New Business Ventures is a non-profit private corporation that assists small businesses in finding financing in addition to several other services. Their phone number is (317) 634-8418.

The Indiana Statewide Certified Development Corporation also makes fixed-rate loans to small businesses. Their number is (317) 253-6166.

Minority business assistance programs are available from the Gary Minority Business Development Center (219) 883-5802, the Indiana Department of Commerce Minority and Women Business Development Division (317) 232-8820, The Indiana Department of Highways' Equal Employment Opportunity Section, Disadvantaged Business Enterprise Program (317) 232-5093, the Indiana Regional Minority Suppliers Development Council (317) 923-2110, and the Indianapolis Minority Business Development Center (317) 687-0272.

Iowa

The Iowa Business Development Credit Corporation provides numerous services in addition to financial assistance. Call them at (515) 282-2164.

Iowa's Community Development Block Grant is divided into three programs — Economic Development Set-Aside, the regular block grant program and the Public Facilities Set-Aside. Details about the programs and requirements are available by calling (515) 281-4167.

The Community Economic Betterment Account, which is funded by state lottery money, provides financing to create or retain jobs. For more information call (515) 281-4167.

The Financing Rural Economic Development program provides financial assistance to small rural companies. Their number is (515) 281-3752.

The Linked Deposit Program provides financial assistance to small businesses. Call the State Treasurer's Office at (515) 281-6859 for more information on this program.

The Iowa Product Development Corporation invests in Iowa innovation. For detailed information call (515) 281-5292.

The Self-Employment Loan Program provides loans to low income business owners. Call (515) 281-7237.

The Iowa Small Business Loan Program loans funds for purchasing land, construction, building improvements, or equipment. Call the Iowa Finance Authority at (515) 281-4058.

The Small Business New Jobs Training Program provides salary reimbursements of up to 50% for one year of on-the-job training. Information is available by calling the Bureau of Business & Industry Training at (515) 281-3600.

Iowa's Targeted Small Business Loan & Equity Grant Program assists in the expansion of minority and woman-owned businesses. Contact them at (515) 281-3585.

Iowa's minority business assistance programs are administered by the Iowa Department of Economic Development. The Targeted Small Business Program can be reached at (515) 281-3754 and information on the Equity Grant Program is available by calling (515) 281-3585.

Kansas

You can get information about the Kansas Association of Certified Development Companies by calling (316) 227-6406. They provide both state sponsored and SBA loans.

The Kansas Development Finance Authority provides financing to small businesses. Call (913) 296-6747.

Funds are also available from the Division of Community Development in Topeka. Their number is (913) 296-3004.

Kansas' Division of Existing Industry Development provides financial assistance to small businesses. Contact the Kansas Department of Commerce at (913) 296-5298.

Kansas Pooled Money Investment Board provides low-interest loans to small business owners. Call (913) 296-3372.

If you are looking for venture capital, call Kansas Venture Capital, Inc. at (913) 888-5913.

Kentucky

Kentucky's Commonwealth Small Business Development Corporation provides small businesses with loans for expansion. Call the Kentucky Small Business Development Corporation at (502) 564-4320 for details.

Kentucky also offers loans to craftspersons through the Crafts Guaranteed Loan Program. For information call the Kentucky Development Finance Authority at (502) 564-4554.

The Kentucky Development Finance Authority provides low-interest state loans to supplement private financing. Call (502) 564-4554.

Minority business assistance programs are available from the Kentucky Cabinet for Economic Development, Minority Business Division at (502) 564-2064 and the Louisville Minority Business Development Center at (502) 589-7401.

Louisiana

The Louisiana Economic Development Corporation administers most of the state's loan programs. Contact them at (504) 342-5388.

The Louisiana Small Business Equity Corporation administers three programs, the Equity Leverage Financing program, the Feasibility Studies Financing program and the Industrial Revenue Bond Financing program. Their number is (504) 925-4112.

Minority business assistance programs are available through the Minority Business Development Centers in Baton Rouge (504) 924-0186, Shreveport (318) 226-4931 and the Department of Commerce (504) 342-5363.

Maine

The Finance Authority of Maine direct loans, loan guarantees, and project grants. Call them at (207) 623-3263.

Maine farmers can request low-interest operating loans through the Linked Investment Program of the State Treasurer's office. Call (207) 289-2771 or (207) 623-3263.

Maryland

The Development Credit Corp. of Maryland Department of Economic and Employment Development provides loans to businesses unable to obtain funds from banks and other lenders. Their number is (301) 269-3514.

The Maryland Energy Financing Administration provides loans for businesses seeking to conserve energy, co-generate energy, or to provide fuels and other energy sources.

Maryland's Small Business Development Authority office of the Department of Economic and Employment Development provides financial assistance to small and minority-owned businesses. Their number is (301) 333-6975.

The Maryland Office of International Trade provides grants to help firms sell their goods in the international marketplace. Call (301) 333-4295 to learn about the other services they offer.

Minority programs are available from the Development Credit Fund, Inc. at (301) 523-6400 and the Baltimore Minority Business Development Center at (301) 367-3045.

Massachusetts

The Massachusetts Business Development Corporation is a private corporation that provides six types of loans: working capital, leveraged buyout, second mortgages, government guaranteed loans, SBA 504 loans and long-term loans. Their number is (617) 350-8877.

The Community Development Finance Corporation provides funds to businesses located in economically depressed areas of Massachusetts. For more information call them at (617) 742-0366.

The Massachusetts Industrial Finance Agency provides funding for land purchases, plant construction or updating and equipment purchases. Contact them at (617) 451-2477.

The Small and Entrepreneurial Business Development Division of the Office of Business Development assists small businesses in obtaining R&D funding. Call them at (617) 727-4005.

The Massachusetts Technology Development Corporation is an independent publicly-funded venture capital company that invests in technology-based businesses. If this interests you, call (617) 723-4920.

The Massachusetts State Office of Minority and Women Business Assistance assists minority- and women-owned businesses of obtaining public contracts. Their phone number is (617) 727-8692.

Michigan

The Michigan Department of Commerce offers numerous loan programs through the Michigan Strategic Fund. Call (517) 373-7550.

The Michigan Department of Commerce Office for New Enterprise Services provides information and referrals for state financing. They can be reached by calling (313) 769-4664.

The Manufacturing Development Group, while not directly providing financing, does offer assistance programs to help small businesses locate financing. Call the Michigan Department of Commerce at (517) 373-6378 for more information.

The Michigan Product Development Corporation assists small businesses in getting financing from the Michigan Strategic Fund. Their number is (313) 474-331.

The State Research Fund provides grants to Michigan businesses who cooperate with Michigan schools in certain technology areas. Call the Michigan Energy and Resource Research Association's Small Business Development Center at (313) 964-5030.

If you are looking for venture capital, call the Venture Capital Division of the Department of Treasury at (517) 373-4330.

Minority assistance programs are available from the Detroit Minority Business Development Center (313) 961-2100, the Michigan Minority Business Enterprise office of the Department of Commerce (800) 831-9090, and the Michigan Women Business Owners Services office of the Department of Commerce (800) 831-9090.

Minnesota

The Community Development Division of the Minnesota Department of Trade and Economic Development offers numerous programs to assist small businesses. Contact them at (612) 297-2515.

The Export Finance Division of the Minnesota Department of Trade and Economic Development provides financial assistance to small companies in the exporting area. They can be reached at (612) 297-4283.

Minnesota Project Innovation promotes technological innovation, creates private sector financing opportunities, and assists small businesses in obtaining Federal grants. Phone them at (612) 448-8810.

Minnesota minority business assistance programs are available through the Minneapolis/St. Paul Minority Business Development Center (612) 333-3600 and the Minnesota Chippewa Tribe Minority Business Development Center (218) 335-2252.

Mississippi

The Certified Development Company of Mississippi, Inc. administers the SBA 503 Loan program and the Mississippi Small Business Loan Guarantee program. Contact their Jackson office at (601) 359-3039.

The Mississippi Department of Economic Development Finance Division provides financial assistance to small businesses in the form of SBA 504 loans and loan guarantees. Their phone number is (601) 359-3437.

The Mississippi Venture Capital Clearinghouse matches small businesses with private venture capitalists. For more information call their Jackson office at (601) 982-6513.

Minority assistance programs are administered through the Jackson Minority Business Development Center at (601) 362-2260 and the Mississippi Minority Supplier Development Council at (601) 352-0161.

Missouri

The Missouri Corporation for Science and Technology is a private non-profit company that provides seed capital for new advanced technology businesses. Call them at (314) 751-3906.

The Missouri Department of Economic Development's Finance Program provides both direct loans and loan guarantees to small businesses. They can be reached at (314) 751-0717.

The Missouri Agricultural and Small Business Development Authority makes direct loans to small businesses. Call them at (314) 751-3359.

The Missouri Department of Economic Development promotes job creation and capital investment in small businesses. Their phone number is (314) 751-4962.

The Missouri Department of Economic Development Enterprise Zone Program provides tax benefits to economically underdeveloped areas. Contact them at (314) 751-5979.

The Missouri Industrial Development Time Deposit Program provides inactive state funds to back short-term bank loans made to small businesses. Phone them at (314) 751-4241.

Rural Missouri, Inc. packages SBA 503/504 loans. They may be reached at (314) 635-0136.

Minority assistance programs are administered by minority business development centers in Kansas City (816) 221-6500 and St.Louis (314) 621-6232 and by the Missouri Department of Economic Development Minority Business Assistance Office (314) 751-3237.

Montana

Montana's AG Finance Program provides funds to rural youth, youth organizations, and first-time farmers. More information is available by calling (406) 444-2102.

The Beginning Farm Loan Program provides financial assistance for first-time farmers or ranchers. Call the Montana Department of Agriculture at (406) 444-2402 for all the details.

Montana's Community Development Block Grant Program assists low and medium income individuals. A portion of this money is set aside for economic development projects. Call (406) 444-3757 to see if you qualify.

The Montana Department Of Agriculture AG Finance program provides loans to rural youth and youth organizations. (406) 444-2402.

Montana's Business Assistance Division of the Department of Commerce assists small businesses in obtaining financing through private and state sponsored programs. Their phone number is (406) 444-3923.

The Montana Community Finance Company offers SBA 504 loans in the state. Their number is (406) 443-3261.

The Office of Development Finance manages several loan programs including the Federal Guaranteed Loan Program, the Business Loan Participation Program, the Economic Development Linked Deposit program and the Montana Capital Company Program. Call the Board of Investments at (406) 442-1970 to get information about each program.

Nebraska

The Business Development Corporation of Nebraska provides small businesses with SBA loans for fixed assets. Call (402) 483-0382.

The Community Development Division offers financial aid for rural development. Contact them at (402) 471-3762.

Contact the Nebraska Department of Economic Development at (402) 471-4167 for information about The Community Development Block Grant Program and direct loans and loan guarantees available through local Economic Development Districts.

Nebraska's Investment Finance Authority is a private non-profit agency that provides loans for farm property, manufacturing facilities, residential and health-care programs, and small businesses. They can be reached at (402) 477-4406.

Nebraska's Department of Economic Development Economic, Development Administration offers direct loans and loan guarantees. Their phone number is (402) 471-3780.

Nebraska's Investment Finance Authority provides industrial development revenue bonds for financing industrial, manufacturing, and waste treatment projects. Their number is (402) 477-4406.

Nevada

The Department of Commerce offers the Industrial Development Revenue Bond Program to help businesses expand or build new facilities and the Venture Capital Bond Program that provides venture capital financing to small businesses. Their phone number is (702) 885-4250.

The City of Las Vegas Loan Program provides direct loans, loan guarantees, and interest supplements to small businesses. (702) 386-6551.

The Nevada Financial Development Corporation is a private financial organization providing various Federal loan guarantee programs to small businesses. Their phone number is (702) 323-3033.

Nevada Office of Community Services which can be reached at (702) 885-5978 oversees The Small Business Revitalization Program which provides assistance with SBA 504 loans for fixed assets and 7(a) loan guarantees. They also administer the Nevada Revolving Loan Fund which is used to finance small business expansion and the Urban Development Action Grant program..

The Nevada State Development Corporation offers three financing programs, the SBA 503/504 loan program for fixed assets, the SBA 7(a) program for loan guarantees, and the American Development Finance Enterprise Capital Fund which helps finance business expansion projects. Their number is (702) 323-3625.

Nevada's department of Commerce Industrial Development Revenue Bond Program helps companies expand or build new facilities through the use of tax-exempt financing. More information is available by calling (702) 885-4250.

Nevada Financial Development Corp. provides credit to supplement conventional lending sources. Call them at (702) 323-3033.

The Commission on Economic Development allows some businesses to defer payment of tax on capital equipment within the state. For more information call (702) 885-432.

The Las Vegas Minority Business Development Center provides minority assistance programs. Contact them at (702) 384-3293.

New Hampshire

The New Hampshire Industrial Development Authority provides several financial assistance programs, ranging from establishing credit to securing loans. Through the Industrial Development Revenue Bond Financing they can provide up to 100% financing for business facilities, land, or equipment. The Guarantee Plan for Real Estate guarantees first mortgage loans for existing New Hampshire companies or companies relocating into New Hampshire. The Guarantee Plan for Machinery and Equipment will provide up to 35% of the loan amount for new equipment. Call (603) 271-2391 for specifics.

Granite State Capital, Inc. (603) 436-5044 and VenCap (603) 644-6100 are small business investment corporations in New Hampshire.

New Jersey

The Corporation of Business Assistance provides SBA 503/504 loans for fixed assets such as land, buildings, or equipment. Contact them at (609) 633-7737.

The Division of Rural Resources of the New Jersey Department of Agriculture provides financial assistance to farmers. Their phone number is (609) 292-5511.

The New Jersey Economic Development Authority has financing available for land acquisition, buildings, and machinery. They also have a Guaranteed Loan Program, a Direct Loan Program, a Pre-shipment Working Capital Loan Program for Exporting, and a Loan Program Directed to Small Retail Businesses. Their number is (609) 292-0187.

The Set-Aside and Certification Office's Financial Assistance Grant Program assists woman- and minority-owned businesses participate in local grant programs. Their phone number is (609) 984-9835.

New Jersey's Local Development Financing Fund provides supplemental financial assistance to small businesses. Call (609) 633-6659.

The New Jersey Economic Development Authority arranges long-term financing for manufacturing facilities, land acquisition, and business equipment purchases. Their phone number is (609) 292-0192.

Minority business assistance programs are available from the New Brunswick Minority Business Development Center (201) 247-2000, Bu-

III. Raising Money to Finance Your Venture

reau of Hispanic Enterprise (609) 984-9668, the Office of Minority Business Enterprise (609) 292-0500, the office of Women Business Enterprise (609) 292-3862, and the Newark Minority Business Development Center (201) 623-7712.

New Mexico

The Business Development Corporation of New Mexico is a private state-chartered company that provides financing to businesses for equipment, new products, and market development. Contact them at (505) 286-1316.

The Development Training Programs of the New Mexico Economic Development Department provide state-sponsored funds for training New Mexico workers. Their phone number is (505) 827-0300.

The state-sponsored Economic Incentive Loan Program offers loans for small businesses. Contact them at (505) 262-2247.

The New Mexico Research and Development Institute provides state funds to advanced-technology businesses. Call them at (505) 827-5886.

The Albuquerque Minority Business Development Center provides minority assistance programs in the state. Their number is (505) 843-7114.

New York

The Corporation for Innovation Development is a venture capital fund for technology-based small companies. Contact the New York State Science and Technology Foundation at (518) 474-4349.

The New York Business Development Corporation is a private company that provides both SBA and New York State / U.S. Small Business Administration Initiative loans. The SBA direct program provides funding for fixed assets such as land, buildings, and equipment. The other program is a revolving loan fund for small businesses. Contact their Albany office at (518) 463-2268.

New York's Empire State Certified Development Corporation provides both direct loans and loan guarantees to small businesses. They also administer the Rural Development Loan Fund, the Long-Term Economic Development Fund, the Export Program, and the Regional Economic Development Partnership Program. Call their office at (212) 818-1700.

The Empire State Certified Development Corporation provides SBA 503/504 loans for the purchase of fixed assets such as land, buildings, and equipment. Their phone number is (518) 463-2268.

New York's State Department of Economic Development Project STAMP (State Training and Manpower Program) offers small businesses located in one of New York City's five boroughs an incentive to hire and train disadvantaged individuals. Contact them at (718) 596-4120.

The New York State Urban Development Corp. provides incentives in six areas: downtown development, industrial development, minority business development, university research and development and planning special projects. Their phone number is (212) 930-0200.

The New York State Small- and Medium-Sized Business Assistance program provides loans to small businesses for re-tooling and modernization. Their phone number is (212) 930-0285.

Minority business assistance programs are available from Minority Business Development Centers in Brooklyn (718) 522-5880, Buffalo (716) 855-0144, Manhattan (212) 779-4361, Queens (718) 699-2400, and Rochester (716) 232-6120, and the New York Minority and Women's Business Division (212) 827-6180, and also the Opportunity Development Association Business Development Center (718) 522-5620.

North Carolina

The Frank H. Kenan Institute for Private Enterprise runs the Investment Contacts Network which provides computerized matching of small businesses and venture capitalists. For more details, call them at (919) 962-8201.

North Carolina's Small Business Development Division acts as a clearinghouse for information about financing and numerous other areas pertinent to small businesses. Contact the Small Business Development Division of the Department of Commerce at (919) 733-7980.

The North Carolina Technological Development Authority makes grants to small businesses and oversees the North Carolina Innovative Research Fund which provides equity financing. Their number is (919) 733-7022.

Northeastern North Carolina Tomorrow, a program sponsored by Elizabeth City State University provides grants and loans to small businesses. Contact them at (919) 335-3491.

Minority business assistance programs are run by the state Minority Business Development Centers in Cherokee (704) 497-9335, Fayatteville (919) 483-7513, Raleigh/Duram (919) 833-6122, and the North Carolina Department of Commerce, Minority Business Development Division (919) 733-2712.

North Dakota

The state-operated Bank of North Dakota offers several innovative lending programs for promoting business within the state. The Small Business Loan Program provides financing to non-farming small businesses. The Risk Loan Program grants financing to businesses with a higher degree of risk than a conventional lender would accept. The Export Loan Program provides loans to importers who want to buy North Dakota products. You may contact the Bank Of North Dakota at (701) 224-5685.

The Fargo Cass County Economic Development Corporation provides SBA funding to small businesses. You must create one new job for each $15,000 borrowed. Call them at (701) 237-6132.

North Dakota Small Business Loan Services administers the state's SBA 504 loan program.

Ohio

There are several small business investment corporations in Ohio. Among them are A.T. Capital Corp. (216) 737-4970, Banc One Capital Corp. (614) 248-5832, Center City MESBIC, Inc. (513) 461-6164, First Ohio Capital (216) 687-1096, and SeaGate Venture Management, Inc. (419) 259-8526.

Minority business assistance programs are administered by the Ohio Minority Business Development Centers in Cleveland (216) 664-4152, and Columbus (614) 645-4764, and the Minority Development Loan Program (614) 644-7708, the Minority Construction Contract Bond Assistance Program (614) 644-7708, the Ohio Minority Business Development Program (800) 282-1085, and the Minority Office of Contract Procurement Assistance (800) 282-1085.

Oklahoma

The Capital Resources Network assists small businesses in securing loans through conventional sources. Contact the Capital Resources Division of the Department of Commerce at (405) 843-9770.

111

The Oklahoma Development Finance Authority (405) 848-9761, and the Oklahoma Industrial Finance Authority (405) 521-2182 both offer financial assistance to small businesses.

The Central Oklahoma Economic Development District provides assistance to small businesses in obtaining financing. Their number is (405) 273-6410.

The Southwestern Oklahoma Development Authority administers and operates state and federal programs on a substate level. Contact them at (405) 562-4884.

Minority assistance programs are available through the Minority Business Development Centers in Oklahoma City (405) 235-0430, and Tulsa (918) 592-1995, and the Oklahoma Indian Minority Business Development Center (405) 329-3737.

Oregon

The Oregon Business Development Fund provides financing to small businesses. Contact the Oregon Economic Development Department at (503) 373-1240.

The Oregon Certified Development Company provides SBA loans for land, buildings, and equipment. Their phone number is (503) 373-1240.

Oregon Resource and Technology Development Corp. (ORTDC) provides investment capital for early-stage business finance. Their phone number is (503) 246-4844.

The Oregon Resource and Technology Development Corporation provides investment capital for new small businesses for their research and development activities. They also sponsor the Northwest Capital Network which offers computerized matching of small businesses with private investors. They can be reached at (503) 378-6359.

Oregon sponsors a special fund for minority and women-owned businesses. For more details about this fund, contact the Oregon Economic Development Department at (503) 378-6359.

The Oregon Department of Transportation administers a goal program for minority, disadvantaged, and women-owned business participation in contracting for highway and bridge construction, engineering, architectural, and environmental consulting services. Their phone number is (503) 378-8077.

Minority assistance is also available from the Portland Minority Business Development Center at (503) 245-9253.

Pennsylvania

The Office of Enterprise Development oversees the Appalachian Regional Commission and the Enterprise Development Program. These two organizations provide various financing options. Call them at (717) 783-8950.

The Ben Franklin Partnership program sponsors five privately managed venture capital funds to assist small businesses engaged in technology-based ventures. Call (717) 787-4147 for more information.

The Pennsylvania Capital Loan Fund provides low-interest loans to small businesses that will result in new jobs. Call them at (717) 783-1768 for the details.

The Pennsylvania Industrial Development Authority provides low-interest loans to small businesses. Contact them at (717) 787-6245.

The Industrial Development Authority provides low-cost funding for small businesses. Their phone number is (717) 783-1108.

The Pennsylvania Department of Commerce's Business Infrastructure Development Program provides financing for infrastructure improvements such as sewer and water systems, waste disposal facilities, transportation facilities, and fire and safety facilities. They may be reached at (717) 787-7120.

The Pennsylvania Economic Development Financing Authority also provides financing to new and small businesses. Call (717) 783-5831.

Pennsylvania Department of Commerce's Bureau of Domestic Commerce works with new companies to find buildings or sites for startup or expansion projects. Their phone number is (717) 787-6500.

The Pennsylvania Energy Development Authority finances research and development of energy technology projects. Phone them at (717) 783-9981.

113

Minority assistance programs are available through the Pennsylvania Bureau of Minority and Women Business Enterprises (717) 787-7380, the Pennsylvania Minority Business Development Authority (717) 783-1127, and the Minority Business Development Centers in Philadelphia (215) 629-9882 and Pittsburgh (412) 921-1155.

Rhode Island

The Department of Economic Development offers several financing programs for small businesses. Call them at (401) 277-2601.

The Rhode Island Industrial Building Authority provides financial assistance for construction or renovation of facilities or for the purchase of equipment. Contact them at (401) 277-2601.

Call (401) 277-2287 for information about the Rhode Island Investment Fund. They provide and SBA loans for fixed assets and/or working capital.

The Ocean State Business Development Authority issues SBA loans for land, buildings and equipment. Their number is (401) 277-2601.

The Rhode Island Partnership for Science and Technology offers grants to businesses for applied research. For all the details, call (401) 277-2601.

The Rhode Island Partnership for Science and Technology also offers support for Small Business Innovation Research applicants. They help applicants obtain grants to help defray application and proposal costs. Their phone number is (401) 277-2601.

The Rhode Island Port Authority and Economic Development Corporation provides loans for construction, acquisition, plant renovation or machinery. Their phone number is (401) 277-2601.

Venture Capital Club, Inc. matches small businesses with private investors. For more information call (401) 232-6111.

South Carolina

Several Certified Development Companies in South Carolina offer SBA loans to small businesses. Contact the US Small Business Administration office in Columbia at (803) 253-3119 for a complete list.

The Jobs Economic Development Authority through the Carolina Investment Corporation provides loans to small businesses. Preference is given to less developed areas of the state. Their number is (803) 737-0079.

Minority assistance programs are available through the Minority Business Development Centers in Charleston (803) 724-3477, Columbia (803) 256-0528, and Greenville (803) 271-8753.

South Dakota

The Agricultural Loan Participation Program provides loans through local lenders and the South Dakota Department of Agriculture's Rural Development Office. Applicants must derive at least 60% of their income from farming. Contact them at (605) 773-3375.

The Economic Development Finance Authority provides fixed-rate financing for land, buildings and equipment. For more information, call (605) 773-5032.

The South Dakota Revolving Economic Development and Initiative Fund (REDI Fund) provides permanent financing for land, site improvements, construction, equipment, trade receivables, inventory, and work-in-progress inventory. Their toll-free number is (800) 843-8000.

The Enterprise Initiation Higher Education Program works with the state's colleges and universities in providing funding for applied research activities. Approved applicants are awarded a contract which reimburses the cost of the research activities. Contact the Governor's Office of Economic Development at (605) 773-5032 for all the details.

The Revolving Economic Development and Initiative Fund provides loans to start-ups, small businesses or companies wishing to relocate in South Dakota. Contact the Office of Economic Development at (605) 773-5032.

Minority assistance programs are available through the South Dakota Business Opportunity Centers (for the Rosebud Sioux and Yankton Sioux tribes) in Rosebud (605) 747-2651, and Yankton (605) 384-3641.

Tennessee

Financing is available in Tennessee through a number of small business investment corporations. These include American Health Capital Associates, L.P. (615) 377-0416, Chickasaw Capital Corp. (901) 523-6404, Finan-

115

cial Resources, Inc. (901) 527-9411, International Paper Capital Formation, Inc. (901) 763-5951, Tennessee Venture Capital Corp (615) 244-6935, and Valley Capital Corp. (615) 265-1557.

Minority assistance programs are available through the Nashville Minority Business Development Center (615) 255-0432, and the Tennessee Office of Minority Enterprise which has offices in Nashville, Chattanooga, Knoxville, and Memphis (615) 741-2545.

Texas

The Texas Capital Fund provides loans for land, buildings, equipment and working capital. You must reside in certain rural areas to be eligible. Contact the Department of Commerce at (512) 320-9555 for details.

There are several Certified Development Corporations in Texas providing SBA loans. Call (800) 888-0511 for a complete list.

The Industrial Development Corporation Act provides financing for industrial and limited commercial projects. The Rural Development Act provides loans for up to 40% of expansion costs for companies in certain rural areas. The funds may not be used for working capital or inventory. Contact the Department of Commerce at (512) 472-5059.

Loans for manufacturing and industrial enterprises are available to companies located in rural areas, rural cities, or counties that are predominantly rural in character. Preference is given to food and fiber processing businesses. Contact the Texas Department of Commerce at (512) 320-9649 or (512) 472-5059.

The Texas Loan Program provides loans for products that contain at least 25% Texas-produced components. Loans may be used for raw materials, inventory, marketing, or equipment. Call (512) 320-9443 for more details.

The Product Commercialization Fund provides direct loans to small businesses for new products or processes. Call (512) 320-9678.

The Texas Department of Commerce publishes the *Texas Sources of Capital* which lists numerous alternative financing sources in the state. For a free copy, call The Small Business Division at (800) 888-0511.

Minority assistance programs are available from the Minority Business Development Centers in Austin (512) 476-9700, Beaumont (409) 755-

0565, Brownsville (512) 546-3400, Dallas/Fort Worth (214) 855-7373, El Paso (915) 592-2020, Houston (713) 650-3831, Laredo (512)725-5177, McAllen (512) 687-5224, and San Antonia (512) 224-1945, and the Texas Department of Commerce's Office of Business Development (512) 472-5059.

Utah

Utah has three Certified Development Companies that provide small businesses with SBA loans for land, buildings, and equipment. Call the Desert Certified Development Company in Salt Lake City at (801) 266-0443, Provo Central Utah Certified Development Company in Provo at (801) 374-1025, or the Historic 25th Street Certified Development Company in Ogden at (801) 629-8397.

The Utah Innovation Center provides many services for new companies within the state including match-up of small companies with private money sources. For more information contact the Utah Innovation Foundation at (801) 584-2520.

The Utah Technology Finance Corporation provides funds for high-technology research contracts and program grants to Utah-based small businesses. Their phone number is (801) 583-8832.

Minority Business Assistance Programs are available from the Salt Lake City Minority Business Development Center (801) 328-8181, The U.S. Department of Commerce IMPACT: Minority Business Program (801) 328-8181, Utah Office of Asian Affairs (801) 538-3045, Utah Office of Black Affairs (801) 538-3045, Utah Office of Hispanic Affairs (801) 538-3045, and the Utah Office of Indian Affairs (801) 538-3045.

Vermont

The Vermont Industrial Development Authority offers several programs to assist small businesses. These include both direct loan programs and loan guarantees. Their phone number is (802) 223-7226.

The Vermont Job Start program loans money to low-income state residents to start new businesses. Contact the Office of Economic Opportunity at (802) 241-2450 for a complete list of the qualifications and restrictions.

Virginia

The Office of Small Business and Financial Services assists small businesses in locating both private and government sources of funds. Contact the Virginia Department of Economic Development at (804) 786-3791.

The Rural Virginia Development Foundation provides several financing options for businesses starting in rural areas. Call (804) 786-3978.

The Small Business Financing Authority assists small businesses in obtaining financing. They over see several programs; the Industrial Development Bonds program and the Taxable Bond Program both provide funding for land, buildings, and equipment, while the Working Capital Loan Guarantee Program provides loan guarantees to small businesses. Their phone number is (804) 786-3791.

Minority assistance programs are available from Minority Business Development Centers located in Newport News (804) 245-8743, Norfolk (804) 399-0888, and Richmond (804) 648-0200, and the Tidewater Regional Minority Purchasing Council, Inc. (804) 627-8471, the Virginia Minority Business Enterprise (804) 786-5560, and the Virginia Regional Minority Supplier Development Council (804) 780-2322.

Washington

The Department of Community Development's Finance Program assists small businesses by combining private financing with federal and state "gap financing" loans. Contact them at (206) 753-4900.

The Industrial Revenue Bond Program provides financing for the acquisition, construction, or expansion of manufacturing facilities. Information is available through the Department of Trade and Economic Development at (206) 586-1667.

The Small Business Export Finance Assistance Center in Seattle is a non-profit state-sponsored company that assists small companies with the financing of exports.

The State Umbrella Bond Program provides low-interest financing for small businesses. For more information, call the Department of Trade and Economic Development at (206) 586-1667.

Washington Department of Community Development administers the Development Loan Fund which provides for financial assistance in distressed areas, particularly for low and moderate income persons. (206) 754-8976.

Minority business assistance programs are available from the Seattle Minority Business Development Center (206) 728-0177, the Washington Department of Trade and Economic Development Business Assistance Center (800) 237-1233, and the Washington Office of Minority and Women's Business Enterprise (206) 753-9693.

West Virginia

The West Virginia Certified Development Corporation provides small businesses with fixed-rate loans pursuant to the SBA 504 program. Their number is (304) 348-3650.

The West Virginia Economic Development Authority funds low-interest loans for land, buildings, and equipment. The focus of the program is on the creation of new jobs through manufacturing firms. They may be reached at (304) 348-3650.

The Treasurer's Economic Development Deposit Incentive program provides low-cost loans to small West Virginia businesses to create or preserve jobs. Call them at (304) 346-2623.

The West Virginia Industrial and Trade Jobs Development Corporation supplements other financial incentive programs to help small businesses create new jobs. Contact them at (304) 348-0400.

The International Development Division of the Governor's Office of Community and Industrial Development identifies international bankers to assist companies with financial problems. For more information call (304) 348-0400.

Wisconsin

The Bureau of Development Financing oversees several state programs. The Wisconsin Development Fund-Economic Development Component program focuses on funding for job creation in low and medium income areas. The Customized Labor Training Fund finances small businesses wishing to expand or introduce new products. The Technology Development Fund provides financing for research and development activities. The Employee Ownership Assistance Loan Program provides financing and assistance to employees interested in purchasing a business. The

Major Economic Development Projects Program provides both loans and grants to small businesses willing to locate in Wisconsin. Call (608) 266-3075 for information on all these programs.

The Bureau of Expansion and Recruitment provides assistance to small businesses in locating financing. Call (608) 266-0165.

The Wisconsin Business Development Finance Corporation provides SBA loans for land, buildings, and equipment. Their telephone number is (608) 258-8830.

Wisconsin Community Capital, Inc. provides loans for job creation activities in low-income areas of the state. Contact them at (608) 256-3441.

The Wisconsin Housing and Economic Development Authority offers several financing programs including the Business Development Bond program, the Linked Deposit Loan Program, the Business Energy Fund and the Venture Capital Fund. Call (608) 266-9991 for more information about each program.

Minority business assistance programs are available from the Milwaukee Minority Business Development Center (414) 332-6268, the Wisconsin American Indian Economic Development Program (715) 346-2004, the Wisconsin Bureau of Minority Business Development (608) 266-8380, and the Governor's Committee on Minority Business (608) 266-8380.

Wyoming

The Wyoming Economic Development Block Grant program provides low-interest loans for the creation or retention of low and medium income jobs. Their phone number is (307) 777-7287.

The Economic Development Loan Program provides both direct loans and loan guarantees to small businesses. Call (307) 777-7287.

The Wyoming Export Incentive Program provides limited financial assistance for research in determining the feasibility of foreign markets for Wyoming products.

For SBA loans contact the Wyoming Industrial Development Corporation at (307) 234-5351 and the Wyoming State Treasurer at (307) 777-7408. You should contact both offices since each offers its own program.

The Wyoming Job Training Administration provides loans to support worker training. The funds can be used for either on- or off-site training programs. You can be reimbursed up to 50% of the individual's salary during the training period. Call (307) 777-7671 for more information.

The State Linked Deposit program provides small businesses with a five-year fixed rate interest subsidy. The funds can be used for land, buildings, equipment, livestock, and capital. Their number is (307) 777-7408.

Federal Minority Business Development Agency

In addition to the numerous minority assistance programs included in the above state-by-state listings, the federal government provides six regional offices whose goal is to increase opportunities for racial and ethnic minorities through the formation of minority owned and managed firms.

The Atlanta office's number is (404) 347-4091 and serves Alabama, Florida, Georgia, Kentucky, Mississippi, North Carolina, South Carolina, and Tennessee.

The Chicago office can be reached at (312) 353-0182 and serves Illinois, Indiana, Iowa, Kansas, Michigan, Minnesota, Missouri, Nebraska, Ohio, and Wisconsin.

The Dallas office serves Arkansas, Colorado, Louisiana, Montana, New Mexico, North Dakota, South Dakota, Texas, Utah, and Wyoming. Their phone number is (214) 767-8001.

Connecticut, Maine, Massachusetts, New Hampshire, New Jersey, Rhode Island, and Vermont are all handled out of the New York office at (212) 264-3262.

The San Francisco office at (415) 744-3001 serves Alaska, Arizona, California, Hawaii, Idaho, Nevada, Oregon, and Washington.

The Washington D.C. office serves Delaware, the District of Columbia, Maryland, Pennsylvania and West Virginia and can be reached by calling (202) 377-8275.

BIRD Funds

The **Israel-U.S. Binational Industrial Research and Development Foundation** (BIRD) will finance up to 50% of the development costs for promising technology-related product development that will involve some sort of joint venture between an Israeli company and a U.S. one. For more information, contact the BIRD Foundation, 3 Tevuot Ha'aretz St. P.O. Box 39104, Tel Aviv 61390, Israel or phone 972-3-470710. Their fax number is 972-3-498341.

Accounts Receivable Financing

Usually your bank will lend you money secured by your outstanding accounts receivables. The receivables must be less than 60 days past due and the customers themselves must pass as being credit worthy. Banks will usually advance 65-80% of the face value. You pay down the financing as customer's checks come in. You are charged interest only on the outstanding balance.

Factoring Receivables

This is a way to turn your receivables into cash. Normally you might wait 30 days or more for invoices to be paid; specialized companies known as *factors*, look at your customer's credit (not yours), and can pay you the bulk of what's owed within a couple of days. You'll receive the balance, minus administrative costs and fees, after the customer pays. Factors actually buy your receivables. Most factors want companies to sign contracts promising them a certain amount of business over time. Their rates usually are not cheap. Expect fees of 4% to 7% of the value of the invoice. Your accountant should be able to help you locate factors in your area.

Customer Financing

If there was ever a stigma in asking customers to assist with the financial needs of your business, it seems to have faded away in the current financial environment. Everyone understands that bank credit is tight, and when you can get it, expensive. If you explain to your customers that by paying their invoices promptly, you can keep your costs down and pass the savings on to them in the form of lower prices, they will understand. Explain to them that by paying 50% of the purchase price when they place the order and the balance immediately upon receipt of the goods, you eliminate your need for short term bank financing and you will offer them further preferential pricing. You can reduce their prices, maintain your profits and solve your needs for short term cash all in one.

Leveraged Buy Out

This technique, long used by large corporations, is available to almost anyone wishing to purchase a business. With an LBO you use the assets of the company you wish to purchase as collateral for the loan. Virtually every asset can be used; receivables, inventory, raw materials, and equipment. This is an expensive kind of financing—the bank will usually charge you 2-3% over prime, but under favorable conditions, you may be able to secure as much as 70% of the acquisition cost.

Bartering

If you are short on cash but long on products or time, consider trading your excess inventory or services for items that you need. You can go directly to a trading partner or use a barter exchange service to assist you in finding the type of products or services you need. Be aware that the IRS considers the value of the products or service bartered and treats it like cash for tax purposes. To locate an exchange in your area, contact **International Reciprocal Trade Association**, 9513 Beach Mill Road, Great Falls, VA 22066, (703) 759-1473; or the **National Association of Trade Exchanges** in Euclid, Ohio (800) 733-6283.

Venture Leasing

Venture leasing companies rent equipment to brand new companies in return for pricey rental rates and a piece of the company's equity. One company that offer this type of arrangement is Comdisco, Inc. of Rosemont, Illinois.

Entrepreneurial Services

Ernest & Young's Entrepreneurial Services Division headquartered in Dallas offers a variety of advisory services for growing companies through offices in 22 cities. Look in your phone book to see if they have an office near you. They have helped a number of young companies locate capital after being turned down by conventional lenders.

Franchisor Financing

If you are still unable to obtain funds, you might consider purchasing a franchise where the franchisor offers financing. There are over 250 franchises that offer this feature.

Surety Bond Guarantees

The U.S. Small Business Administration can guarantee bonds for contracts up to $1.25 million. They will cover bid, performance, and payment bonds for small and emerging contractors who cannot obtain surety bonds through the regular commercial channels.

Businesses in the construction and service industries can meet the SBA's size eligibility standards if their average annual receipts, including those of their affiliates, for the last three fiscal years do not exceed $3.5 million. Any contract bond is eligible if the bond is:

- Covered by the contracts bonds section of the Surety Association of America Rating Manual,
- Required by the invitation to bid or by the contract, and
- Executed by a surety company that is determined by SBA to be eligible to participate in the program and is certified acceptable by the U.S. Treasury (Circular 570).

Some non-competitive negotiated contracts are eligible if they are in accord with appropriate federal regulations.

Contact your local SBA office listed in the telephone directory under U.S. Government or call the SBA Answer Desk at (800) 827-5722.

Other Important Sources of Information

Bank Financing for New and Growing Businesses. This handy 17 page booklet is available through some banks. If your bank is unfamiliar with it, you can order it directly from Suttmiller & Associates, 11516 N. Port Washington Road, Meduon, WI 53092 for $3.00.

The Catalog of Federal Domestic Assistance. This publication is updated twice a year by the U.S. Government Printing Office and describes every federal money program in detail. You can order it for $38.00 by calling (202) 783-3238.

The Directory of State and Federal Funds. This comprehensive publication lists state and federal funding sources and also gives you tips on how to apply.

Finding Private Venture Capital for Your Firm. Written by Robert Gaston (John Wiley, 1989, $55.00), this insider's guide lays the groundwork for finding the deal that's right for you. Look for it in the library first.

Getting Yours. This book by Matthew Lesko (1987; Penguin Books; New York; $10.00) lists sources of government money and shows you how to write a winning proposal.

Money Sources for Small Businesses: How you can find private, state, federal, and corporate financing. Written by William Alarid (Puma, 1991, $19.95), this book is a comprehensive source of information with state-by-state listings of programs and alternative money sources.

Your Business Plan includes step-by-step instructions for preparing a business plan that you can take to your bank. Available from Oregon Small Business Development Center Network, 99 West 10th Avenue, Eugene, Oregon 97401-3017 or by phoning (503) 726-2250. $14.95

*Take away my people
but leave my factories
and soon grass will grow
on the factory floors.
Take away my factories
but leave my people
and soon we will have a
new and better factory.*

Andrew Carnegie

Chapter 4

Building
Your Staff

You cannot do everything and expect to grow your company at the same time. Even modest success can overwhelm you unless you hire staff and delegate responsibility. Unfortunately most entrepreneurs hire incorrectly. They tend to surround themselves with employees who have similar backgounds and views. Technical people hire technical people, accounting people hire accounting people, etc. This is a natural condition since it is much easier to communicate with people who think like we do. The problem is that a balance of skills is absolutely essential to effectively compete in the business arena.

Unbalanced organizations survive for a while based on the strength of their product, or because of a window of opportunity presented by the market. Inevitably external conditions change, and there is no one in the company who can anticipate or deal with the situation.

You should involve people who have very different backgrounds from you in your organization, *and listen to their input*. If you are a heavily sales-oriented organization, get some good technical and administrative people. If you are technically oriented, you need "bean counters" and "sales types."

How Much Should You Pay

Establishing salary levels doesn't have to be a seat of the pants decision, nor does it have to require an elaborate research effort. One easy way to determine salaries is to look in the Help Wanted section of your local newspaper and see what everyone else is paying for similar positions.

Actual salary surveys are far more precise, and a surprising amount of information is easily available, provided you know where to look. Several or all of the publications listed below may be available from your local or branch library.

The U.S. Bureau of Labor Statistics has collected a great deal of salary information that it issues in the form of inexpensive reports. These surveys are your best starting points for determining prevailing pay rates for your employees.

The bureau's *Area Wage Surveys* are detailed, well-researched reports designed to bring employers up to date on local job market conditions for dozens of common occupations, such as office, technical, and maintenance jobs. Each survey is published in booklet form for a particular geographical area. A complete list including prices is available from the U.S. Government Printing Office, Washington, DC 20402. Each survey includes an appendix that breaks down jobs according to skill and responsibility levels. This information is further grouped by the company size and type of industry, and tells you the actual number of employees surveyed to arrive at the figures in each category.

If you are interested in establishing comparative scales for employees with a higher level of skills, the Bureau of Labor Statistics also has available an annual *National Survey of Professional, Administrative, Technical, and Clerical Pay*. This book is also available through the U.S. Government Printing Office and provides nationwide salary averages for 21 occupations broken down into 91 work levels. The jobs surveyed include, among others, auditors, attorneys, computer operators, personnel directors, and secretaries.

Since salary levels often depend on conditions in a particular industry, you may be able to use a third Bureau of Labor Statistics series of surveys that refine salary data even further. The Directory of Occupational Wage Surveys is an index, available free of charge that lists studies of 32 manufacturing and 17 non-manufacturing industries ranging from refuse hauling to hotel and motel management. Even if your particular industry isn't covered by a bureau study, there will probably be points of comparison with the ones that are covered that can help you further.

There are literally hundreds of specialized salary surveys prepared by periodicals and by professional and trade associations that provide information on a narrow slice of the job market. Every spring, for example, *Datamation* magazine surveys salaries for data processing employees, broken down according to more than 50 different job descriptions from managers to entry level employees. The *National Society of Professional Engineers* located at 2029 K Street NW, Washington, DC 20006 compiles current data on salaries for its members according to job type, level of experience, industry, and region. The *College Placement Council* at P.O. Box 2263, Bethlehem, PA 18001, issues five annual reports on the salaries offered to recent college graduates, as reported by 161 colleges.

Such surveys can give you detailed, reliable information—but often they reflect compensation levels for larger firms where data is easier to obtain. It's important to check company sizes and the number of employees covered by the survey before relying too heavily on the data in such surveys.

The American Management Association at 135 West 50th Street, New York, NY 10020, phone (212) 586-8100, publishes two books that offer in-depth information about compensation plans and practical strategies for smaller companies; *Compensating Key Executives in the Smaller Company*, by Theodore Cohen and Roy A. Lindberg, and *Salary Management for the Nonspecialist* by Stanley Henrici. The AMA's quarterly journal, *Compensation Review* is also a source for current trends and research reports.

Compensating salesmen and sales managers is often a special problem, since pay is closely tied to commissions or other performance-related standards. A book by John W. Barry and Porter Henry, *Effective Sales Incentive Compensation* (McGraw-Hill) offers a detailed analysis of various types of plans for sales employees.

Developing Esprit De Corps

Smart business owners realize their employees are among their most valuable assets. You cannot afford to have unproductive workers on your payroll or to have talented employees leave because they aren't satisfied. "Numerous studies have clearly shown a link between excited and challenged employees and performance," says Richard E. Boyatzis, professor of organizational behavior at the Weatherhead School of Management at Case Western Reserve University in Cleveland.

Boyatzis offers three key principles for creating an effective and challenging work environment.

1. *Strive for Clarity.* People need to know the reason the business exists. To get the real mission of your business across to your employees and help them to adopt your business philosophy, you need to share your vision and dreams for the business.

2. *Make sure everyone is involved.* "Involvement is the best way to achieve clarity," says Boyatzis. Involve your employees in decision making and keep them informed about what's going on in all areas of the business. Share problems as well as victories. You'll be pleasantly surprised by their creative solutions and willingness to endure personal hardship to overcome obstacles.

3. *Develop a system for rewarding and recognizing employees who contribute to your business.* Often, entrepreneurs can't pay big salaries, so they must develop creative methods to accomplish this important task. Employees like to know you value their efforts and how they have contributed to the success of your business. A simple thank you note or letter goes a long way.

Respect your employees and treat them as professionals. Everyone has an important role in the overall success of your company. Stress teamwork. People who pull together will always outperform those who don't, and they will have more fun doing it. Hold your team together by stressing common objectives and mutual assistance. Work hard to pull loners into the group.

Offer competitive salaries and benefits. You will probably not be able to afford to offer your employees complete medical, life, dental, and eye insurance when you first start. Your accountant should be able to help you locate cost effective group plans which your company can join. Involve your employees in the choice. Let them know how much you can afford to spend on insurance. They may want a certain plan and be willing to personally pay the additional cost to get it. If you can't afford certain coverage such as dental, there may be employees who are willing to pay the entire cost of the policy to get the coverage. Many employees may be covered under their spouse's insurance plan. Offer your employees 50% of the cost of your plan if they can prove that they are covered by another plan and they opt to not be covered by you. You both save money.

Offer everyone in your company the opportunity to advance. If they are willing to work to learn the necessary skills and you have an opening in the area they want to get into, give them the opportunity to grow. If someone has the desire to advance and you don't satisfy this need, they will most likely leave your organization.

Give credit where credit is due. Projects usually involve many people. Make sure you thank everyone involved in a successful project and not just the person in charge. When a job is well done, let the customer know who did it. Give your employees their moment in the spotlight. Send a thank you note to their spouse when someone does a good job—include a box of candy or theatre tickets or a gift certificate to a nice restaurant.

> **One of the fastest ways to de-motivate your employees is for you to take all the credit yourself.**

My experience shows that generally employees are more motivated to work hard and stay with your firm if you give them some control over their own work and work environment. An effective leader knows that one cannot continually second guess employees or put too many restrictions on their freedom.

A good training program often helps attract and retain quality employees, but unless you provide a challenging work environment, your training dollars may end up working for your competitor. Don't expect to keep all your good employees; you're bound to lose a few.

But when valuable employees are lost, all is not necessarily lost. Often, you get excellent employee and customer referrals from former employees who appreciate being treated well and the training and challenging environment you provided. I have also had good employees leave and return to my company after an unpleasant experience with a new employer. Don't ever burn any bridges. Employees have the right to move around and you must respect this right.

While you may not be able to compete with large firms in terms of compensation and benefits, you can compete in other ways. You can separate yourself from the crowd by developing a business based on values of employee respect, recognition, and even recreation. Have monthly barbecues where you set up a grill in your parking lot. Make it a pot luck affair where some employees bring salads, others bring deserts, etc. and you supply the main course. Invite your customers. Have picnics where the whole families are involved.

Offer employees a bonus for perfect attendance or no sick time taken. A couple hundred dollars at the end of the year or a couple of extra days of vacation the following year show your appreciation.

Keep your workplace clean and organized. While clean, well-lighted work areas, lunchrooms, and restrooms may not automatically lead to higher productivity, dirty, dingy areas rapidly result in dissatisfaction.

Celebrate employees' special occasions. Put up a hand-written banner on their birthday and work anniversary. If you can afford it, give each employee their birthday off. Send hand-written thank you cards.

Give employees business cards within a week of joining your firm. Seeing their name in print confirms their acceptance.

Show off your business and employees by having employees conduct tours of your facility to prospective customers.

How to Motivate Employees

Motivating and managing your employees will be one of your greatest challenges. In fact, people problems left unresolved can destroy morale, productivity and profits. If you see a problem, it is your responsibility and duty to react quickly and correct it.

So how do you get unmotivated employees to be more productive? I've often heard the best way is to "Kick 'em in the pants." While I don't disagree, I feel there are various ways to administer this "kick."

Negative Physical Kick. This is a literal application of the term and has been frequently used in the past. This technique has three major drawbacks: (1) it is inelegant; (2) it contradicts the precious image of benevolence; and (3) since it is a physical attack, you might just get kicked back. Therefore, I don't recommend this approach.

Negative Psychological Kick. This "tongue lashing" is superior to a physical kick but still has some problems. Even though it appeals to the higher centers of the brain, is less likely to invoke a physical backlash, and usually invokes movement, it does little to create motivation.

Positive Kick. If I say to you, "Do this for me or the company, and I will give you a reward, an incentive, more status or a promotion," are you motivated? Probably. We have long known that it is easier to pull a rope than push it. The same is true for employees. Enticing them to do something works much better than forcing them to do it. And as employees become increasingly self-motivated, it becomes less necessary for the organization to motivate them; they will kick themselves.

Let's examine the pluses and minuses of several different forms of positive kicks:

1. ***Shorter hours.*** This certainly motivates people because they get more time off. But it's not a win-win solution. The employee wins but the company suffers. Letting employees go home when their work is done can sacrifice speed for quality, not something that you, as the owner, are particularly excited about. A variant to time off that often works is the establishment of off-hours recreational programs — sports leagues such as bowling, softball, basketball, volleyball, etc., card playing groups, fishing trips, ...

2. ***More pay.*** This works to some extent, but it has been proven over and over that money is not the best way to motivate people. Employees certainly deserve fair pay, but paying more doesn't necessarily motivate them to work any harder. However, giving monetary bonuses for outstanding performance motivates employees and rewards behavior you want to encourage.

3. ***More or Better Fringe Benefits.*** The cost of fringe benefits has reached almost 25% of a person's wages and yet companies still cry for higher productivity and more motivation, so this doesn't seem to be the answer either. You will find that both the economic nerve and the lazy nerve of most people have insatiable appetites; the more someone gets the more they want. Additional pay and/or benefits are no longer viewed as rewards but as rights. And once something is given, the clock can never be turned back. However, giving your employees a voice in choosing benefit options (such as choosing between two health insurance providers) can be a motivator. If you can't afford certain options, consider offering a shared-cost plan where the employee contributes a percentage of the cost for the new service.

4. ***Better Communications.*** Not just the dissemination of information by management, but listening to what employees have to say and openly discussing issues. When employees can openly voice their concerns and participate in the business, they become more motivated. Show employees the big picture — explain that they are not just tightening a nut, but they are building a car.

A study published in the *Harvard Business Review* resulting from 12 separate investigations (involving lower-level supervisors, professional women, agricultural administrators, men about to retire from management positions, hospital maintenance personnel, manufacturing supervisors, food handlers, military officers, engineers, scientists, housekeepers, teachers, technicians, assemblers, and accountants) shows that while certain things may upset employees, correcting these items does not necessarily motivate them. For instance, employees may not like the company policy regarding time off for jury duty, but modifying this policy will not motivate them to work harder, it will simply eliminate a dissatisfaction. They came up with a list of factors that affect one's attitude toward one's job. The items which lead to job satisfaction (or employee motivation), listed in order starting with the highest motivators are:

>Achievement
>Recognition
>Work Itself
>Responsibility
>Advancement
>Growth

And the items which may lead to unhappiness with the job (but if corrected do not necessarily motivate the employee) are:

>Company Policy and Administration
>Supervision
>Relationship with Supervisor
>Work Conditions
>Salary
>Relationship with Peers
>Personal Life
>Relationship with Subordinates
>Status
>Security

Listed below are some examples of ways to implement these ideas.

>Remove some controls while retaining accountability. *This increases responsibility and personal achievement.*

>Increase the accountability of an individual for their own work. *This increases responsibility and recognition.*

>Grant additional authority to employees in their activity; give them more job freedom. *This increases responsibility, achievement and recognition.*

>Introduce new and more difficult tasks not previously handled. *This increases growth and learning.*

>Assign individuals specific or specialized tasks, enabling them to become experts. *This increases responsibility, growth, and advancement.*

> "The best executive," said Teddy Roosevelt, "is the one with sense enough to pick good people to do what needs to be done, and self-restraint enough to keep from meddling with them while they do it."

Things to Consider Before Hiring Employees

Don't overstaff. Most people utilize their time better when they're busy than when they don't have enough to do. The time spent on the task usually grows or shrinks according to the time allotted to it. Before you hire a new employee, make sure your existing staff couldn't assume the added responsibilities.

Once you've decided you need another employee, write a job description of the new position so you know exactly what experience, educational background, and other qualifications you are looking for. Don't just hire bodies, hire individuals qualified to fill the position you have open.

Remember that what you really need in a service business are *people who like people*. Regardless of what you are selling, it all comes down to people buying from people. Hire people that you are proud to have representing your company.

Where to Find Job Candidates

The first and least expensive way to find new employees is to ask your current employees if they know anyone who is looking for work. If your employees are good workers, chances are pretty good that their friends will be also.

The next best source is to contact prior employees. Contact good ex-employees (the ones you didn't want to lose) three to six months after they leave your organization to see if their new position is working out. They may be too embarrassed to call you but might jump at the opportunity to come back.

Advertise in your local newspaper's Help Wanted section. Running ads every day of the week is usually a waste of money. Run your ad on just Saturday and Sunday, but avoid holiday weekends. Pick up a recent copy of a Help Wanted section and scan the ads. When you find one that looks good to you, write your ad using a similar style or wording. Ask for the candidates to send you a resume or letter stating their qualifications and salary requirements.

Contact your local unemployment office and list your open position with them. The position is posted but no screening is done by the unemployment office. Be prepared for both under and over-qualified individuals to respond to your posting.

Call an employment agency. These companies take on much of the legwork of recruitment, but they can be expensive, charging up to 25% of the new employee's *annual* salary in fees.

If you run a retail operation, you might try soliciting new employees from your customers. Send a letter to all your retail customers letting them know that you have an opening. You might be surprised at the response. After all, the people already know about your store and like it or they wouldn't shop there.

Another source of potential employees is the human resource department of corporations that are downsizing. Often they have placement services for their displaced employees.

How to Interview Job Candidates

Take the time and the effort to recruit and hire the best possible individual for each job opening in your company. Don't hire anyone until you've interviewed at least four people (and preferably ten) for the position—you will find that the more people you interview, the better employees you end up with. Be very selective; it is much easier to hire someone than to let them go. When you hire the wrong person, you waste your time, their time, and your money.

Make sure the candidate clearly understands the position which you are trying to fill. Ask what similar positions they have held. Don't ask yes / no questions. Instead of asking "Have you ever worked in a retail store before?", ask "What positions have you held in retail stores in the past? What were your duties? What were your responsibilities? What part of your job did you like the best? What did you like the least? How did your boss treat you? Why did you leave? Would you go back to work for them again? Why or why not? Describe the ideal boss for me." These questions start them talking and give you more insight into their personality and abilities.

Take the time to jot down a few questions before the interview starts. This will help you stay on track. Interviewing takes a lot of time, but it is time well spent if you keep focused during the interview. If you see the person is wrong for the position, don't feel bad or embarrassed ending the interview early—be polite, but end it. Prolonging the interview just wastes everyone's time.

Let the job candidate do most of the talking. Too many entrepreneurs get overly excited when talking about their company and spend most of the interview convincing the candidate that their company is wonderful and trying to talk the applicant into working for them. When the interview is over, they realize that they know little or nothing about the applicant who was just in their office for 45 minutes.

When considering job candidates, focus on past accomplishments rather than just credentials. Pay more attention to achievements than job functions. Check business references carefully.

Immediately after the interview, jot down your impressions of the individual. Include such items as appearance, friendliness (if relevant to the particular job), poise, stability, personality, conversational ability, alertness, knowledge about the general work field, experience, drive, and your overall impression. Do this immediately after the interview because after a few days, you'll forget who was who.

Here's a big secret: Hire people who are smarter or better at a particular task than yourself. You may say, "I know that." But as Confucius said, "To know and not to do, is not yet really to know." Your actions will show how well you understand this principle.

Companies that attract a high proportion of peak performers are run by individuals willing to give power to gain power, not by people who collect and hoard power in order to squelch others. David Ogilvy, founder of the advertising giant Ogilvy and Mather, reinforced the importance of this principle among his executives by sending a Russian doll to each person newly appointed to head an office in the Ogilvy and Mather chain. The doll contains five progressively smaller dolls. The message inside the smallest one reads: "If each of us hires people who are smaller than we are, we shall become a company of dwarfs. But if each of us hires people who are bigger than we are, Ogilvy and Mather will become a company of giants."

When you find the right person, you'll know it. If you haven't found the right person, keep looking. Don't get discouraged, persistence pays. I cannot overstress this point—*good employees are absolutely essential to your company's success.*

Part-Time Employees

An excellent way to keep costs down is to use part-time employees to assist you with seasonal work loads. Keeping part-time employees motivated can be a challenge. Here's how Tom Cavalli, Vice President and CFO of Bulk International does it. He pays his part-time employees a bonus if monthly sales goals are met in his retail stores during the holiday season. The part-time employees play an important part in these sales. Part-timers can earn from $.50 to $1.00 per hour bonus in addition to their $4 or $5 per hour wage. One of the nice things about this program is that it is self funding.

Consider using a part-time bookkeeper instead of hiring someone full-time. Most small business bookkeeping can be done by someone working just two or three days a week.

Employee Performance Evaluations

Establish a policy of regular employee evaluations. Employees want and need to know where they stand. If they're doing a good job, they want the recognition and praise. If they are unsure of their performance, they want to know how you feel. My suggestion is to formally review employee performance every six months, with salary reviews once a year. *Semi-annual performance reviews do not eliminate the need for daily reprimands and/or praisings.* Problems should be immediately addressed and corrected, and performance that pleases you should be immediately recognized and encouraged.

The purpose of these periodic performance reviews is monitor employee growth and progress on a more general scale. The process can be far easier and more beneficial if you:

- Have established (and mutually agreed upon) performance standards and/or goals by which to evaluate the employee. The employee either has or has not met these standards or accomplished the goals.

- Concentrate on the performance and not the person during the review. You can criticize the performance without belittling the individual. Be completely honest with the employee, and encourage them to openly express their feelings.

- Provide the employee with the opportunity to excel and grow. Encourage employees to take on more responsibility and provide them with a growth path. Set goals for the next review.

- Coach your employees and teach them how to do better. Encourage them to come to you when they have a problem.

- Tie compensation increases to specific performance criteria. If they have accomplished all their goals, then they deserve a large raise; if they haven't, then the size of their raise should reflect your displeasure with their performance.

Independent Contractors

There are several advantages to hiring independent contractors. You eliminate the need to keep track of payroll taxes and the filing of the tax forms and you don't have to pay unemployment or worker's compensation insurance. In order for individuals to qualify as independent contractors, they must:

- Work for others in addition to you
- Set their own hours
- Provide their own tools
- Work on their own instead of being directly supervised by you
- Work for you less than 20 hours per week

If you claim an individual as an independent contractor when they are really an employee, you are taking a big liability risk. Federal and state taxing authorities will impose heavy fines in addition to back taxes if you are found in violation.

Using Consultants

Properly selected and utilized, consultants can be very cost effective and beneficial for small companies. The ability to hire specific expertise by the hour (even though the fee may seem high) is great for limited budgets. Consultants can direct their attention fully to the project at hand because they are free of the time consuming daily operating responsibilities that occupy management.

Finding the right consultant takes as much care as hiring a key manager, even though the relationship may last only a few days or weeks. Unfortunately, consulting is an unregulated business in which anyone can hang out a shingle.

First get recommendations from your colleagues who have used consultants for similar needs. Do not assume that a consultant will be good at doing task B just because he or she got a rave review for doing task A. Make sure the consultant has experience doing exactly what you want done. When interviewing consultants, ask for several references where the individual did the same type of work you are requesting. Call the references and ask questions such as: Did the consultant solve the problem he or she was hired for? Was it solved in a timely manner? Did the initial estimate match the actual cost? What do they feel is the consultant's strongest point? In what area did they seem weakest? Would they hire this consultant again?

Make sure the consultant is truly independent and does not have ties to any vendor or service organization they recommend. Ask them to disclose all the firms from which they receive fees of any sort. Be especially suspicious of consultants whose fees seem unusually low.

Take the time to prepare before the consultant arrives for the interview. Know exactly what you want this person to do. Since consultants are project or task oriented, the more precisely you can define your desired result, the better. The best consultants are the ones who listen and ask lots of questions, not the ones who are constantly trying to impress you. Ask them to present you with a fixed bid for their services or at least a "not to exceed" clause. When they know they are working within a budget, consultants tend to be more focused (and usually less expensive).

Once you've selected a consultant, following these guidelines can increase their effectiveness.

- **Bring the consultant into the project early.** Consultants can often guide initial decisions and planning efforts or provide a quick solution to an immediate problem.

- **Define the task in detail.** If both sides are clear on what is expected, the chances for success increase.

- **Provide the consultant with whatever they need.** This may be some of your employees' time. It may be company records. It may be your ideas or approval. Once you've hired the consultant, make sure they get all the support they need.

- **Monitor their progress.** You can expect more if you inspect more.

- **Verify their results.** The ultimate decision to implement the consultant's recommendations rests on your shoulders. Make sure you're completely comfortable with the results before you act.

To locate a consultant, look in the *Consultant and Consulting Organization Directory*, published by Gale Research, (313) 961-3707. This directory is available in most libraries.

How to Select an Attorney

You are going to need the services of an attorney from time to time. Try to find one with whom you feel comfortable. Having a lawyer you know, trust, and can call on in emergencies, can provide a great deal of peace of mind, even if you prefer to handle most matters on your own.

How do you find an attorney?

- Word of mouth is the best place to start your search. Ask friends, neighbors, business associates, members of trade organizations, customers, accountants, and your banker for attorneys they know and respect. Be sure, however, that the recommendation is based on a prior business relationship with the lawyer and not on a personal one.

- Contact your city, county, or state bar association, which will be listed in the white pages of your telephone directory under the name of the city, county, or state in which you live, i.e. Alameda County Bar Association. Most bar associations have a lawyer referral and information service that will assist you in your search. Not all referral services screen lawyers before listing them, but most do have lawyers listed in their records according to their areas of expertise. Some communities have legal services directories listing attorneys, their specialties, training, and sometimes even their fees. Ask the local bar association if such a directory exists in your area and how to obtain one.

- Check the Yellow Pages — for areas of specialty, hours, and locations. You may also obtain information by looking for lawyer advertisements in newspapers and on the radio and television.

- If you live or work near a law school, contact the dean's office, describe your needs, and ask if the school or individual faculty members are able to recommend someone.

Below are some questions you should ask your prospective attorney:

Will you meet with me to get acquainted before I hire you?

Many lawyers will meet with you once without charge, as long as you make it perfectly clear that you do not expect any free advice during this get-acquainted session. Pick an attorney that talks to you in a language you understand — not "legalese." Here are some questions to ask at that first meeting.

What percentage of your business is devoted to general business practice?

Attorneys, like doctors, are often specialized. Choose an attorney in general practice who handles commercial matters. This general practitioner is very capable of keeping your legal affairs in order, is usually cheaper, and can refer you to a specialist when the need arises.

It is wise to use the services of a specialist for matters such as serious criminal offenses, workers' compensation cases, and bankruptcies, etc. If you need expert advice, pay the extra cost and hire a senior attorney with significant experience in the matter before you. Poor advice and/or representation from an inexperienced or incompetent lawyer can end up costing you far more in the long run.

If something goes wrong between us, will you consent to binding arbitration?

Most state bar associations have arbitration committees which, for a fee, well settle disputes that you may have with your lawyer about fees. By agreeing to binding arbitration, both attorney and client agree to present their cases to an outside panel and to abide by its decision in the dispute.

Negotiating Fees

Most fees are agreed upon through discussions between clients and lawyers. If you cannot afford what the lawyer asks, say so. Fees are negotiable. Shop around until you find a lawyer who is willing to work within your budget. If necessary, you may want to discuss working out a payment plan if you do not think you can afford a lump fee.

Here are some questions to ask about fees:

What services do you provide for a flat fee?

Often, you will be able to pay a set fee for straight-forward tasks such as composing a deed, will, or incorporation.

What are your hourly rates?

Depending on the experience and reputation of the lawyer, you could pay from $20 to $300 per hour. Make sure the hourly fee is understood from the very beginning.

Do you bill by the minute, in tenth of hour, or quarter hour increments?

It is very common for lawyers to bill in tenth or quarter hour increments. For example, if your lawyer charges by the quarter-hour and you are on the phone for only five minutes, you will still be billed for a full quarter-hour of the lawyer's time.

Do you require a retainer for your services?

A retainer is similar to a downpayment for services to be per-formed. (No retainer is preferable.) If a retainer is required, be certain you know exactly what services are and are not covered by this retainer. Ask that the retainer be applied to the balance owed. Also insist the lawyer agree to refund the balance to you if the retainer exceeds the cost actually spent on your matters.

Do you accept contingency fee arrangements?

If you are under financial pressure or cannot raise enough money to hire a lawyer on an hourly basis, (for legal case work such as a lawsuit) request a contingency fee arrangement. Under this arrangement, the lawyer collects a percentage of any amount of money you win as a result of the case being decided in your favor. If you do not win the case, the lawyer does not receive a fee. Since you may have to pay court costs, which are different from lawyers' fees, be wary of statements that there will be "no charge" if you do not win.

Ask whether the lawyer computes the contingency fee before or after the expenses for handling the case are disbursed. You may collect more money if expenses, such as court costs or witness fees, are deducted before the contingency fee is computed.

145

The customary contingency fee is 33 percent of the settlement award, although fees range from 25 to 50 percent. Some lawyers offer a sliding scale in which the percentage changes depending on how long it takes to settle the case, and/or how much the award is.

If the sliding scale is based upon how long it takes to settle, the lawyer may collect 25 percent if you settle before trial, 30 percent if there is a trial, and 40 percent if there is an appeal. Or, the sliding scale may be based on the size of the amount, with the lawyer generally receiving a lower percentage as the amount increases. You should discuss the sliding fee option with your attorney to negotiate the best price.

Make sure you get your agreement in writing.

Attorneys are very expensive. One way to control their costs is to use them less. Another is to get a written estimate or top limit on the fees you will be charged before you have them begin working on anything for you. Remember that they bill by the hour and tend to overcomplicate everything they work on. Insist on monthly *itemized* invoices and review them carefully. If you feel your money isn't being spent wisely, say something!

You also have several legal assistance options if you cannot afford legal fees, but need a lawyer's help. The federal government's Legal Services Corporation funds offices across the nation to serve low-income clients. Legal Aid Societies and other public legal assistance programs in your county or city also may be able to help you. If you live near a law school, see if it has a legal clinic serving the community.

Lastly, don't assume that attorneys are always right; trust your gut feelings and question their actions and judgment. If you disagree with what you are being told, get a second opinion. And if you have a complaint about your attorney, contact the local bar association or the national headquarters, the American Bar Association, at (312) 988-5158.

Why Hire a CPA?

They can provide you with many services beyond the typical record keeping and tax preparation duties.

- They can help you set up your internal record keeping.
- They can help you locate a good accounting package to run on your office computer.
- They can advise you on lease / buy decisions.
- They can help you write a business plan.
- They can help you set up a retirement account.
- They can help you get a loan.
- They can help you analyze the profitability of your business and make possible suggestions for improvement.
- They can recommend other professionals such as business consultants and attorneys.

When shopping for an accountant, look for one that has experience in your field. Most industries have special tax considerations, so it's nice to have an accountant that already has this knowledge. Start out with a small accounting firm and have them handle both your business and personal taxes. You will be more important to a small firm and will get more personal attention.

Find an accountant that uses and is familiar with computers. You are missing a tremendous opportunity and competitive advantage if you don't fully utilize this technology.

Other Important Sources of Information

Hiring the Best. If there's one book you read on the topic, make it this one by Martin John Yates (Bob Adams, 1988, $9.95).

Employees: How to find and pay them. This 18 page publication from the Small Business Administration will provide you with answers to some basic questions about interviewing, using temporary services, and establishing fair pay. It costs about $1.00. Call (800) 827-5722.

The Desktop Lawyer. This reference tool comes with two binders and eight diskettes containing over 175 legal forms and over 35 checklists designed to walk you through every conceivable transaction in which you might become involved. It is published by The Open University and is available from the author: Laurence J. Pino, Pino & Dicks, 24 South Orange Avenue, PO Box 1511, Orlando FL 32802 (407) 425-7831.

The view that an industry is a customer-satisfying process, not a goods-producing process, is vital for all businessmen to understand. An industry begins with the customer and his or her needs, not with a patent, a raw material, or a selling skill.

Chapter 5

Marketing Your Product or Services

How important is marketing? No matter how good your product or service is, its fate in the marketplace will be determined largely by how you expose it to the consumers. However, no amount of marketing can make up for a poor product or poor service. There's an old story about a president of a dog food company who was angrily addressing his subordinates, saying his dog food brand had great packaging, great ads and a good price. Why, he bellowed, wasn't it selling? An underling gave him the simple answer: Dogs won't eat it.

Marketing is one of the most challenging activities in the world of business because it requires making choices that will please others. Most people find it hard enough to decide what's best for themselves. How much more difficult to anticipate and choose what others will want, enjoy and appreciate! Successful effective marketing certainly takes special talents and skills. More than that, it demands exceptional sensitivity and familiarity with your consumers.

A poorly focused marketing plan translates into wasted money. There are many firms that can offer you assistance in this area. Most will be happy to show you what they can do for you and itemize how much it will cost. Look in the yellow pages under Marketing Consultants or Sales Promotion Services. Ask for references. Call each reference to see if prior customers are happy with the services they received. Ask if they feel that they got their money's worth and would use them again.

Free Media Coverage

One of the quickest and most effective ways to publicize your business is through free local media coverage. Convince your local newspaper to do a story based on your product or services. Mention of your new business in a local newspaper is more valuable than advertising. More people read articles than ads.

Take advantage of the many hidden publications in your community such as special publications for seniors, singles, business associations, junior colleges, and weekly advertising supplements. Simply write a brief article about your new business and send it to the editor of each of these publications. Sometimes it's easier to get your article published if it contains a newsworthy event, such as sponsoring a fund raiser, a fashion show, a unique swap meet, a free grand-opening barbecue, a community service project, etc.

Customer Retention

Once you gain an account, you must do everything in your power to keep it. **Customer retention is the key to profits and growth.** According to an article published in the *Harvard Business Review* in 1990, "Companies can boost profits by almost 100% by retaining just 5% more of their customers." Think about it—you can *double* your profits with just a *five percent* increase in retention. Studies also show that for service-type businesses costs can drop by as much as two-thirds from the first to the second year because customers know what to expect from you and you become more familiar with their particular needs. As time passes and loyalty grows deeper, your customers will even be willing to pay a premium because of their confidence in your company. In fact, you probably know someone who is willing to pay more to stay at a hotel they know and trust rather than chancing it with a less expensive unknown.

Before you spend lots of time and money trying to solicit new business, make sure you are taking care of your existing clients. It is much cheaper to keep an existing customer than to find a new one. Treat your customers with dignity, respect, and honesty. A satisfied customer is also your best sales person. According to a 1990 study, up to 60% of your new business can be the direct result of referrals.

Five Rules for Creating Powerful Advertising

If you can't afford professional help, and you want to create some ads or flyers on your own, here are some helpful rules to follow.

1. **Quickly grab the reader's attention.** People are busy and seem to always be in a hurry. You have only a second or two to catch the reader's attention. David Ogilvy, the advertising guru, states that "The *headline* represents eighty cents of your advertising dollar." This means that you should spend eighty percent of the time you spend on your ad developing your headline. This message should be relatively short and in bold type to grab the customer's attention quickly. *It must tell how your product or service benefits the customer.* It's been proven in hundreds of advertising tests that the way to get somebody to read something (or to buy something) is to promise a great benefit. Don't expect people to read your ad unless you quickly and effectively communicate this benefit to them.

2. **Use subheads that outline what you are saying.** Most people who read your ad will only read the headline and subheads. Therefore, your subheads must walk the prospect through your sales pitch. If your products or service offer four main benefits, it's logical that they should be brought out in the subheads. *Focus your subheads on benefits to the reader not on product features*. One way to ensure you are phrasing your subheads correctly is to insist that they contain the word "you." Ken's Widgets help you... or Using Don's Tree Service means you...

151

3.   **Use eye-catching graphics that support your promise.** If you promise fast service, show what makes your service fast or show a race car to support this concept. If you stress convenience, display a customer being shown a product, or short check-out lines, or on-site delivery, etc. Above all, the graphics should pull the reader's eyes into your ad and support your headline.

Many larger copy shops can help you with "stock" graphics or photographs if you don't have your own. They can also typeset the copy and help you with the layout. Look in the yellow pages under Desktop Publishing.

4.   **Write copy whose subject is the reader and whose hero is your product or service.** Make your ad mainly about your customers—about their problems and their needs. Explain in detail why your product or service is unique among all the alternatives—why it is better than the competition; all the time *stressing benefits over features.* Think of your product as the hero that shows up to "save the day." *As with the subheads, make sure the word "you" shows up more often than your product name.*

Don't write copy that is too clever. In general, use the same standards in writing copy that would apply in a conversation with a customer.

Make sure your copy is clear, understandable, and short. It is better to stress one point very clearly than to confuse the reader with four poorly presented ideas. Since you have to assume that most readers have little time and less patience, your ad must be crystal clear. Revolve your ad around one single, powerful idea.

5.   **Make sure your ad calls for action.** The purpose of your ad is to sell your product or service. What is it that you want someone to do once they have scanned or read your ad? If you want a phone call, then conclude your ad with a prominent subhead: *To start saving money today, phone*

123-4567. If you want them to come to your store, try *Bring this ad to our store at ... and receive an additional 10% discount on your first purchase.*

If your ad doesn't clearly and quickly communicate your product's benefits, you will be wasting your money—people just won't take the time to read it.

Where to Advertise

Target your advertising where you get the best return on your advertising dollars. If you have a business that caters mostly to your local neighborhood or community, you can print inexpensive flyers at a local copy shop and hand them out door-to-door. This ensures that everyone in your local area at least receives the information.

Advertising in your local newspapers gives you wider coverage at a higher cost. Your ad will be seen by lots of people, but not everyone will be a potential customer. Consider advertising in inexpensive local publications that are delivered to every home in your community. You may find that they pull better and cost less. Experiment.

Placing an ad in the yellow pages of your local phone book is good for almost every business. When people want a service and don't know where to go, often they go to the phone book first. Don't scrimp on your ad in the phone book. Make it as large as you can comfortably afford.

If you have a product that is of interest to only specific people, then mailing advertisements directly to your target market is very effective. You can expect to hear back from 1 to 3 percent of the people you contact through direct mail.

You can obtain specific mailing lists from numerous companies. They can select by categories such as industry type, zip code range, and annual sales volume. Check with the reference librarian in your local library for a book of companies that rent these lists. One such company is American Business Lists at 5711 South 86th Circle, P.O. Box 27347, Omaha, NE 68127. Call them at (402) 331-7169 for a free catalog. They assemble their lists from listings in the phone books. Each business is then called to obtain the owner's name, annual gross revenues, number of employees, and other pertinent information.

If you market to a specific group of people, you can quite possibly benefit from advertising a magazine that is widely read by your potential market. Start with a single small ad as a test. If you get good response, try a larger ad. A good, well-targeted ad should be able to pull .1 percent (1 out of a thousand) of the total circulation.

Pursue radio and television advertising with extreme caution. The ads are expensive, the coverage area is enormous, and you may be disappointed with the results. This type of advertising works well for auto dealerships and large mass merchandisers, but represents a poor advertising investment for the majority of small businesses.

Five Marketing Basics

1. Your objective is to influence, not impress, the buyer.

2. Be brief. The more you say, the less impact it has.

3. A product's benefits are only as good as their perceived value. Always stress benefits over features.

4. Develop a plan. An accurate plan that is poorly executed is better than a vague plan executed with precision.

5. Do something. We more often regret those things we should have done than those we actually did.

How to Price Your Products or Services

This one decision probably affects your overall success or failure more than anything else. Pricing is a marketing tool that can be creatively used to build your business.

First you need to decide what you want your pricing to do. Do you want to increase sales? To maximize profits? To deter competition from entering your niche? To establish a particular image?

The items you must consider when establishing your price are:

1.   What is the cost of your product. Be sure to add your overhead costs (sometimes referred to as burden) to the price you pay for your products. You must amortize your building rent, utilities, depreciation, employee wages, taxes and benefits, phone bill, postage, ...all other costs of running your business... (don't forget items that are only billed periodically like insurance premiums and year-end accounting fees) onto the cost of your inventory. The easiest way to do this is to calculate your average monthly costs less merchandise and divide this number by your monthly merchandise costs.

For example: You purchase $50,000 worth of products a month and all your other monthly expenses come to $18,000. Dividing $18,000 by $50,000 gives you .36 (36 percent). This is the burden you must add to the cost of each product you buy to calculate its true cost. To an item that costs $17.47, you must add $6.29 overhead ($17.47 times .36) to arrive at a true cost of $23.76. This is the minimum amount you can sell this item for and break even. If you desire to make a 10% pre-tax profit then your selling price would be $23.76 + $2.38 or $26.14.

For a service business such as bookkeeping services, desktop publishing services or teaching, treat the salaries of the individuals involved as the raw material cost. For example, you have 6 bookkeepers (including yourself) that bill out their time on an hourly basis. Your total salary cost for these individuals (including part of your salary cost since you bill out a portion of your time also) is $15,000 per month. All your other expenses (including the portion of your salary not allocated to direct billing) cost you $4,050 per month. The overhead percentage would be $4,050 divided by $15,000 = .27 or 27%.

You're not done yet. How many hours do you realistically expect each individual to bill each month? A month is calculated as having 22 days time 8 hours or 176 hours. The typical bookkeeper may bill 6 hours per day times 22 days per month or 132 hours. Divide that individual's salary (say $2,000) by 132 hours to arrive at their effective cost per hour. $2000 divided by 132 = $15.15 per hour. Now add the 27% for overhead ($15.15 times .27 = $4.09) to arrive at a true hourly cost of $19.24. Again add to this figure your 10% profit ($1.92) to arrive at a billing rate of $21.16. This would provide you with a monthly profit of $1,500 ($15,000 @ 10%).

Your overhead percentage will change monthly as you sell more products or add additional costs. Over a period of time you will be able to establish a standard percentage to use.

2. How will the customer perceive your costs? Are you providing good value? Will the customer perceive the cost of the product or service you are selling as too high or will they be willing to pay more for it? For specialty services such as performing an energy analysis on a family home, do a survey and ask potential customers what they feel would be a fair price for this service, and would they be willing to pay that price? Their answers may surprise you. They may be willing to pay two, three, or four times what you were going to charge. Here the consumer is paying for the value of the service and not for the hourly wage of the individual performing the service.

3. What is the competition charging? You must be competitive with the marketplace. Are you providing more or less service than your competition? Is the customer willing to pay extra for this extra service? It is all a game of *customer perceived value*. Do your customers feel your price fairly reflects the value they are receiving? If not, you must adjust your price or change their perception.

Customers want and are usually willing to pay extra for "the personal touches" from remembering their name to courtesy, friendliness, and an attitude of sincere caring.

Building Prospect Lists

In most business-to-business sales programs, you make the first contact by telephone or through direct mail. In either case, you need to develop comprehensive prospect lists.

Your first step should be to visit your public library. There you will find excellent directories such as the *Ward's Business Directory*, which lists companies by size and state, along with state industrial directories. Industry specific trade publications can be located by using the *Standard Rate and Data Service (SRDS)* and the *Gale Directory*. For instance, to target architects, you search *SRDS* for the trade publications that cover that industry. Then contact those publications for issues that list members by size, location, or other characteristics. You may also be able to purchase or rent rights to all or part of their circulation lists. If you are concentrating in a particular geographic area, ask to select names by zip code, county, or state.

Trade associations often publish directories of their members and may be worth contacting directly. Membership lists can usually be purchased for a nominal fee. If the lists are only available to members, see how much it costs to become an associate member. It may be worth the cost of membership just to get the list.

Consider joining professional and civic organizations to gain access to their rosters. Local business publications can also be an excellent source for developing prospect lists. These regional journals often publish lists of major companies by size.

Once lists from all your sources have been gathered, carefully review them to eliminate duplicates and companies that obviously fail to meet your criteria. Next determine the title of senior people within those organizations who are most likely to be in a position of buying authority. Always try to work with the most senior person possible. You just waste your time selling to individuals who carry little weight within the company. Once these individuals are sold, they often lack the ability to sell the idea or product to their management.

Now you must call the prospect companies to obtain the appropriate individual's name if you don't already have it. Most receptionists are helpful when asked politely, "I'd like to send some information to your vice president of marketing. Can you tell me to whom I should address it?" Make sure you make it clear that you want to send literature and not speak directly to the individual at that time or the receptionist may be less cooperative.

It's easier to maintain and use your prospect lists if you keep them on a computer. There are several good software packages available to assist you in this task. Most allow you to attach notes and other information to each prospect and many have "tickler" systems built in to further organize your selling activities. Insist on the ability to automatically merge the names into letters or mailing labels. This simplifies and speeds up the task of addressing the mailings.

When it's time to send out your mailing, consider calling the prospects first and asking them to watch for your material. "Look for a white envelope with a picture of a tree in the corner." Or even better, ask their permission to send it. If you only mail to people who want your literature, you save postage and get a more qualified lead.

A few days after you've mailed your literature, call the recipients to see if they have any questions or would like more literature or a demonstration. Follow-up phone calls can increase your response rate from two to tenfold.

Selling to The Government

Many government contracts are "set aside" or reserved for small businesses. You will receive lots of literature from government agencies once you've requested information about contracts. It may seem overwhelming at first, but if you get your foot in the door and find the right niche, you could have steady work for a long time. For more information contact one or more of the following:

1. Look up and visit the nearest General Services Administration (GSA) Business Center if you live in the vicinity of Atlanta, Boston, Chicago, Dallas, Denver, Fort Worth, Hous-

ton, Kansas City Missouri, Los Angeles, San Francisco, Seattle, New York, Philadelphia, or Washington. Look in the phone directory under "United States Government." Or you may write to GSA, 18th and F Streets NW, Washington, DC 20405. Ask for a sample copy of the *Commerce Business Daily (CBD)* and ordering information. This publication is the government's official journal of needs, bid opportunities, and related information.

2.   Contact the Office of Small and Disadvantaged Business, The Pentagon, Room 2A 340, Washington, DC 20301-3061, and ask for procurement information for small businesses.

3.   Write or visit your state capitol building, county courthouse, or city hall, and speak to the purchasing and supply department. Request information about becoming a prospective contractor and ask for a registration form.

4.   Write your senator or representative and ask when the next seminar on selling to the government will be held. Members of Congress frequently sponsor such sessions.

Civic Organizations

Organizations such as the Kiwanis Club, Rotary, Lions Club, and the Chamber of Commerce are wonderful places to meet other local business owners and potential customers. Several have regular luncheon or breakfast meetings. Once you are a member, you have access to the organization's roster for your direct mail advertising.

Deliberate Customer Turnover

In a service type business you will find that the 80/20 rule often applies. Twenty percent of your customers will generate eighty percent of your business. You will also find that twenty percent of your customers will generate eighty percent of your problems and headaches. If these two groups are the same, you need to work on improving your product or service. More than likely you will have a customer that is generating more problems than profit. In these situations it is better to approach the customer and end the relationship as amiably as possible. In the long run both you and the customer will be happier. In this light, it is desirable to turn over five to ten percent of your customers per year. Replace small unprofitable customers with new profitable business. This is a great way of increasing your profits and still stay "small."

Win/Win Philosophy

I will assume you want to be in business for a long time. The secret of longevity is to enter every dealing with a win/win philosophy. Your prices must be good for you and good for your customers. Your wages and benefits must be good for you and good for your employees. The prices you receive from your suppliers must be good for you and good for them. This philosophy creates strong, long-term relationships. Relationships start to sour only when the scale begins to tip too far to one side or the other.

Low wages are good for you and bad for the employee (win/lose). What happens? Production drops. Employees quit. You have high turnover, waste lots of time training new employees, and build a bad reputation. You lose. Win/lose just changed to lose/lose. How about if you treat your employees fairly in the first place? "Fair" means an even balance, tipped neither to the left nor the right. Your turnover goes down, your employees are motivated, your production goes up, the business grows, you offer even better benefits, and on and on and on.

You drive your supplier's prices down so low that they barely make any profit on your account. (win/lose) What happens? The first time there is a shortage of product, guess who'll get cut—you or a more profitable account. Don't kid yourself. You'll be out in the cold. Or maybe you'll be part of the five percent of the customers your supplier decides to let go this year. You lose. Instead, what if you established a win/win relationship from the start. You are a good account for the supplier; you get great service, you get promotional considerations, you get co-op advertising money, you get leads, and on and on and on. Everyone wins.

You have a market with no competition so you overcharge your customers for everything you provide. (win/lose) What happens? Some enterprising individuals decide to start a business directly competing with you under one of two motives—you're making a lot of money so they can too or they're upset at the way they've been treated by you. They take part of your customers; you end up lowering your prices to compete against them and now you only have half as much business. You lose. What if your initial pricing was fair and reasonable? The incentive for a competitor to enter your arena would not be there and you would enjoy the lion's share of the market forever.

I hope you get my point. If not, any success you have will be short lived.

Other Important Sources of Information

Guerrilla Marketing Attack. This book by Jay Conrad Levinson (Houghton Mifflin, 1989, $8.95) effectively lays out the many options for small companies who can't afford to hire an advertising or public relations agency.

Pricing Your Products and Services Profitably. This SBA publication is available for $1.00 by writing SBA Publications, P.O. Box 30, Denver, CO 80201-0030 or by calling (202) 205-6743.

Small Business Marketing. This book is bent toward retail, but it is good for anyone just learning about topics such as media buying and advertising. It is available from the Oregon Small Business Development Center Network, 99 West 10th Ave., Eugene, OR 97401-3017 or by phoning (503) 726-2250. The cost is $14.95.

The Wall Street Journal on Marketing. This book, written by Ronald Alsop and Bill Abrams (Dow Jones-Irwin, 1986) is a collection of the Journal's "Marketing" columns and other feature articles. It covers the broad functional areas of marketing and provides insight into changing consumer behavior, new products, advertising styles and campaigns, packaging and promotion, retailing and distribution, selling services, the world market, and corporate strategies.

While no one should quit because the going gets rough, it may be wise to take a moment to see if there isn't an easier way to reach the same destination.

Chapter 6

Effective Management

Having a title after your name and putting yourself at the top of the organizational chart doesn't make you a good manager. It just makes you the boss. Management combines technical and administrative skills with vision, compassion, honesty, and trust. Unfortunately, too many managers take themselves too seriously and too few take management seriously enough.

Just because you're in charge, don't feel that you have the right to boss people around like they are your slaves—you are not in business for the power trip, or if you are, you won't be for long. You are in business to make money, and you can't do that without your employees' support. Treat your employees with dignity, respect, and total integrity, and they will want to help you succeed.

If your business fails, you will have no one to blame but yourself, but if you are successful, your employees will deserve most of the credit. Once you really, truly appreciate this concept and grasp how important your employees are to your ultimate success, you will understand the essence of management. You must create an environment that fosters personal and financial growth for both yourself and your employees.

One of the first things you must learn is that you can accomplish much more by directing the activities of others than by doing everything yourself. The Chinese proverb states that "The eye of the master can do more than his hand."

Most entrepreneurs like to be "the expert" in every aspect of their business. If you don't release this attitude, you will always be small — both personally and financially. Don't make all the decisions. Delegate tasks, responsibility, and authority to others. Give them guidance initially, but eventually give your employees the freedom to do their job. It's just plain poor management if you must make all the decisions. What if you get seriously ill for 30 or 60 days? Will your company survive your illness? I know too many business owners who have worked for years and years without ever being able to take a vacation (They're always going to take a *big* vacation next year.) Think about it; is that the life you want? If you get in this position, you have no one to blame but yourself.

Good leaders understand that true leadership consists of only seven basic concepts, which have pretty much remained unchanged throughout time.

1. *You must take risks.* If you never take a risk, you aren't really leading, you're just supervising.

2. *You must be innovative.* You won't usually find answers to your critical problems in textbooks. You must have the ability to think creatively.

3. *You must take charge.* Complacency doesn't cut it. You must take control and lead your organization. You must have both a vision and a plan.

4. *You must have high expectations.* The higher your expectations, the greater your results will be.

5. *You must be positive.* A positive, upbeat attitude creates an atmosphere where you have fun and things get done.

6. *You must get out in front.* Lead by example. Lead by pulling, not by pushing. There is a world of difference

between walking the walk and just talking the talk. You as the leader must "walk the walk."

7. ***You must care for your employees.*** Proper management involves caring for people, not manipulating them.

Sixteen Roadblocks to Noteworthy Achievement

Napoleon Hill discusses the psychological attributes of success and failure in his book *Think and Grow Rich* (Fawcett Crest, 1960). He states that a lack of persistence is "the real enemy which stands between you and noteworthy achievement." Hill sums up this lack of persistence as failure in 16 possible areas:

1. Failure to recognize and to define clearly what one wants.

2. Procrastination, with or without cause.

3. Lack of interest in acquiring specialized knowledge or skills.

4. Indecision, the habit of "passing the buck" on all occasions, instead of facing the issues squarely.

5. The habit of relying upon alibis instead of creating definite plans for the solution of problems.

6. Self-satisfaction.

7. Indifference, usually reflected in one's readiness to compromise on all occasions, rather than meet the opposition and fight it.

8. The habit of blaming others for one's mistakes, and accepting unfavorable circumstances as being unavoidable.

9. Weakness of desire due to neglect in the choice of motives that imply action.

10. Willingness, or even eagerness, to quit trying at the first sign of defeat.

11. Lack of organized plans placed in writing where they may be analyzed.

12. The habit of neglecting to move on ideas or to grasp opportunity when it presents itself.

13. Wishing instead of doing.

14. Compromising instead of dealing with issues head-on.

15. Searching for all the shortcuts; trying to get without giving a fair equivalent.

16. Fear of criticism — failure to create and implement plans because of what other people will think, do, or say.

Success vs. Attitude

There is a direct correlation between your attitude and your ultimate success. Your commitment toward accomplishing your goal is merely a reflection of your attitude. We all know what success is — it's accomplishment... "I did it." Here are the other rungs on the ladder of success.

10.	Determination	I will do it.
9.	Knowledge of Power	I can do it.
8.	Willingness	I will try to do it.
7.	Faith in Self	I think I can do it.
6.	Lack of confidence	Do you think I can do it?
5.	Desire	I wish I could do it.
4.	Inability	I can't do it.
3.	Indifference	I don't care if I do it or not.
2.	No Desire	I don't want to do it.
1.	Stubbornness	I won't do it.

20 Ways to Increase Employee Performance

1. *Establish clear expectations.* Make sure your employees understand what their job is and what you expect of them. When you give out assignments, spell out as many details as possible. Don't make any assumptions.

2. *Delegate responsibilities.* There is a difference between telling a person to do something and making them *responsible* for its successful execution. Give them the task and

then you must let go. Chances are that the employee will do the project in a slightly different manner than you would have, but you must give them this freedom if you want them and the company to grow. Be certain they understand exactly what responsibility they have. This is particularly important in group projects. Make sure the individuals within the group all have clear cut responsibilities.

3. ***Face up to unpleasant tasks.*** If you have unpleasant tasks that your employees must do, face up to the situation and give them the assignment anyway. Accept the fact that not all projects that your employees must perform will be pleasant for them.

4. ***Monitor your employee's use of their time.*** Employees can abuse the time they should be spending on their job by excessive socializing, conducting personal business during business hours, or just wasting time by doing nothing. In the worst case, this lost productivity can force overtime. Monitor your overtime policies carefully.

5. ***Learn to say "no" tactfully.*** Whenever you must refuse an employee's request, be it for a raise, time off, or whatever, make sure you decline the request in a way that doesn't alienate the employee. Always give the individual an explanation for your decision.

6. ***Keep your employees informed*** on all issues that might affect them. If you don't spread the truth, your employees will become distrusting and rumors will fly. Experience shows that rumors are almost always worse than any bad news you might be holding back.

7. ***Keep meetings to a minimum.*** It's been said that a company's success is inversely proportional to the number of meetings it holds. Make sure meetings are really necessary before you call them. Keep your meetings short and to the point. (Hint: Stand-up meetings tend to be shorter than sit-down meetings.) Set a time limit for each meeting. Have

167

a written agenda allotting a predetermined amount of time to each subject and follow that schedule. Distribute this agenda a few days before the meeting so everyone will come prepared to discuss the important topics. Start and end meetings on time. Don't wait for late arrivals—start without them, or better yet, lock the door and don't let them in, and then *you* make the decisions that affect them or their department. Never hand out support material at the beginning of a meeting. If you do, people will be reading the material when they should be listening to you. After the meeting prepare a written document recapping decisions reached and action items to be accomplished (with names and specific due dates).

8. ***Explain the economics of business to your employees.*** It is important that they understand how much product or service must be sold to pay for each business expense.

Here's an example to show the point. Let's take an employee who earns $30,000 per year. To determine the total cost to the company, we must add the cost of benefits and company-paid taxes which equals $13,800 (46 percent of wages according to the U.S. Department of Commerce). We will assume that your company earns 5 percent after tax profit and is in the 50 percent tax bracket.

To determine how much sales revenue is needed to pay for this employee's wages, the calculations go like this:

Salary and benefits	**$43,800**
Tax deduction (50%)	**-21,900**
Cost of salary and benefits (after taxes)	**21,900**

Divide this number by 5% (.05), the after tax profit percentage and you get **$438,000**. This dollar figure represents the gross sales necessary to pay for one employee earning $30,000 per year and maintain your 5 percent after-tax profit. This is truly a shocking statistic to most people. *One of the secrets of success is understanding that when you purchase something, you pay for it with profits, not gross income.*

Here's another example to make this point clearer — let's assume you want to buy a stapler that costs $10.00. You will pay for it by selling some of your Widgets which sell for $10.00 each. If you sell one of your Widgets for $10.00, you cannot use *all* this revenue to buy the stapler, since you must pay for the Widget, which costs you $6.00, and an additional $3.50 will be used to pay for fixed costs (building rent, payroll cost, etc.). This leaves you with only $.50 (5 percent profit) to go toward the cost of the stapler. This means you will have to sell 20 Widgets to have enough profit to buy the stapler. ($10.00 divided by $.50). Twenty Widgets sell for $200.00 ($10.00 X 20). So the $10.00 stapler really costs you $200.00 in sales.

Most people neither understand nor appreciate this until you explain it to them.

9. *Rotate job responsibilities* to the extent that it is practical. This minimizes boredom and provides for cross-training within your organization. You will appreciate the cross-training aspect of this during vacation time and when employees are ill. Job rotation also allows you to compare individual employee job performance as they move from position to position.

10. *Get rid of the "bad apples"* regardless of how talented or competent they may be. I am specifically talking about individuals with bad attitudes, poor work habits, or who set a poor example for other employees. It only takes a few of these types to erode the productivity of an entire department or company. Be fair, they should be given the opportunity to shape up, but if they don't ...

11. *Promote from within* whenever possible. This doesn't mean that you should never consider bringing in an outsider. You must use your best judgment, depending on the position and availability of promotable employees. As long as it is your "policy" to promote from within whenever possible, this in itself builds morale.

169

12. ***Lead by example.*** You should exemplify the standards you expect your employees to follow, especially in areas of punctuality, appearance, courtesy to customers and other employees, and willingness to work extra hard when the need arises. Few things will motivate employees more than to see the boss pitching in when the pressure is on.

13. ***Treat each employee as a unique individual***, but retain consistency in your general approach to supervision. The way you handle each employee will vary based on their unique personality and position, but make sure the rules and regulations are fairly enforced throughout the organization.

14. ***Praise often.*** Be sincere and praise in public. Praise those actions or activities that you want to encourage, and don't worry about over-praising. Most people respond to praise by working harder. It's far better to over-praise than to under-praise.

15. ***Criticize in private.*** When employees aren't performing to your standards, let them know, but do it in private and with tact. Focus criticism on the activity and not the individual.

16. ***Talk to employees who quit.*** An exit interview with a departing employee can provide you with insight into company problems which you may not even know exist. Listen to both sides of the story before taking any rash actions.

17. ***When you make a mistake, admit it.*** If you don't, you are just encouraging your employees to conceal their mistakes from you. Employees respect honesty and humility more than perfection.

18. ***Look for problems and ways to improve everything.*** Never assume that your employees will verbalize concerns on their own and don't assume that employees will come running to you when they screw up. You must actively seek

problem areas. Encourage comments, observations and suggestions. People closest to the activity invariably have efficient and creative solutions for most problems. Focus on fixing the problem, not blaming someone.

19. ***Stretch your employees.*** When given the choice to give an assignment to someone who is slightly over-qualified and someone who is slightly under-qualified, give it to the under-qualified person. This will help the individual grow, increasing their own self-worth and their value to the organization.

20. ***Assign a deadline to every project and monitor the progress.*** Tasks just take longer when there is no deadline. Make sure deadlines are realistic and all parties agree that they are reasonable and attainable.

When Things Aren't Going Quite Right

Sometimes there will be problems and you just won't be able to spot them. Maybe moral is low or business is slower than normal for no apparent reasons. Your employees may see the problems but are afraid to confront you. Having your employees answer a questionnaire (anonymously if desired) may highlight the problem and point you in the direction of a solution. See Appendix C for a sample questionnaire.

Time Management

There will be many demands on your time and if you're not organized and protective of your time, you will find yourself at 5, 6 or 7 o'clock in the evening wondering where the day went. Here are some things that have helped me get control of my time.

1. ***Organize yourself.*** Make and prioritize a to-do list of everything you have to do. Take a moment and read Appendix D at this time. Make copies of the form and start using it today—in fact start right now—make and prioritize a list of everything you have to do. I *guarantee* you will feel better and more organized.

171

2. ***Prioritize your tasks.*** Think how each task on your list contributes toward your business goals. Concentrate on the most important items first. Its not how much you accomplish, but *what* you accomplished that counts.

3. ***Work smarter not harder.*** Don't try to crowd every minute of the day with tasks. If you do, you will simply create tension within yourself and your overall productivity will decline.

4. ***Schedule your tasks to take advantage of your most productive time.*** Realize that you have certain times of the day when you are most productive. Plan to do important or difficult tasks at this time.

5. ***Schedule unpleasant tasks early in the day.*** If you have a particularly unpleasant task to do, do it first thing in the morning. That way you get it done early and can move on to more pleasant activities. Once it is done, you will get a surge of energy that will propel you through the rest of the day. If you put the task off, you will either consciously or subconsciously dwell on it — this dark cloud will hang over your head and rob you of energy and enthusiasm until the task is completed.

Having a written to-do list is the single most effective time management technique I have found. Having numerous loose slips of paper laying everywhere or post-it notes stuck to everything in sight does little to help you get or stay organized. You misplace notes, lose phone numbers, and can't find important messages. Using a to-do list and staying focused on your most important tasks will double your productivity and effectiveness.

Use your to-do list to record daily information such as important calls and phone numbers, notes to yourself, and follow-up reminders. Turn the sheet over and write more detailed information you don't want to forget on the back. Use a yellow highlighter to mark the items you finish. It's amazing how good you feel at the end of the day when the sheet is covered with yellow ink—and the sense of accomplishment you feel knowing you've spent your time wisely.

At the end of the day before you go home, make a new list for tomorrow, transferring the unfinished items to the new page. Make twelve file folders labeled January through December. Drop yesterday's list in the appropriate folder. This way you can go back through a whole year's lists if necessary. It's surprising how often you'll need a phone number or try to remember someone's name and then recall that you talked to the person a couple months ago. Within a few minutes you can find the information. What a tremendous tool!

I now use and carry a Pocket Day-Timer calendar. I find this smaller format works better for me personally. But I use it the same way as I used the larger pages. To obtain a free catalog of the Day-Timer time-management calendars, contact Day-Timers, Inc., One Day-Timer Plaza, Allentown, PA 18195-1551.

Other Important Sources of Information

The Portable MBA. This book by Eliza G. C. Collins and Mary Anne Devanna (John Wiley & Sons, 1990, $24.95) presents a series of concentrated seminars on everything from accounting to marketing to quantitative techniques, taught by a team of leading business thinkers from America's top schools, including Columbia, Harvard, Wharton, Stanford and M.I.T.

In Search of Excellence. This classic by Thomas J. Peters and Robert H. Waterman, Jr. (Warner Books, 1983) is full of lessons from America's best-run companies.

All I Really Need to Know I Learned in Kindergarten. This book by Robert Fulghum (Villard Books, 1989) is must reading for everyone.

The Double Win. Dr. Dennis Waitley's book describes how to get to the top without putting others down. This book outlines the philosophy I have followed for years. I believe the win/win philosophy is one of the basic secrets leading to true success. Berkeley Books, 1985.

173

It is harder to conceal

ignorance than to

acquire knowledge.

Andrew Glascow

Chapter 7

Automation

Business owners are discovering that the computer is becoming as crucial to their businesses as the calculator or telephone. The advent of affordable desk-top computers provides small business owners with computing power that only a few years ago was beyond the financial reach of all but the largest corporations. What an advantage you have over those who only a few years ago had to do everything by hand!

Small businesses and small computers are ideally suited for each other. For small businesses in the 90's, working smarter will be critical. Every business, regardless of its size, is managed with information. Orders, invoices, contracts, letters, expense figures, inventory reports, sales figures — the list is virtually endless. You as a small business person face the same challenges as big business: how to grow despite labor and skills shortages, how to cope with the cost of money, new tax legislation, and the constant need to keep up with change.

Today the computer is the answer of choice, and in the near future, the computer will become an answer of necessity. Just as you can't now conduct business without a phone, the day isn't far off when you won't be able to do business without a computer. Necessity or not, how do you buy something you may not fully understand?

What is a Computer?

Computers are really nothing more than information processors. With them you can store, retrieve, change, analyze, monitor, and report your company information in all its various forms.

A computer is told what to do through a set of instructions — sometimes called a *program*, sometimes called *software*. Software tells the computer what to do and how to do it. Without software, a computer can't do anything.

The physical part of the computer is called *hardware*. Hardware consists of the components you can actually touch — the monitor, the computer with all its electronic components, the printer, keyboard, mouse, etc.

Processors are represented by numbers — 286, 386, 486, etc. Generally speaking, the larger the number the faster the machine. A computer's processing power is also affected by its internal clock speed. This speed is designated in *megahertz* (MHz) — 25 MHz, 33 MHz, 50 MHz, etc. The larger the number the faster the computer can process data. Think of the computer as a car with the processor representing the size of the engine and the clock speed representing how fast the engine is running. When you look at computers, the sales people will talk in terms of these two numbers. A 486 based computer running at 50 MHz might be referred to as a 486/50.

Buy a computer right away. The sooner you start taking advantage of the management information that computers can provide, the more money you will make or save. Buy your machine from a reputable source and buy proven software that conforms to your business. And buy all the computer you can afford, because you will continue to find new ways to use it.

176

What Can a Computer Do For Me?

It can help improve profits, the service you offer, and the quality of the work you do. It can help you manage your money and time. It can help you run your business and keep your business from running you.

A computer can help you get your bills out on time, do your payroll, pay your bills, keep track of your inventory, assist you in preparing professional-looking letters and proposals, and keep track of your appointments and work schedules. With the right software, computers can do all this and more.

A computer helps you work more efficiently by performing many of your tasks faster, cheaper, and more accurately. A computer increases your effectiveness by providing you with management information and freeing up your time. Giving you time to concentrate on critical business issues. Time to plan. Time to innovate.

In small businesses, accounting and word processing represent the largest uses of computers. Other common applications include: database/file management, spreadsheets, desktop publishing, education, personal finance, budgeting, planning, presentation graphics, project management, design work (CAD/CAM), and job training. The truth is, computers can help you do almost any job better, faster, and more accurately.

What Can a Computer Do For My Business?

It will take some time and effort to set your business up on a computer. But it has been found that there isn't much loss of productivity if you take it one step at a time.

You will need to decide which jobs you want the computer to do. Some jobs such as billing, inventory control, accounts receivables, accounts payable, payroll, and general ledger are pretty much the same regardless of the line of business you're in. Other tasks, such as finding the right coverage for a client if you are an independent insurance agent, are industry-specific. The good news is that all these applications are readily available with off-the-shelf software.

What Does Integrated Software Mean?

Integrated software referrs to groups of programs that share common data. Most integrated accounting packages let you use the same data for different jobs in different parts of your business.

Take inventory control, for example. When the item code and quantity are entered as an order, the computer checks to see if the items are in stock. If so, the quantity is subtracted, giving you a new quantity on hand. If that falls below a specific minimum quantity, the computer can automatically produce an order for more of them.

By analyzing the numbers, inventory control programs can maintain a high level of customer service while holding cash investment to a minimum. The computer can spot what is selling to make sure that the bin is full, and what isn't so you can move to reduce inventory.

Once merchandise is shipped and invoices are cut, the computer can help keep accounts receivable to a minimum. To aid in managing your cash flow, the computer will automatically generate collection notices, calculate late or finance charges, and put a credit hold on filling further orders when accounts lapse beyond an acceptable period.

Using the information captured in billing, inventory control, and accounts receivable, the computer can analyze sales. For each item sold, the computer can list the customer, customer location, and sales person. By analyzing the numbers, the computer can help you adjust sales territories and product mix to better respond to your customer's needs. The computer can also analyze current sales and compare them to previous levels, so you can accurately track the performance of individual sales people and products as well as your business as a whole.

At the same time, your computer can generate customer information to help your salespeople plan more productive sales calls and travel arrangements. By analyzing customer buying patterns, the computer can also help you detect trends and new market directions.

Clearly, all this information should flow to your general ledger. As the information flows electronically within the computer, you greatly reduce accounting steps, avoid losing information, and minimize errors.

The general ledger, the summary of all your business journals, needs to be posted at the end of each accounting period. The advantage of the computer is that while you run the business, it does the posting. How? By reading the general ledger account number that you have assigned each transaction.

When the computer has everything in order, it prints transaction listings and journals, and it posts each journal entry to the proper place in the general ledger and on the financial statements.

Once this information is in the computer and the bills are out, you can generate graphs and charts and conduct spreadsheet analysis. Graphs and charts can portray in pictorial format what may lie buried in the data. With spreadsheets you can play what-if analysis (for instance, what if you raised the price of a product by 10 percent or what effect will a tax revision have on your bottom line?)

The accessibility of spreadsheets has contributed to a new trend in entrepreneurship. The advantage — an extremely powerful advantage — is that new products, new services, and new ways of doing business can be systematically tested before spending the money and committing your business.

Three other areas where computers can benefit your new business are in the areas of word processing, desktop publishing, and business management systems.

Word processing programs can help organize your words like accounting programs help organize your numbers. For example, if you type a letter with a typewriter and find you left out a sentence, you have to retype the entire letter. With word processing, you find the spot on your computer screen and type only the new sentence. The computer takes care of shifting everything else down.

Many programs help you edit, revise, and change text in seconds. You can move words in phrases, phrases in sentences, sentences in paragraphs, even paragraphs between pages and between reports. You can do mass mailings by merging names and addresses from your customer or prospect lists with "boiler plate" letters.

With word processing software, the computer can check the spelling, find a word, number pages, add footnotes, combine different typestyles, align your words in columns or justify your margins if you want squared off paragraphs.

Desktop publishing applications can help you publish what you write in-house, with professional design and typography. Without the cost of middlemen, you can lay out your document, select the type font, and do all the composition work. Your payback in time and money saved is immediate. (This entire book was produced using a home computer, laser printer, and desktop publishing software — the book was delivered to the printer in camera-ready format just as you see it.)

Desktop publishing can be used to create newsletters, advertisements, catalogs, brochures, flyers, proposals, overhead transparencies, training guides, and more.

Business management systems can now help you manage your office routines — your calendar, telephone, notepad, and in-and-out box. These benefits can all be delivered by generic ready-to-use computer programs. They are usually self-instructing, and most are designed to get you up and running in a short period of time.

If they fit your business, the dividends of computerizing with ready-made programs are immense. If they don't, you still have two choices. You can modify prepackaged programs to fit your business needs (This means you will have to hire a programmer) or you can buy industry-specific programs.

There are many programs written from the specific rather than the generic vantage point. Instead of a general accounting system, for instance, you may want a retail accounting system, or a retail accounting system for a camera store. There are specific systems for farmers, advertising agencies, doctors, lawyers, printers, service stations, bakeries, etc., etc. There is probably a system specifically designed for your line of business. It may take more effort to computerize your business with this type of system, but the benefits to you may be greater.

While generic programs are usually found in computer or software stores, industry applications can be found by working with a third-party programmer, industry remarketer (IR), value added reseller (VAR), through an industry association that specializes in your type of business, or through a consultant.

Evaluate your choices carefully to determine which provides you with the best of what you need, both in terms of price and performance.

How to Choose the Right Software

With dozens of products in every category and new ones arriving all the time, how do you choose the right software for your particular needs? First, check with business colleagues. Buying software is like buying clothes. You want something that closely fits *your* needs. It is better to over-buy than to under-buy. Trying to fit into a jacket that is too small just doesn't work. The same is true with software. Make sure it does everything you want and need up front.

For generic applications such as spreadsheets and word processors, you can go to a reputable computer store that offers demonstrations of competitive products. Explain to the salesperson what you want to do and have them make recommendations to you. Ask why they recommend the particular product over all the others they sell. Ask to see the first chapter of the documentation to see how easy it is to understand. Ask about any limitations this product might have.

Computer magazines regularly review these software packages. Look for articles that compare several competitive products rather than reviews of a single product. The product comparisons will allow you to evaluate features side by side. If you can't find a current review at the magazine store, try your local library. Look through back issues of the computer magazines until you find what you want—but don't go back any farther than six months or the information will be outdated.

Where to Buy Software

If you are new to computers, buy from a local computer store that offers after-sale help and possibly even training. Even if you pay a slight premium, it's comforting to know that they will be there to help you.

If you are an experienced user, consider shopping mail order. You can often save significant money by utilizing this no-frills option. Always compare the prices to those at your local computer stores. If the difference is not significant, you should support your local economy.

How to Buy a Computer

Choose your software before buying your hardware. Often the software will dictate the size and speed of computer you need. Don't shop on price alone. Ask the sales person about service, support, and education classes available. Look for a sales person who listens to you and the questions you ask before jumping into the sales pitch.

You should begin to shop with an idea of everything you want your computer to do. You also need to know the volume of information that the computer must retain. For accounts receivable, this includes how many customers, open invoices, and orders you receive each month. For inventory, it's how many products you stock. For accounts payable, it's how many vendors, open invoices, and checks you print per month.

You can buy your computer from a local computer store, a discount store selling computers, by mail order, or through a reseller. Both industry remarketers (IR) and value added resellers (VAR) buy computers at established discounts and add significant value — typically incorporating hardware, software, and support — and sell "total solutions" that are often for a specific need or are industry-oriented. Whether you buy from a store or an IR/VAR generally depends on whether or not you decide to use generic programs or solution-tailored programs specifically for your industry or business.

Stores often advertise and should be easy to locate. Most IRs and VARs advertise in industry trade publications or through direct-mail.

Working with Value Added Resellers

Check out VARs and IRs with the same scrutiny that you check out any other professional with whom you will work. Try to review at least three competing products before you make your purchase decision. Plan on spending at least a couple hours evaluating each company's software. Have the sales representative show you every feature of the system and explain why this particular system is better than someone else's. Again, it is better to buy a system that already does everything you want (or more) than to buy one that is too small, even if the vendor promises to add the features you need at a later date.

Below is a good checklist to follow when working with VARs or IRs.

❑ Have the reseller demonstrate the software at your site or arrange for you to visit a customer's site.

❑ Ask the reseller ...
How long have you been in business?
How many customers do you have?
How large is your staff?
What were your gross sales last year?
How many offices do you have?
Where is your support group located?
How large is your support group?
Where do you train my staff, at my location or yours?
How much training is included with the system?
How many people can attend the training classes?
Do you have a toll free phone support line?
What are your phone support hours?
Who is your largest user? (Make sure it won't be you.)

❑ Ask the reseller for five business references that are approximately the same size as your organization. Then ask to see the entire customer list and ask if you can select five more references at random from the entire list. See if the number of names on the list equals the number of customers the vendor told you they had.

❏ Talk to the references. Here are some questions to ask them:
> How long have you used the software?
> Which modules do you use? (receivables, payables, etc.)
> How many employees do you have? (same size as you?)
> What do you think of the quality of the software?
> What do you think of the quality of the support?
> What do you think of the quality of the training?
> How many updates do you receive per year?
> How many bugs are in the software?
> How responsive is the vendor to fixing bugs?
> How long does it take them to fix bugs?
> What features of the software do you like best?
> What would you like to see changed in the system?
> Do you feel this software is the best on the market?
> In your opinion, which software is the next best?

❏ Does the system meet all your needs?
> Reporting—daily, weekly, monthly, and on-demand
> Accounting needs
> Tax reporting
> Auditing
> Financial analysis and reporting
> Managements reporting
> Sales and marketing

❏ Do you get the source code to the system?
> If not, insist that a copy of the source code be deposited in an escrow account and it be updated with every new release of the software. Both companies should sign an escrow agreement allowing you access to the source code should the reseller go out of business or stop supporting the product.

❏ How much does the system cost?
> Is this an all-inclusive cost or are their other hidden fees?
> How much does monthly support cost?
> How much do program updates cost?
> (And how are they updated?)
> Pay 1/3 of the amount as a down payment.

Pay 1/3 of the amount when the system is installed.
Pay 1/3 when you are satisfied with the system.

❑ How much does extra training cost?
Where is it held?
How often is it held?

❑ Ask for a thirty day, **no cost** evaluation period.
Run parallel—no matter how painful. What this means is that during the testing period you will have double work. You will continue to do the functions that will be automated the same way you always have and you will also do them on the new computer system. Then compare the results of your old systems with the computer. They should balance. If they don't, find out where the problems are before you commit to buying the system.

❑ Read the sales contract very carefully. If you don't like parts of it, have it modified or rewritten by your attorney.

Some Problems a Computer Can't Solve

A computer generally won't save you money by eliminating employees. It will create new ways of doing things. Providing your secretary with a word processor doesn't mean the number of letters produced per day will increase, but the letters will probably go out with fewer spelling and grammatical errors. If you were billing monthly, you may find that with a computer you can bill weekly and speed up your cash flow.

A computer won't solve employee problems or poor internal procedures. If your receivables are always wrong because the clerks at the counter are sloppy or careless, automation won't help. Automating inaccurate information will still provide you with the same wrong answers.

A computer can't solve a problem if you don't know what the problem is. Suppose a competitor is luring your accounts away and you rationalize that it is because of the competitor's computer system. So you run out and buy one of your own. You'll probably be disappointed. You'll have the machinery, but you don't know what problem you're trying to solve.

185

...

A computer won't make you a better manager. Having lots of information doesn't guarantee that you'll make better decisions. They will be more informed decisions, but not necessarily better.

Computers don't always tell the truth. They just do what they are told, so if something doesn't look right, question it.

Computer Consultants

If you know little or less about computers, you may be money ahead to hire the services of a computer consultant. Before doing so, re-read the section on "Using Consultants" in Chapter 4.

You can locate a computer consultant by contacting the Independent Computer Consultants Association, at either (800) 438-4222 or (314) 997-4633. Another source is the *Consultant and Consulting Organization Directory*, published by Gale Research, (313) 961-3707. This directory is available in most libraries.

Site Preparation

When designing the area for your computer system, you should give special consideration to electrical requirements, telephone access, lighting, and security.

Electrical Requirements

Even though today's computers can be plugged into any normal electrical outlet, I recommend that you have your electrician install an *isolated 20 amp circuit* specifically for your office computer equipment. When you purchase your computer you should also purchase a surge protection device (surge protector). Plug this surge protector into the isolated outlet and then plug your computer components into the surge protector. This will isolate your computer from all but the most severe electrical spikes. If you have a modem in your computer, purchase a surge device that also isolates electrical spikes coming from the telephone line.

Electrical power spikes can both destroy data stored in your computer and cause physical damage to your computer equipment. Placing your computer on an isolated circuit minimizes the chances of spikes generated by other office equipment damaging the computer. Items such as electric typewriters, microwave ovens, copy machines, coffee pots, electric motors and personal heaters can all cause these spikes.

Telephone Access

Install a phone next to your computer. If you must call for technical assistance on a computer problem, it is handy to be able to sit at the computer while you are on the phone.

Lighting

Your computer should be situated so that you are neither looking directly into a window nor have a window directly behind you. Either of these conditions cause eye strain when viewing the monitor. The bright light coming from a window in front of your computer will cause you to squint while light from behind will create annoying glare on your screen. If you notice glare from your office lighting, try tilting the monitor to eliminate it or, as a last resort, purchase an anti-glare screen for your video display.

Security

Place your computer system where it is not easily visible from any window. Remember that the true value of the computer system is not the cost of the hardware or the software, but the value of all your company information stored inside it. Protect it accordingly. I recommend purchasing a small fireproof storage box in which to store your data backup diskettes or tapes. This should be located in a different room than the computer itself.

Make sure you back up your data on a regular basis — preferably daily. Keep your month-end back-ups for at least a year.

The basic need of every company is to make a profit. Only then can it provide jobs and earnings for employees.

I. W. Abel

Chapter 8

Financial
Strategies

Running a business brings many rewards—independence, community prestige and personal satisfaction, but true entrepreneurs never lose sight of the need to make a profit. Profits pay for employees, benefits, and give you the money you need to "give back to the community." Most entrepreneurs realize the importance of cash, and make at least some effort to know their cash position on a fairly current basis. (If they are wrong, their bank will help keep them on track by returning their checks.)

Cash vs. Accrual Basis Accounting

You can keep your books on either a cash or accrual basis. The prevalence of cash basis accounting reflects this intuitive understanding of the importance of cash (setting aside the use of cash basis accounting to juggle tax liability). Unfortunately many companies utilizing cash basis accounting are essentially bankrupt and do not know it because they still have cash in the bank. The benefit of accrual based accounting is that it gives you a leading indicator of your cash position in the near future. If you start showing losses on a pure accrual basis, you might have time to do something before your cash position reflects your losses.

The basic difference between cash and accrual accounting is in the way you "book" revenue and expenses. With cash accounting, sales are posted to the financial statements when the money is *received*, not necessarily when the sale is made. If the buyer buys on credit, you don't post the amount (for financial statement purpose) until you receive the payment. Likewise, you post expenses to the financial statements when you *pay* the bill, not when you receive it. You can see why it is called cash-based accounting—the financial statements reflect *cash* received and *cash* paid out. The tax advantage of cash-based accounting arises from your ability to pre-pay invoices at the end of your tax year to reduce your current taxable income. This will, however, come back to haunt you in later years. When you prepay expenses this year, you have less expenses next year (since you paid them this year)—which means you will show more profit next year. This will force you to pay more taxes or again pre-pay more expenses next year. This is a vicious cycle once you start it. Work closely with your accountant when determining the best tax strategy for you and your business.

With accrual-based accounting, revenue is posted to the financial statements when the sale is made and expenses are posted when you receive the bill, without regard to when the payments are received or the bills are paid.

Easy on The Spending

Be prudent with your initial spending. It's not necessary to start with a custom executive leather chair and a slate topped walnut desk. Avoid Taj Mahalitis—the urge to outfit a fledgling business in a grandiose style.

It's much better to start small and lean. Think about every penny you spend. Nice office space, original artwork, and expensive furniture only serve to feed your ego and contribute nothing to your profits. Your first few years will be your toughest anyway; why burden yourself with unnecessary debt? Work smart and spend your money wisely. Slow and steady wins every time.

Equipment — Lease vs. Buy vs. Rent

Few companies can afford to pay cash for large purchases, but those who do pay cash generally pay the least for their equipment since they avoid the steep finance charges associated with bank loans or leasing. However, saving money on equipment may not be your highest priority. The money used to purchase the equipment may generate a better return on investment (ROI) if used in other areas such as marketing or sales. Also, if the equipment you are planning to buy is likely to become obsolete fairly quickly, you may not want to own it.

> **It's not necessary to buy all new equipment—the savings can be substantial on used items.**

When you purchase equipment for cash, you do not generally get to deduct the entire cost of the equipment as a business expense that year. The equipment must be *depreciated* over its expected useful life. For example, suppose you pay cash for a piece of equipment that costs $5000. The IRS guidelines may determine that the useful life of this item is five years. Depending on the type of depreciation chosen, you may only be able to deduct a maximum of $1000 during the first year. If the item was purchased with this year's profits, you would still have to pay taxes on the other $4000 even though you spent the money and no longer have the cash available! This is a somewhat complicated area of accounting and there are various depreciation options available to you. Be sure to check with your accountant before you make any major purchases.

The advantages of paying cash are:
- It is generally your least expensive option.
- It enables you to depreciate the equipment.

The disadvantages of paying cash are:
- Cash is usually in short supply at most companies.
- Your cash might be better spent somewhere else.
- You are exposed to the risk of obsolescence since you actually own the equipment.
- You may end up having to pay taxes on money you no longer have.

For the majority of small companies that can't or don't want to pay cash, borrowing or leasing may be your only alternatives. In general, since interest rates are usually less on loans than on leases, borrowing is the least expensive of these two options, but that really depends on the creditworthiness of your business and the relationship you have with your banker.

Borrowing usually requires a down payment which uses part of your available cash. This cash might be put to better use elsewhere. You will own the equipment in the end, but it may be obsolete by the time you pay it off. It's hard to throw away working equipment even if it is obsolete. But if it is not replaced, older equipment may become a drag on your operations in a few years.

The advantages of borrowing money to buy equipment are:
- It is generally less expensive than leasing.
- It enables you to depreciate the equipment.

The disadvantages of borrowing money to buy equipment are:
- It uses a credit line that could be used elsewhere.
- It represents a liability on your balance sheet.
- You are exposed to the risk of obsolescence since you actually own the equipment.
- Bankers are becoming more and more conservative when it comes to lending to small businesses.

Leasing equipment is generally the most popular choice since it usually requires no money down (other than maybe first and last month's lease payment). Many lessors offer flexible payment schedules which can mean even lower monthly payments. If you ask for it, some companies will offer payment schedules that fluctuate based on your seasonal cash flow. When leasing directly from the manufacturer, insist that your lease allows you to trade up to newer or better equipment mid-term with no penalty.

Leases are written so that the equipment has a *residual value* at the end of the lease. This is the amount you will have to pay for the item, should you decide to purchase it at the end of the lease. This may range from "fair market value" to a fixed dollar amount that can vary from several thousand dollars down to just a dollar.

At the time you negotiate a lease, the leasing company can fairly accurately predict the remaining value of some items, like a car, but will have more difficulty in calculating the value for items that become quickly obsolete, such as copiers or computers. Consequently, leasing companies factor these unknowns into your monthly payment. For an item that will have little or no remaining value at the term of the lease, you will end up paying close to the entire cost of the equipment, plus the leasing company's interest charge throughout the lease period.

If there is any uncertainty on the part of the leasing company, you can bet that they will base their calculations on a minimal residual value (meaning higher monthly payments to you) and establish the value for purposes of the paperwork at "fair market value." In this scenario, the leasing company always wins. If, at the term of the lease, the equipment still has significant value and you want to purchase it, you must pay that higher "fair market value" even though your monthly payments were calculated based on the assumption that the equipment would have minimal value. Should the equipment be relatively worthless at the end of the lease, the leasing company is covered since they have already passed virtually the entire cost of the equipment on to you through your monthly payments.

Therefore, it is to your advantage to establish the actual residual value of the equipment up front and put that *exact dollar amount* in the lease paperwork. This provides a fair correlation between the monthly payments and the residual value.

There are two kinds of leases: finance leases and operating leases. In an operating lease, the ownership of the equipment usually reverts to the leasing company at the term of the lease. Most leases for office equipment are of this type. Payments on this type of lease are treated as operating expenses and are deducted directly from operating revenues. The lease does not appear as a liability on your balance sheet the way that a loan purchase for the same equipment would. This makes it easier for you to borrow money in the future (less long-term debt).

Finance leases require you to purchase the equipment at the end of the lease period for a percentage of the original purchase price or for a nominal amount. Since in this type of lease the ownership eventually passes to you, the equipment is treated as a depreciable asset, and the lease will appear on your balance sheet as a liability.

If you choose to lease major equipment, you should require the following terms and conditions to be placed in the lease.

1. **The right to add new, used, or third-party upgrades with or without financing from the original lessor.** If your lease prohibits you from obtaining competitively priced upgrades for your equipment, your only alternative may be to upgrade through the original lessor at prices they dictate. This is especially important where the manufacturer of the equipment is leasing to you directly.

2. **The right to sublease the equipment.** Most leasing companies will allow you to sublease the equipment if you no longer use it. You should check to ensure this provision is written into your lease.

3. **The right to reconfigure subleased equipment.** Make sure you have the right to modify the equipment as necessary for you to sublease it. Some leases will only allow you to sublease the equipment as originally configured.

4. **The right to sublease to other leasing companies.** Some leasing companies consider it reasonable to restrict you from subleasing to other leasing companies even though they say they will not "unreasonably withhold" their consent. Unless you have the time and contacts required to release your equipment directly to another end-user, you should include a provision to allow you to sublease to other leasing companies.

5. **The right to return the equipment with like parts at the end of the lease.** As parts wear out or as you replace them, make sure you have the right to replace these parts with "like parts." This allows you to purchase replacement parts from third parties which can sometimes save you substantial amounts. Make sure that you do not have to

replace all these parts with original equipment if you exercise your option to return the machinery at the end of the lease.

Leases are typically very technical in nature and should be reviewed by either your accountant or attorney before you sign them.

The advantages of leasing are:
- You are protected from obsolescence since you are under no obligation to purchase the equipment at the term of the lease.
- The asset may not be carried as a liability on your balance sheet.
- You can get 100% financing—no down payment.
- If the equipment has a significant residual value, your monthly payments will usually be less than with borrowing.
- Leases can generally be written to allow you to upgrade the equipment or replace it with equipment of higher value during the term of the lease with no penalty (your payments will increase to cover the new value). As an example, approximately 60% of all computer leases are renegotiated mid-term.
- Leases directly from the equipment manufacturer can be written to also include equipment maintenance.

The disadvantages of leasing are:
- It is generally the most expensive way to buy equipment.
- You must generally pay a penalty if you cancel the lease midterm.

Another option is to rent the equipment. Equipment that is only occasionally required should be rented on an "as needed" basis. This is especially true of any equipment required for seasonal work or where your need for specific equipment may vary by job. Don't polish your ego with a fleet of pretty trucks or other equipment that you can't keep busy 100% of the time. It's better to polish your pocketbook with wise cash and asset management.

The advantages of renting are:
- You pay on an as-needed basis.
- You can rent exactly what you need; no more, no less.
- You are not responsible for major maintenance — if it breaks on the job, you just call the rental company for another unit.

The disadvantages of renting are:
- The equipment may not be available when you need it.
- You have to schedule for pickup and delivery of the equipment.
- The hourly cost of use is higher than if you own the equipment, provided you can keep it busy all the time.

Extending Credit

Extending credit to customers is a delicate issue. To "lure" some customers, it may be necessary to extend credit terms. The secret is to balance the liberalness of extending credit with the amount of bad debt it generates — if you are too generous and extend credit to everyone, you may end up writing off substantial amounts as uncollectable; if you are too tight with credit, you may lose some potential sales. A general rule is to start out granting credit terms carefully, and as you get more comfortable with the paying habits of your customers, you can loosen up a bit. If you write off *no* bad debt, then you are probably too stingy with your credit. Check with your accountant to determine an acceptable amount of "bad debt" for your business type.

You should be able to obtain general "credit application" forms from a local stationary store. You are also entitled to run a credit check on anyone (individual or company) who applies for credit from you. Several credit bureaus such as those listed below will supply more extensive credit information for a fee payment in advance.

ABI Network
5711 South 86th Circle
Omaha, NE 68127
(402) 593-4650

Computer Science Corporation Credit Services
652 Northbelt, Suite 133
Houston, TX 77060
(713) 878-4840

Dun & Bradstreet, Inc.
Dun's Dial Credit Reports
(800) 362-2255

Equifax
1600 Peachtree St., NW
Atlanta, GA 30309
(404) 885-8000

Trans Union Credit Information Co.
555 W. Adams Blvd
Chicago, IL 60661
(312) 258-1717

TRW Information Services Division
505 City Parkway, West
Orange, CA 92668
(714) 385-7000

Ask for credit references from the prospect's bank. Ask the bank how long the prospect has had a checking account. Do they bounce checks? If so, how often? See if they have they borrowed money from the bank. If they have, how good is their repayment history?

The National Association of Credit Managers at 8815 Centre Park Drive suite 200, Columbia, MD 21045, (410) 740-5560 offers educational programs, trade references, seminars, and publications. Call them for a free brochure of their services.

Credit Cards

Industry experts claim that taking charge or credit cards can increase a company's business from 10 to 50 percent, depending on the type of business and its clientele. But it's not always easy to become a credit card merchant. It is fairly easy to establish an American Express merchant account by calling (800) 528-5200. The same is true for Discover which offers merchant accounts by calling (800) 347-6673. Visa and Master Card are more difficult to obtain. Below are three avenues for you to pursue.

1. ***Try your bank.*** Ask to speak with an officer. If your bank resists, offer to buy a $1000 CD to be pledged against potential credit card losses. This will sometimes reassure them that handling your business will be both safe and profitable. If your bank still refuses, try other banks in your area.

2. ***Join a business organization or trade association that offers access to Visa and Master Card accounts as a member service.*** To find a trade association in your field, check the *Gale's Encyclopedia of Associations* in your local library.

3. ***Contact an independent sales organization (ISO) or bank agent.*** These companies act as intermediaries between banks and small businesses. They sell you the credit card processing equipment and charge you a fee on top of the bank's transaction fee. You can expect to pay an ISO several hundred dollars more for their credit card processing terminal than you would through other sources. Likewise, you'll pay between 4 and 7 percent in transaction fees, compared to 2 to 5 percent with a bank. Still it's better than not accepting credit or charge cards.

Here are some ISOs to contact if you need their assistance.

Bancard (800) 666-7575 or (303) 530-0264
Cardservice International (800) 456-5989 or (818) 593-3500
Data Capture Systems (605) 341-6461
Datacap (818) 331-1003
International Bankcard Systems (303) 691-2513
R. E. Mulhern Co. (800) 245-2558

Invoices vs. Statements

Many large accounts only pay "bills" or "invoices." If your billing document happens to say "statement," it may not get paid. My suggestion is to use "invoices" for all billings.

Include terms on your invoices. It's typical today for most businesses to allow 30 days for payment, although "due on receipt" is a close runner up for small companies. Ten and fifteen day terms are also becoming more popular. My suggestion is to use "TERMS: NET 10 DAYS."

Invoice your customers promptly. If it's practical to do weekly invoicing, by all means do it. The sooner you invoice, the sooner you'll get paid. Having money tied up in receivables doesn't pay the rent.

If a client is late paying an invoice, call them and ask if there was a problem with the goods or services. If there is no problem, politely ask them when you can expect payment. This works much better than demands. If your customer is having financial problems and needs more time to pay the invoice, work with them to the extent you feel comfortable, but remember that you are not a bank and having your funds tied up in receivables costs *you* money.

> NOTE: If there was a problem with the invoice, make it "right" with the customer. If the customer is unhappy with the quality of the product, offer to exchange it and give him or her a voucher good for 10% off the next order (for the inconvenience), or offer to write off half or all of the amount. When you treat your customers correctly, they develop tremendous loyalty. Often when treated right, customers are so astonished that they have to tell their friends. What a great source for new business!

Lastly, keep good records. Accounts receivable is a perfect application for a computer. It may even justify the cost of the purchase.

How to Find a Bank

Talk to business associates, your accountant, consultants, and business groups. If possible get specific names of bank executives and lending officers to contact. Personal introductions can be enormously helpful, especially when you are just starting out.

When talking to the banker, ask what they look for when establishing credit lines and in granting loan approval. What does the bank like to see in the way of ratios (more on this later) and other information, and does he or she have examples of how they like to see it presented? What interest rates will you be charged on your loans? What can you do to get a better rate?

Shop around, but don't burn any bridges.

Talking to Your Banker

Do you know what bankers really hate? Surprises. If you tell your banker in November that you are going to make $250,000 profit for the year and then come back in February and say that you lost $150,000, your banker is going to think "How can this person run a company?"

Be completely honest with your banker. Develop a relationship where your banker trusts you and knows that you always tell the truth. If you run into a problem and are losing money, talk to your banker early—especially if you are going to rely on his or her help to pull you through. Explain to your banker what happened, what you are planning to do to get through it, and what you're going to do to ensure that it doesn't happen again.

If something really good happens, call your banker and say, "We just got this big new order and thought you'd like to know." It's just a matter of staying in touch and developing a strong relationship with your bank.

You may not need to borrow money today, but when you do you'll be happy that you established and nurtured this relationship over the years.

You'll make a much stronger impression on your banker or other investors by wearing conservative business attire when making your initial presentation. Including a picture of your facility and a group shot of your employees with your application shows the banker that he or she is dealing with real people and not just numbers. Spreadsheets and supporting graphs produced on your computer lend credibility to your figures. If you don't have the facilities to create these, ask your accountant for assistance.

Personal Loan Guarantees

If you're looking for a new business loan, don't be surprised when your banker leans across the desk and asks for a personal guarantee as one form of collateral. Before you sign, you should understand that not all guarantees are alike.

With an *unlimited guarantee*, you stand behind the entire loan amount or credit line. That means that if the business defaults, you'll be expected to personally make good on all deficiencies. Bankers push for this type of guarantee.

A *limited guarantee* is less encompassing than an unlimited guarantee. With this type of guarantee you only personally guarantee part of the debt. For instance, the company borrows $50,000 but you only personally guarantee $25,000.

A *joint and severable guarantee* is one in which more than one person is guaranteeing the loan. This is common for partnerships where the bank wants both partners to guarantee the debt. In the case of a $50,000 debt, both parties are responsible for the entire amount. It does *not* mean that each of you is responsible for only $25,000.

Most guarantees are written to stay in effect until the loan is completely paid off. Some agreements spell out conditions under which the personal guarantee can be eased or removed entirely. One of these is a *time guarantee* where you only personally guarantee the debt for a specific period of time.

Make sure you get the type of guarantee you want in writing at the time the loan or credit line is established. Once the paperwork is signed, it is very difficult, if not impossible, to get it changed.

Resist your banks attempts to have your spouse co-sign your notes. They like to do this to gain clear access to jointly-owned property should you run into problems. Banks like security; they want you to wear both a belt and suspenders. If you politely resist on this issue, they will usually give in.

Plan for Your Retirement From Day One

As a self-employed individual or partnership, you can use one of two tax-deductible retirement plans. The two plans are known as the Simplified Employee Pension (SEP) plan and the H.R. 10 (Keogh) plan.

A SEP is a written plan that allows you to make contributions toward your own and your employees' retirement without getting involved in the more complex Keogh plan. But some advantages available to Keogh plans, such as the special averaging treatment that may apply to Keogh plan lump-sum distributions, do not apply to SEPs. Under a SEP, you make the contributions to an individual arrangement (called a SEP-IRA), which is owned by you. SEP IRAs are set up for each qualifying employee. You are not required to make contributions every year. But, if you make contributions, they must be based on a written allocation formula and must not discriminate in favor of highly compensated employees. When you contribute, you must contribute to the SEP-IRAs of all qualifying employees who actually performed personal services during the year for which the contributions are made, even if the employee dies or is terminated before the contributions are made. Contributions are deductible within limits, and generally are not taxable to the plan participants.

A Keogh plan is a retirement plan that can only be established by an employer. A sole proprietor or a partnership can set up a plan. An individual partner can not. The plan must be for the exclusive benefit of employees (for Keogh plan purposes, a self-employed individual is both an employer and an employee) or their beneficiaries. As an employer, you can usually deduct, subject to limits, contributions you make to a Keogh plan, including those made for your own retirement. The contributions (and earnings and gains on them) are generally tax-free until distributed by the plan.

Your Keogh plan can include a cash or deferred arrangement (401(k) plan) under which eligible employees can elect to have you contribute part of their before-tax pay to the plan rather than receive the pay in cash. (As a participant in the plan, you can contribute part of your before-tax net earnings from the business.) This amount, called an elective deferral (and any earnings on it), remains tax free until it is distributed by the plan.

Retirement plans are complicated and will require the assistance of your accountant. If these options are too cumbersome or costly for you, consider simply setting up a separate savings account for your retirement. Contributions to this account will *not* be tax-deferred, but you can still accumulate significant wealth through this regular savings plan. *The secret to building financial security in your retirement years is consistent regular contributions to your retirement account.*

Think of your retirement as a monthly expense. Write your first check each month to your retirement account. Do this from day one. Promise yourself that you won't touch this money for any reason until you are at least 59 1/2—it is only for your retirement. Being self-employed means that *you* are responsible for funding your own retirement plan. As an employer, you also have a responsibility to provide for the retirement of your employees. Don't count on Social Security providing for you or your employees in old age.

If you invest just $100 a month, every month, into your personal tax-deferred retirement account earning 10% interest, you will create a retirement nest-egg of $74,524.44 in 20 years, 129,781.93 in 25 years and 220,328.76 in 30 years.

Invest $455 per month in this same personal account every month and you will have over $1,000,000 in thirty years. Remember though, that you must also contribute for each of your employees when you contribute for yourself into a tax-deferred retirement account. If you can't afford this level of funding for yourself and all your employees, consider setting up a tax-deferred company plan with smaller monthly contributions and a personal non tax-deferred account into which you deposit an additional amount each month to make up the difference.

To create a $1,000,000 retirement fund in a *non tax-deferred account* you would have to invest $755 per month at 10% for thirty years (assuming 25% taxes). This money would be tax-free at this point since you have already paid all the taxes on it.

I cannot over-stress the importance of *immediately* starting this retirement program. Don't put it off till next year because if you do, you'll just keep putting it off, and off, and sooner than you think, it will be too late. This is one of the big secrets of financial independence that most new business owners overlook. Don't be one of them.

Interpreting Financial Statements

When you hear the term "financial statements," someone is generally referring to two documents, the balance sheet and the income statement, also referred to as the "Profit and Loss Statement" or "Operating Statement." See Appendix E for sample financial statements.

What is a balance sheet? A **Balance Sheet** is a financial report that shows all your *assets* (everything valuable that you own) and all your *liabilities* (how much you owe and to whom). Subtract the liabilities from the assets and you have your *net worth*.

The balance sheet is considered a statement of the "financial position" of the company as of the date noted in the heading of the document. This document is a snapshot of this information at a specific point in time. The balance sheet shows neither how the company arrived at its current position nor where the company is heading. Information from the balance sheet is analyzed to produce "business ratios" which will be discussed in the next section.

An **Income Statement** shows if you are making or losing money during a span of time known as an accounting period. It shows *gross sales* (how much you sold your product or services for), less *cost of goods sold* (how much you paid for the product you sold). This gives you your *gross profit*. From this figure you subtract all your expenses for the accounting period (refer to the example in Appendix E) to arrive at your *Net Profit or Loss*. If this amount is a positive number, you made money; if it's a negative number, you lost money. Net Profit or Loss is also referred to as your *"Bottom Line."*

By comparing several successive months' income statements, you can spot trends in the profitability and growth of the business. For this reason, income statements are generally produced for both the current month and year-to-date. I suggest you create income statements that compare this month to the same month last year and this year-to-date to the corresponding year-to-date figure from last year. This further assists you in spotting trends.

Key Business Ratios

Business ratios are primarily broken into three categories; profitability ratios, liquidity measures and ratios, and asset productivity ratios. The most common profitability ratios are return on equity, return on total investment, and return on total assets. Liquidity measures and ratios consist of working capital, current ratio, and the acid test ratio. The asset productivity ratios are net fixed assets to total assets, long-term debt to equity, net worth to total assets, and current assets to total assets.

The figures being used in the following examples are coming from the balance sheet sample in Appendix E and a YTD net income figure of $146,687.

PROFITABILITY

> **Return on Equity** (Net Income / Total Equity)

$$\frac{146,687}{682,730} = .2149$$

Ten percent (.1000) is considered good and 15% to 20% (.1500 to .2000) is considered excellent. This measure is considered one of the most important measures of profitability. It tells you how profitable your venture is in terms of your total capital contributions plus capital you've reinvested in the venture as accumulated in retained earnings.

Return on Total Investment (Net Income / Loans + Equity)

$$\frac{146{,}687}{(146{,}222 + 682{,}730)} = .1770$$

This measure tells you how much your venture earned on all the dollars invested in it, whether they be debt dollars or equity dollars. An increase in Return on Investment (ROI) over time is considered favorable to investors.

Return on Total Assets (Net Income / Total Assets)

$$\frac{146{,}687}{881{,}768} = .1664$$

Profit margins can be increasing, but profitability can still be poor because total assets are excessive. The return on total assets is an excellent measure of overall profitability.

LIQUIDITY

Bankers and others often want to know, "How liquid is your venture?" This question refers not only to the amount of cash on hand but also to the amount of current assets that are available for the venture's operations over the short term (next 12 months or less).

Working Capital (Current Assets - Current Liabilities)

$$\begin{array}{r} 659{,}887 \\ - 52{,}815 \\ \hline 607{,}072 \end{array}$$

A healthy venture should have positive working capital (current assets should exceed current liabilities). There are two reasons:

1. You should not use long-term money to pay for short-term obligations.

2. You want to have something left over to pay for expansion. Positive working capital means current assets are already available to pay for new obligations incurred from growth.

Current Ratio (Current Assets / Current Liabilities)

$$\frac{659,887}{52,815} = 12.4943$$

Many analysts feel it is too difficult to judge a venture's liquidity by just looking at a total dollar figure. Instead, they want to know how many dollars of current assets exist compared to current liabilities. Once a venture is relatively stable, the consensus is that a healthy liquidity position is one that sees at least two dollars of current assets for every one dollar of current liabilities. This would represent a number of 2.000.

Acid Test Ratio (Cash + A/R) / Current Liabilities

$$\frac{(222,212 + 312,782)}{52,815} = 10.1296$$

This measure is used to access the solvency of a venture in terms of its ability to respond to a crisis or take advantage of sudden opportunities that require cash. The general rule is that this figure should be at least 1.000.

ASSET PRODUCTIVITY

A number of different asset and debit ratios are used that help tell us how productive our assets are employed. The basic notion behind asset and debt ratios is to see if a venture is properly capitalized given the relationship between assets, between assets and debt, and between interest generated by debt versus projected profits.

Net Fixed Assets to Total Assets (Net Fixed Assets / Total Assets)

$$\frac{221{,}881}{881{,}768} = .2516$$

This measure tells you what portion of your total assets are considered fixed assets. The size of this ratio is dependent upon the extent to which capital (fixed) assets are required by the business. You should watch for trends in this number — it should remain relatively stable.

Long-Term Debt to Equity (Long-Term Debt / Total Equity)

$$\frac{146{,}222}{682{,}730} = .2142$$

This ratio shows the extent to which you (the owner) are committed to the business by comparing the amount invested by creditors to that invested by the owners. The general rule is that there should be one dollar of long term debt for each two dollars of equity. This means that this figure should remain at .5000 or less.

Net Worth to Total Assets (Total Equity / Total Assets)

$$\frac{682{,}730}{881{,}768} = .7743$$

This ratio reflects the proportion of total assets provided by the venture's owners. A high ratio is desirable to potential creditors who see a good offer of the owner's investment to protect them against future losses.

Current Assets to Total Assets (Current Assets / Total Assets)

$$\frac{659,887}{881,768} = .7484$$

This reflects the portion of total assets that are comprised of current assets. If the ratio is too high, there may be problems with the way current assets are managed.

Other Important Sources of Information

Understanding Cash Flow. A must for a newcomers to cash flow, this 10 page pamphlet can be picked up at your local Small Business Administration office for about $1.00. Call (800) 827-5722 for the office nearest you.

The Art of Business Credit Investigation. This book explains how to collect and verify credit information and includes an extensive list of resources. Written by Peggy Mound and available from Advanced Verification Services (612) 469-3196 for $26.50.

Small Time Operator. This best selling small business guidebook by Bernard Kamoroff, C.P.A. is highly recommended. In addition to general business information, it contains a complete yet simple bookkeeping system, with step by step instructions, and a full year's set of ledgers. Available from Bell Springs Publishing (707) 984-6746 for $14.95.

Coopers & Lybrand Guide to Growing your Business. The chapter on accounting systems and controls alone, explained in everyday English, justifies the $23 price tag. Available from the offices of Coopers & Lybrand. Call (212) 259-2244.

Strategies for Getting Charge Card Merchant Status at Your Bank. This 50 page booklet gives a good introduction for people who have just butted their heads against their bank's reluctance to issue them a merchant credit card account. It is available form John Cali at (800) 392-9445 for $21.95.

If you believe in the unlimited

ability to improve the quality of

what you offer and if you behave

with total integrity in your business

dealings then all the rest of that

stuff, market share, growth, and

profitability will take care of itself.

Frank Purdue

Chapter 9

Miscellaneous Information

On Choosing A Name

Choose a name that means something to your customers. For example, Gene's Landscaping Service tells more about what your business does than Gene Dailey & Associates. Do you really want your name in the company name? Having your name in print is good for the ego, but under certain situations it may actually hurt your business. Some larger firms are not comfortable working with small companies, and when Gene shows up from Gene's Landscaping, it has a different impact than when Gene, the president, shows up from Diablo Landscaping.

However, Betty's Corner Bookshop sounds warmer and more personal than The Book Store. Think of the image you want to project and choose accordingly.

Negotiating a Building or Office Lease

When looking at business space ask what type of rental or lease arrangements the landlord offers. Most landlords will want you to commit to a five year obligation, but it is prudent to try to negotiate only a one to three year lease initially. You should, however, write a provision into the lease whereby you have first choice to re-lease the property at the expiration of your current lease. Make sure you also put in a formula stating how the new lease rate will be calculated when you renew. If this is omitted, you may end up paying higher than prevailing rates for the privilege of not having to move. When it comes time to renegotiate your lease, start 9 to 12 months before your current lease expires. It takes this long to shop around and for the landlord to construct any required "tenant improvements."

Does the landlord want you to pay separately for utilities, janitorial service, routine building maintenance such as exterior painting, roof repairs, parking lot repairs, landscape maintenance, water charges, electricity fees, taxes, recurring and special assessments, real estate taxes, insurance, etc? How much will these extra costs add to your monthly fee? Is there a ceiling on these fees or are they completely open ended? If there is a fee ceiling, make sure you get it in writing.

A lease that includes all these items in the monthly lease payment is known as a *full service* or *gross lease*. A lease that requires the tenant to pay for some or all of the real estate taxes in addition to the rent is known as a *net lease*. A *net-net lease* (double net lease) requires the tenant to pay for rent, real estate taxes, and insurance. A *net-net-net lease* (triple-net lease) additionally passes on all the costs for operating the building, including repairs and maintenance — external or internal, structural or nonstructural, ordinary or extraordinary. You can, however, write a provision into your lease that limits your responsibility in these respects. For example, you may want the option to cancel the lease if these costs exceed a certain amount.

Are the payments fixed for the term of the lease or do they increase over time? What basis is used to determine the amount of the increase? Is there any ceiling on the monthly amount?

Most landlords will modify their space to specifically meet your needs. The costs of this renovation (tenant improvements) will be added into your monthly payments. Make sure the monthly payment you are being quoted is *all inclusive* of these costs.

Some landlords will offer you a period of free rent to entice you to lease from them.   To be able to accurately compare the costs of different properties, calculate the total amount you will pay over the term of the lease and compare these numbers.

For example, Landlord One has space available on a three year lease for $1500 per month but will give you seven months of free rent. Landlord Two has similar property for $1200 per month on a three year lease with no free rent. Which is the better deal?

Total cost for option one is $1500 times 29 months (36 - 7 free months) = $43,500.

Option two is $1200 time 36 months = $43,200.

Option two is the better deal from a "total amount spent" standpoint. But if the free months are the first seven months of the lease, meaning that I wouldn't have to start making lease payments until the eighth month, I would choose option one. This option allows me to use my cash that I would normally spend for rent on inventory and other start-up costs.   Note, however, that many "free rent" offers spread the free months over the life of the lease.   For instance, two free months up front, two free months after one year, and the final three free months as the last three months of the lease.

If you are strapped for start-up cash and the landlord doesn't volunteer option one, ask them to consider it. Many times they will — possibly in exchange for a longer term lease.

What type of a security deposit is required and when do you get it back? Under what situations would you not get it back? Does the deposit earn interest while being held by the landlord?

What type of additional services does the monthly payment include? (Garbage pickup, 24 security or alarm system, use of a common conference room, common restrooms, secretarial services, etc.)

Under what conditions can you get out of your lease, and at what cost?

> Does the lease contain a buy-out provision should you opt to relocate or go out of business? Do you have the option to sublease all or part of the space? Subleasing means that you can lease part or all of your space to someone else if you so desire.

> Does the landlord offer a provision for rolling your lease over to a larger facility should you need it? Try to position yourself so that you will not be stuck in an inadequate facility for several years while waiting for your existing lease to expire.

When negotiating for office space, always have at least two options, working with *two different real estate companies*. Having multiple options ensures you of getting the best possible deal. You will be surprised at how much money you can save by shopping around.

The terms of your lease should spell out what happens if the space isn't ready by your move-in date, and what adjustments to the rent will be made by the landlord. Do not accept a clause whereby the landlord will provide you with "alternative" space if your premises aren't ready, unless the landlord is willing to bear all the costs of relocating your office when the space is finally finished.

Contracts

More than likely, you will enter into one or more contractual agreements related to your new business. If you have a voice in drafting the contract, make it as fair (win/win) as possible. Do not sign any agreement that contains terms you cannot live with. Don't commit to things you cannot do. If the contract is modified, get it in writing. If you have contracts with your customers, remember that it is much cheaper to keep customers happy than to end up in court to settle a disagreement.

Mediation and arbitration are discussed in the next section on Lawsuits and Alternatives. There are standard clauses that can be inserted into your contracts to ensure you take advantage of these alternative dispute resolution options. I recommend that you put both of these clauses in all your contracts.

For mediation, the clause is:

> If a dispute arises out of or relates to this contract, or the breach thereof, and if said dispute cannot be settled through negotiation, the parties agree first to try in good faith to settle the dispute by mediation under the Commercial Mediation Rules of the American Arbitration Association, before resorting to arbitration, litigation, or some other dispute resolution procedure.

For arbitration, the clause is:

> Any controversy or claim arising out of or relating to this contract, or the breach thereof, shall be settled by arbitration in accordance with the Commercial Arbitration Rules of the American Arbitration Association, and judgment upon the award rendered by the arbitrator(s) may be entered in any court having jurisdiction thereof.

It is also wise to put a clause in your contracts which states that the losing party must pay for the attorney fees and costs of the winning party. This keeps both sides from filing frivolous lawsuits. The wording for this clause is:

> In the event any legal action, including arbitration, is instituted to enforce any of the terms of this agreement, the prevailing party shall be entitled to recover reasonable attorney's fees, costs and expenses, including costs, fees and expenses on appeal, paid by the nonprevailing party.

Lawsuits and Alternatives

Avoid lawsuits. Lawsuits cost America's business an estimated $80 billion a year in direct litigation payments according to a study published by the Bush administration's Council on Competitiveness in 1992. And much of that burden falls upon small businesses. In addition to the direct costs involved, litigation consumes enormous amounts of executives' time, physical, and emotional energy. Too often they also result in broken business relationships — a potential loss for all parties.

You have alternatives. Call the other party and arrange a meeting at some neutral location, say at a restaurant for lunch. Try to talk out your differences. You will find that if *you* are reasonable, most people are willing to work things out. There is probably guilt on both sides. Put your emotions aside and work out a fair solution. It costs much less to compromise than to take someone to court.

If you can't work out a solution on your own, suggest using a professional mediator. Often they can simplify the issues and work out an equitable solution. **Mediation** is a voluntary way of settling disputes in which a specially trained neutral individual, with no decision-making authority, helps the disputing parties, in private informal meetings, to negotiate a mutually beneficial settlement. The business owners and not the lawyers control the process. Mediation is fast and usually much less expensive than your other alternatives. Most mediations take one day or less and cost under $2000 with the parties splitting the fees.

A third alternative is **arbitration**. Arbitration is a more widely known process that mediation, but it is far more rigid. It involves a neutral person acting as a judge, working under highly structured rules, listening to evidence, and then handing down a binding decision. Lawyers are normally involved, and usually there is no appeal process. This option is still far superior to, and less expensive than litigation.

You can locate a mediator or arbitrator by contacting the American Arbitration Association, a New York based non-profit organization that promotes mediation and other forms of dispute resolution, at (213) 484-4040, or U.S. Arbitration and Mediation, also a non-profit organization that promotes all types of alternative dispute resolution, based out of Seattle at (800) 933-6348. Both groups have regional offices across the country.

If the dispute degenerates to a lawsuit, work to settle it early. Just because you have been sued, doesn't mean that the issue will end up in court. Nine out of ten lawsuits are settled before trial, and because 85% of the legal costs are incurred before settlement, it makes economic sense to settle early, before the process takes on a life of its own, with abusive depositions, burdensome demands for the production of documents, interrogatories, and endless fee-producing motions.

Before you take someone to court, think if that is what you want to do with your money...and your time. Litigation is a horrible way for civilized individuals to settle their differences. Avoid it.

Bonds and Insurance

As a small business owner you will need general liability, fire, theft, workers' compensation, health, disability and life insurance. Certain business individuals also must be bonded.

General liability insurance usually covers you if you are sued.

Fire insurance covers your building and property in case of a fire.

Theft insurance covers your building and property in case of vandalism or theft.

Workers' compensation insurance covers you in case an employee is injured doing work-related activities.

You should also carry *health, disability, and life insurance.* Health insurance is expensive, but don't cut costs in this area. A single hospital stay can wipe you out if you don't have adequate coverage. Purchase enough disability insurance to be able to hire someone to carry on for you should you become disabled on a temporary or permanent basis. Carry enough life insurance to at least pay off your company debts. If your family is not capable of running the business, make sure they won't be burdened with business debt should something happen to you.

217

A *Bond* is a guarantee of performance. If you are bonded, a company that does work with you knows that if they suffer a loss because of your work, they can recover the damages from the bonding company.

If you don't already have an insurance agent that can help you, look in the phone book under "insurance." Get quotes from at least two different agents, representing at least two different companies.

Tax Deductible Perks

Tax deductible doesn't mean free. Don't think that if you can write something off, it doesn't cost you anything. The money to pay for these perks comes from your profits. Only take advantage of perks to the extent your business can afford them. Don't live beyond your means. Tax laws change every year so check with your accountant to ensure all these options still exist.

- Fly First Class. If the trip is for business purposes, the cost of the ticket is deductible, regardless of whether you travel coach or first class.

- Drive a luxury car. You can get tax breaks for the business driving you do. The rules are the same for an economy or luxury car.

- Visit fancy resorts. Many conventions or trade shows are held in resorts. When attending these shows, your travel and living expenses are deductible and you have access to all the facilities of the resort during your off hours.

- Take your family with you. If the members of your family are involved in your business, their expenses are deductible also.

- Go on a cruise. Many business seminars or conventions are held on cruise ships. If you actively conduct business on one of these business cruises, you can deduct part or all of the cost of the cruise.

- Party with your customers. If the primary purpose of the activity is to conduct business, you can play golf, go to a baseball game, go to a nice restaurant, go to the symphony, go sailing, etc. and most of these expenses are deductible.

- Plan your vacation around a business trip. Extend your business trip with some vacation time and you can still deduct your round-trip cost to your business destination even though you spent part of your time vacationing.

Trade Associations

Belonging to a trade association or professional society that represents your industry can be beneficial in many ways. Many associations offer technical help and expert guidance in such areas as research, marketing, management, finance, labor relations, government regulations, public relations, and problem-solving in general. Association activities are particularly important in helping small business owners solve business problems, meet the competition, make increasing sales, and take advantage of business opportunities.

Trade associations usually offer assistance in the following areas.

Accounting Services
- Provide accounting manuals.
- Publish comparative statements, ratios.
- Publish uniform account classifications and definitions.
- Conduct cost studies.
- Provide accounting forms.
- Provide consulting regarding the installation and maintenance of an accounting system.
- Provide centralized accounting services.

Advertising and Marketing Services
- Provide members with advertising materials.
- Sponsor paid advertising for industry.
- Engage in mutual theme advertising with members.
- Exhibit in shows of other associations.
- Collect and distribute requests for products or services of members.
- Forecast future demands and trends.
- Conduct consumer research for facts regarding buying or selling of products or services.
- Provide members with point-of-purchase materials.
- Conduct studies or provide methods of merchandising.

Education

- Sponsor short courses, clinics, seminars, workshops, or institutes for industry.
- Provide certificates, diplomas, and awards for completion of educational programs.
- Provide tests and manuals for employee training.
- Provide films and cassettes for training programs.
- Cooperate with distributive education programs.
- Provide scholarships.
- Underwrite fellowships or grants.

Employer-Employee Relations

- Conduct surveys concerning wages, work schedules, and fringe benefits.
- Disseminate information on state and national labor relations' issues.
- Hold meetings to discuss employee-employer relations.
- Conduct programs aimed at better health and safety of members employees.
- Conduct personal policy surveys.
- Operate executive referral or personnel placement service.
- Provide information on job evaluation plans, incentives, and aptitude tests.

Government Relations

- Inform members about Federal legislative developments.
- Equip and encourage members to express personal and knowledgeable views on legislative issues to their congressmen.
- Inform members about Federal administrative actions or rulings.
- Inform members about State and local legislative developments.

Publishing

- Publish legislative, technical, and other bulletins as news dictates.
- Publish membership directories.
- Publish handbooks and manuals.

- Publish magazines, trade journals, or newsletters.
- Publish digests of laws.
- Publish directories of suppliers and buyers.

Publicity and Public Relations

- Provide mass media with stories of interest and news releases concerning industry.
- Provide industry and trade journals with information about developments in industry and services of industry.
- Maintain a public relations committee.
- Provide members with news stories which they can use in their own community.
- Provide speeches which members can use in their own community.
- Provide members with public relations films.

Research, Standardization, Statistics

- Conduct studies designed to improve products or services of members.
- Conduct studies to develop new methods and techniques.
- Conduct research on management and personnel performance.
- Conduct research to develop new products or services.
- Cooperate with governmental agencies to review and improve standards and specifications.
- Publish product standards and specifications.
- Study standard types, sizes, grades.
- Study standard dimensional and other tolerances and nomenclature.
- Develop standard operational procedures for office and plant.
- Establish criteria on properties and performance for use in grading, approving, and certifying.
- Disseminate statistical data compiled by governmental agencies.
- Prepare long-term and short-term forecasts.
- Regularly compile and disseminate statistics reflecting such things as orders, sales, production, construction, inventories, employment, operating ratios, and profits.

Cost to You

How much does all this cost? Dues vary according to the group and the amount of services it offers. Generally, dues are a fraction of one percent of the member's annual volume of business. Some associations charge a uniform fee. A few use a combination figure derived from the rate based on volume plus a specific, flat charge. Many groups also have a ceiling on the dues they charge. Most state and national associations bill for dues on an annual basis while local associations usually bill monthly.

Considering the services available, you should regard association dues not as an expense but as a form of investment toward improving your company. Below are some national trade associations.

American Small Business Association
(800) 235-3298

American Entrepreneurs Association
(800) 352-7449

International Association of Business
(800) 275-1171

International Franchise Association
(202) 628-8000

National Association for the Self-Employed
(800) 232-6273

National Association for Private Enterprise
(800) 223-6273

National Association of Women Business Owners
(Affiliated with the World Association of Women Entrepreneurs, in 28 countries.)
(800) 55-NAWBO or (800) 556-2926

National Business Association
(800) 456-0440

National Business Incubation Association
(614) 593-4331

National Federation of Independent Businesses
(Nation's largest small business association with over 500,000 members.)
(202) 554-9000

National Small Business United
(800) 345-6728 or (202) 293-8830

For industry-specific trade associations, check with your suppliers, your accountant, trade journals, and ask the reference librarian of your local library to see a copy of *The Encyclopedia of Associations* by Gale Research or call (800) 877-4253. Also talk to your local Kiwanis Club, Rotary Club, and Chamber of Commerce. They often sponsor business seminars, and their meetings are a great place to meet other business people in your community.

Protecting Yourself Against Embezzlement

You can lose a great deal of money before even suspecting that embezzlement might be going on since, by definition, this crime is committed by someone in a position of trust. The loss may involve a small amount taken by an employee from the cash register, or it may be a considerable sum stolen through an elaborate scheme of juggling the books.

There are three things you can do to minimize the risk of having someone embezzle funds from your organization:

1.   Keep complete and accurate financial records. Incomplete or messy bookkeeping makes it easier for someone to steal money.

2.   Make sure the person who balances the checkbook does not have the authority to sign checks. Make sure the person who deposits customer checks does not keep the customer receivables records. Any individual who performs in these capacities is in the position to embezzle funds.

3. When interviewing employees for these functions, be sure to ask their references about the candidate's trustworthiness, integrity, and honesty. Ask if they would trust this individual with large sums of cash.

Managing Stress

You will undoubtedly have some stressful days. When you feel yourself getting tense and irritable here are a few simple techniques that work for me.

- Take a deep breath. Inhale through your nose. Hold it for about 5-7 seconds and exhale slowly through the mouth.

- Smile. It's amazing how contagious a smile is. When you get a smile back, you realize how good life really is.

- Laugh. Maintaining a good sense of humor helps defeat stress before it takes control of you. Don't ever lose your laugh.

- Talk about it. Don't keep your feelings bottled up inside. If a situation is really annoying you, confront it.

- Take a break. Close your eyes, lean back in your chair, and visualize your favorite spot, wherever that may be. Take a minute to relive a pleasant memory.

- Relax. When we get stressed, all our muscles seem to tighten. Take a moment to relax every muscle in your body—from your forehead all the way down to your toes.

- Exercise. If there is a particular sport you especially enjoy, call someone and set up a game. Take a day off and go fishing or play golf or play tennis or whatever. When you get consumed in the sport, you forget about your problems and whatever it was that caused all the stress in the first place.

- Talk positive. Constant negative talk that rehashes old ground will only re-create and reinforce your stress.

- Take a short walk. It's amazing how a little fresh air and five minutes of exercise will lift your spirits.

Financial Planning

Today, nearly a quarter of a million American men and women earn their living as financial planners. If you decide to hire a financial planner, a good one should analyze your finances and recommend how to improve your financial situation. Successful financial planners may have as many different investment strategies as the clients they serve. Make sure the financial planner you choose works on behalf of your interests and needs.

Your financial planner should assist you in the following ways:

- Assess your relevant financial history, such as tax returns, investments, retirement plans, wills, living trust, and insurance plans.

- Help you decide on a financial plan, based on your age, personal and financial goals, history, and preferences.

- Identify financial areas where you may need help, such as building up a retirement income or improving investment returns.

- Write down a financial plan based on your individual situation and discuss it thoroughly with you, in plain English.

- Review your situation and financial plan periodically and suggest changes in your program when needed.

Before you select a financial planner, you may want to ask yourself these questions:

What are my financial goals today and ten years from now?

Before you ask for advice, it is helpful to know where you want that advice to take you. Factors to consider in analyzing your needs include the size of your family, how much money you expect to need for retirement, and what your budget can afford.

What is my personal investment philosophy?

Do you enjoy risky ventures? Do you seek the comfort of solid, conservative low-risk investments? Or, do you want an investment mix? Be sure to make clear to your financial planner exactly which investment philosophy you are most comfortable with.

How to Select a Financial Planner

There are several ways you can look for a financial planner who will suit your needs. One place to begin is by contacting the International Association for Financial Planning (800) 945-4237, an association of individuals working in the financial planning industry, or the Institute of Certified Financial Planners (303) 751-7600, a professional organization that accredits planners. Both of these organizations can provide you with free information about the financial planning industry as well as the names of members in your area.

Recommendations of friends and colleagues who have had investment success are also a good source for financial planners. But even an investment advisor who impresses one client may be unsuitable for another investor's needs. You are likely to want to select a firm or individual who has the skills and expertise to meet your specific needs. Be certain that any planner you consider has ample knowledge of taxes, insurance, estate and retirement planning, investment alternatives and family budgeting. Check with the Better Business Bureau to determine if any complaints have been lodged against the planner.

When interviewing your prospective financial planner, you may wish to ask the following questions:

What credentials do you have to practice financial planning?

Financial planners come from a variety of backgrounds and, therefore, may hold a variety of degrees and licenses. There are no state or federal regulations for the financial planning industry. Some advisors take specialized training in financial planning and earn credentials such as Certified Financial Planner (CFP), Chartered Financial Consultant (CHFC) or Accredited Personal Financial Specialist (APFS). Others may hold degrees or registrations such as J.D. (Doctor of Jurisprudence) for attorneys, CPA for Certified Public Accountants, or CLU for Chartered Life Underwriters.

Question financial planners carefully about their background and experience. Be wary of individuals who promote various investment items without discussing with you any overall financial planning goal. They may lack the expertise to formulate one.

Are you registered with the federal Securities and Exchange Commission (SEC) or with a state agency?

Anyone who may be giving advise on securities (including tax shelters), use of the stock market, or the value of securities over other types of investments should be registered with the SEC or registered under state laws dealing with investment advisors.

How will you prepare my financial plan?

Financial planners usually prepare financial plans after carefully discussing and analyzing your personal and financial history, your current situation, and your future goals. Some financial planners enter relevant financial information into their computer to generate standard financial plans. This type of plan is often useful, but be certain your unique financial situation is taken into account. Be sure to find an advisor who will give you personalized advice catered to your needs.

How many companies do you represent?

Someone who represents only one or two companies probably is not a financial planner, but more likely a broker or salesperson. It will be to their advantage to sell you only those products offered by the companies they represent. You may want to seek an advisor who can offer you a wide range of choices to suit your needs.

Who will I deal with on a regular basis?

You will want to work consistently with someone who is completely familiar with your account. Many large firms offer a variety of different financial services. Make sure that such institutions provide a comprehensive and coordinated method of referral among the various "experts" who can advise you about your financial plans. Ask how the planner will keep you regularly advised about financial information of importance to you.

How do you keep up with the latest financial developments?

You may want to look for a planner who enrolls in continuing education courses (or, perhaps, teaches in a business school) to keep current on tax and investment strategies. Regular members of the Institute of Certified Financial Planners, for example, are required to complete 30 hours of continuing education every year in order to maintain full membership status.

Will you be involved in implementing the plan you suggest?

Financial planners will develop a plan specifically tailored to your situation and needs. Some planners also will include provisions for updating your plan to adjust to changes in your life, current economic conditions, and tax laws. Your financial planner also can provide for periodic reviews of your plan to show you the progress that is being made in reaching your goals. You should ask if your planner can provide this type of ongoing service and what those services will cost.

Fees

Make sure you get a written estimate of what services you can expect for what price. Compare this estimate with others and select the package of services that best meets your needs at a reasonable cost.

Keeping your Personal Documents in Order

Being self-employed makes it even more important to keep your personal papers and information well organized and easy to locate. In case of a personal emergency, the following list will provide your family with a starting point for the matters that need to be taken care of.

- Birth certificates (both spouses and children)

- Social Security numbers (both spouses and children)

- Marriage licenses; divorce decree or death certificate, in case of a previous marriage.

- Title to all real estate owned, and records showing original cost, cost of all improvements, and (for business or rental property) depreciation taken.

- Tax returns for the past six years.

- Title to cemetery plot or other arrangements.

- All insurance policies, including life, health, casualty, auto, and the name, address, and phone number of your agent.

- A list of the approximate amounts of pension, military, and/ or other benefits you will be entitled to on retirement, or on death of a spouse.

- A list of all assets that you own either separately or with a spouse or other person, with approximate values.

- Location of safe deposit boxes, keys, or passwords.

- Statement for each bank account, retirement account (IRA, Keogh, SEP, 401(k), etc.), mutual fund, and broker or stock account, with banker, broker, or other contact person for each account.

- Your will and living trust documents with the name and address of the attorney who prepared them.

- Names and addresses of your CPA and business attorney.

- Names and addresses of family members, close relatives, and any persons mentioned in your will.

Putting Everything in Perspective

In a national survey, people cited the following factors as their criteria for personal success. They are listed in order from most important to least important.

- Good health
- Enjoyable job
- Happy family
- Good education
- Peace of mind
- Good friends
- Intelligence
- Unlimited money
- Talent
- Luck
- Luxury car
- Expensive home

In 1904, *Brown Book* magazine conducted a contest to see who could provide the best definition of success. Mrs. Bessie Anderson won the prize with: "He has achieved success who has lived well, laughed often, and loved much." Seems some things never change.

One ship drives east, and another west
With the self-same winds that blow;
'Tis the set of the sails
And not the gales,
That decides the way we go.

Like the wind of the sea are the ways of fate,
As they voyage along through life;
'Tis the will of the soul
That decides its goal,
And not the calm or the strife.

Edna Wheeler Wilcox

Chapter 10

Summing It All Up

Balance your life. All work and no play not only makes Johnny a dull boy, but it can make him or her lonely in old age. Set aside time for your family and friends. Leading a well-rounded life will make you a better person which will make you a better boss. Keep a positive outlook. Your mental frame of mind helps to determine your ultimate success.

Always remember the importance of customers. They really want honest, courteous service more than anything else. Don't spend all your energies on getting new customers. Nurture your loyal customers. Long established customers are your most valuable because they buy more, they refer new business, and they are usually willing to pay higher prices. Yet, on average, companies lose about 15% to 20% of their customers each year. By simply cutting the number of customers you lose in half, you will more than double the average company's growth rate. Develop a strategy from the very beginning that puts a major emphasis on customer retention.

The Customer Service Institute of Silver Springs, Maryland compiled the following list of customer rights. Type it up and hang it where all your employees see it every day.

1. The right to courteous, considerate treatment at all times by all members of your organization.

2. The right to receive accurate information about features, applications, prices, and availability of products or services which you offer for sale.

3. The right to have his or her expectations met; that quality, price, and delivery of your product or service will be as represented prior to having made the purchase.

4. The right to be served by skilled, knowledgeable personnel.

5. The right to be promptly and fully informed when your commitment cannot be met as originally stated.

6. The right to complain — and to receive prompt, fair handling and resolution of the complaint on its merits.

7. The right to expect extra effort by your personnel in genuine emergencies, regardless of their cause.

8. The right to expect honesty and integrity at all levels in your organization.

9. The right to expect teamwork from your organization, and never hear the expression, "That's not my job."

10. The right to expect appreciation from everyone in your company — appreciation for the business already given as well as for business to be given in the future.

Don't sell products; sell solutions. Give your customers good value for their money, while maintaining a reasonable profit and your business will prosper.

When you make your customer "first, second and third," as author and consultant Tom Peters once said, you are also doing the same for your employees. It's a cycle of success; good customer service leads to loyal customers, who produce higher profits that make employees want to stay with the company, which in turn produces better customer service.

Marshall Field lists twelve things that we should always remember. His ageless wisdom serves us all well.

1. The value of time
2. The success of perseverance
3. The pleasure of working
4. The dignity of simplicity
5. The worth of character
6. The power of kindness
7. The influence of example
8. The obligation of duty
9. The wisdom of economy
10. The virtue of patience
11. The improvement of talent
12. The joy of originating

"George Bernard Shaw once observed that all progress depends on the unreasonable man. His argument was that the reasonable man adapts himself to the world, while the unreasonable persists in trying to adapt the world to himself; therefore, for any change of consequence we must look to the unreasonable man, or, I must add, to the unreasonable woman.

While in Shaw's day, perhaps, most men were reasonable, we are now entering an Age of Unreason, when the future, in so many areas is there to be shaped, by us and for us—a time when the only prediction that will hold true is that no predictions will hold true; a time, therefore, for bold imaginings in private life as well as public, for thinking the unlikely and doing the unreasonable."

—From *The Age of Unreason,* by Charles Handy (Harvard Business School Press, 1989)

Decide what you really want and develop a plan that will take you there, don't try to do everything yourself, remember that your employees are your most important asset, watch the bottom line, listen to your customers, and take advantage of opportunities.

I wish you the best of luck.

There is no feeling like the feeling of success.

J. Paul Getty

Appendix A

Projected Income Statement

This statement shows **Revenues** (sales), **Expenses** (costs), and **Net Income** (profit or loss) for a specific period of time based on when you *make* the sales and when you *incur* the costs.

Most ventures will start out losing money for at least the first few months. It is important that you produce at least 12 projected income statements, one for each month of the entire first year you will be in business. These Projected Income Statements will show you month by month how your business is progressing, when it will turn its first profit, and when you will recover all your initial costs (your break even point).

Each line on the Projected Income Statement Worksheet that starts on page 249 has an associated line number. A further definition of the information to be placed on each line is provided below. Not every venture will have revenues or expenses for every line. Fill in all lines appropriate for your type of business.

The format used for the Projected Income Statement will allow you to analyze expenses grouped for specific functions; sales, manufacturing and construction costs, warehousing and distribution costs, and general and administrative costs. If your costs seem too high, this grouping may assist you in determining which area is too expensive.

In the Revenue section you will place your anticipated gross sales figure and your estimated "cost of goods sold." You will include all *variable costs* in this section. Variable costs are those costs directly associated with a particular product or job that would not otherwise be incurred if it were not for that product or job. For example, building rent is a *fixed cost* since it remains constant regardless of the number of products you sell. However, the *total cost* of the items you sell varies with the number of items sold — if you sell 5 items that cost $1.00 each, your total cost is $5.00, but if you only sell 1, your total cost is just $1.00 — these varying costs are known as variable expenses.

Revenue

1. **Projected Gross Sales** -- On this line enter the dollar figure that represents your best guess for your total sales for this month. For purposes of the income statement, a transaction is considered a sale when the customer takes legal possession of the product, not when he or she pays for it, even though these two events may occur at the same time.

2. **Less Allowance for Returns** -- Every business will have some returns from customers. Examples of reasons for returns are damaged or malfunctioning merchandise, gift returns, dissatisfaction with the product, promotional returns, etc. Enter your estimate of the dollar value (at the price you sold it for) for the amount of product you expect will be returned this month. If you are unsure what figure to enter here, contact your accountant or local merchants who are engaged in the same type of business for suggestions.

Less Cost of Goods Sold -- This section represents your costs to acquire or produce your products (your costs for the products sold in line 1 less the returns from line 2). Professional service businesses (accountants, consultants, private teachers, etc.) usually do not have any cost of goods sold.

3. **Purchased Products Cost** -- You may be able to use a percentage of the retail price to arrive at this figure. For a retail or wholesale establishment, the cost of the items you sell would be included on this line.

4. **Raw Material Cost** -- Include the cost of all raw material (wood, metal, plastic, nails, screws, bolts, washers, glue, welding rod, paint, decals, etc.) required to produce your final product. Include any freight-in expense and temporary storage fees associated with your raw materials. If you perform construction work and have land cost, include it on this line also.

5. **Purchased Parts Cost** -- For manufacturing or construction type businesses, you would enter the cost of purchased parts or assemblies such as valves, switches, etc. that are integrated into your final product.

6. **Contract Labor** -- Enter the dollar figure for contract (non-employee) labor on this line.

7. **Building Permits** -- If your project requires you to obtain special permits, enter their cost here.

8. **Gross Profit** -- Subtract lines 2 through 7 from line 1 and enter the answer on this line. This number represents the amount of money you have left when you subtract your cost of producing or acquiring your product from your net sales (gross sales less returns). This is the money from which you pay the rest of your bills (your operating expenses).

Expenses

All other costs are listed in this section. These costs are sometimes collectively referred to as operating costs or operating expenses. For purposes of our analysis, we will further break down the costs as shown below:

Selling Expenses -- The costs directly associated with the selling of your products or services — sales salaries, commissions, payroll taxes for sales personnel, sales related travel and entertainment, advertising, promotional, catalog printing and distribution costs, and depreciation expense for your store fixtures (sales racks, counters), etc.

Manufacturing/Construction Expenses -- The fixed costs directly associated with the creation of your product. Any business that buys raw material and makes a product will usually have manufacturing or construction expenses. These costs include salaries and taxes for the manufacturing (or construction) personnel, manufacturing/construction vehicle expense, small tools cost, packaging costs for your finished product, etc.

238

Distribution/Warehouse Expenses -- The costs directly associated with the warehousing and transporting of your product. Costs that fall into this category include distribution and warehouse personnel wages and taxes, depreciation expense on purchased delivery and warehouse equipment, rent or lease payments for non-purchased warehouse and delivery equipment, delivery and warehouse vehicle maintenance costs, delivery and warehouse vehicle expenses (taxes, licenses, fuel, etc.), and freight/shipping charges, etc.

General & Administrative Expenses -- All other costs not specifically allocated above fall into this category. These include such items as office and administrative salaries and taxes, benefits for all employees, rent and utilities, depreciation of office equipment, office supplies, workman's compensation insurance and other non-health insurance fees, dues and subscription costs, business license fees, legal and accounting fees, etc.

If you have expenses that fall into more than one of these categories and you can specifically state how much to allocate to each area, it is OK to split the cost and allocate a portion to each area — just make sure that the entire cost is allocated. If you are unsure how much to allocate to each area, place the cost in General and Administrative Expense.

Selling Expenses

9. **Sales Manager's Salary** -- If you intend to hire a sales manager within the first year, place the manager's salary on this line starting with the appropriate month.

10. **Inside Sales Salaries** -- This is where you place the salaries of your inside sales people. If your sales employees are paid a base salary plus a commission, only include the base salary plus tips on this line.

11. **Inside Sales Commissions** -- If you pay your inside sales force a commission, place the estimated commission amount on this line.

12. **Telephone Sales Salaries** -- If you plan to have telemarketing personnel on your payroll, their salaries should be placed on this line.

13. **Telephone Sales Commissions** -- If you pay your telemarketers a sales commission, place the estimated amount on this line.

14. **Field Sales Salaries** -- More and more retail companies are employing outside sales representatives. These individuals may work going from home to home selling items such as vacuum cleaners or landscaping services or from office to office selling items like janitorial services, vending machines, or computers. If you employ or plan to employ an outside sales force, enter the salaried part of their pay on this line.

15. **Field Sales Commissions** -- If you pay your outside sales force a commission, place the estimated commission amount on this line. If you have outside sales representatives who are paid a commission or fee only, place this estimated amount on this line also.

16. **Payroll Taxes for Sales Employees** -- Contact your accountant to determine how to calculate the figure to place on this line. Remember that only sales-related payroll taxes are entered here. If you have sales agents who are independent (not employees), check with your accountant to determine what tax liability you may have, if any.

17. **Sales Vehicles Depreciation, Lease or Rental Payment** -- Enter the figure on this line that represents the depreciation on any sales vehicles you intend to purchase. If you intend to lease or rent these vehicles, use the monthly lease or rental payment. If you are unsure what figure to enter here or how to calculate depreciation, check with your accountant.

18. **Sales Vehicles - Expenses** -- Enter an amount for day-to-day expendables used with the sales vehicles such as gasoline and maintenance costs.

19. **Sales Related Travel and Entertainment** -- Place all sales related mileage expense, business lunches, airfare and lodging expense, car rental, and promotional entertainment expense such as theatre or sports tickets on this line. Check with your accountant to determine the portion of these expenses that is deductible.

20. **Depreciation - Store Fixtures** -- Your store fixtures (merchandise racks, display counters, cash registers, permanent signs, etc.) must be depreciated over their useful life. The IRS has determined that different items have different useful life spans. You will need to work with your accountant to calculate this figure. Your accountant will need a list of what you expect to buy in this area, when you expect to buy it, the estimated cost, and whether the items will be purchased new or used.

21. **Advertising and Promotion** -- Newspaper ads, temporary window advertising, radio advertising, yellow pages, direct mail printing and postage costs, fees paid to an advertising or marketing agency, etc. would all be included on this line.

22. **Catalog Costs** -- The cost of purchasing or producing your catalog and all distribution costs should be included on this line.

23. **Total Selling Expenses** -- Add lines 9 through 22 and place the total on this line.

Manufacturing/Construction Expenses

24. **Mfg/Const Manager's Salary** -- If you plan on employing an individual in this capacity, enter the monthly salary on this line.

25. **Mfg/Const Employees' Salaries** -- Enter the salaries for all *employees* working in this area. Non-employee contract labor should be included in the cost of goods sold section of the Revenue section.

26. **Payroll Taxes** -- Payroll taxes associated with lines 24 and 25 above.

27. **Mfg/Const Vehicles Depreciation, Lease, or Rental Payment** -- Enter the figure on this line that represents the depreciation on any manufacturing or construction vehicles you intend to purchase. If you intend to lease or rent these vehicles, use the monthly lease or rental payment.

28. **Mfg/Const Vehicles - Expenses** -- Enter an amount for day-to-day expendables used with the above vehicles such as gasoline and maintenance costs.

29. **Mfg/Const Related Travel and Entertainment** -- Place all manufacturing or construction related mileage expense, business lunches, airfare and lodging expense, car rental, and promotional entertainment expense such as theatre or sports tickets on this line. Check with your accountant to determine the portion of these expenses that is deductible.

30. **Packaging Costs** -- The items entered on this line will include boxes, shipping tubes, cushioning material (styrofoam peanuts, bubble-pack, custom box inserts), tape, staples, labels, string, pallets, etc.

31. **Mfg/Const Supplies** -- Enter the cost of supply material required for the production of your finished product such as oil for your equipment, solvents, cleanup supplies, shop rags, disposable paint or dust masks, gloves, goggles, ear plugs, etc.

32. **Small Tools** -- This line includes items such as hand tools, paint gun nozzles, welding tips, etc.

33. **Total Mfg/Const Expense** -- Add lines 24 through 32 and enter the total on this line.

Distribution/Warehouse Expenses

34. **Distribution/Warehouse Manager's Salary** -- If you plan on employing an individual in this capacity, enter the monthly salary on this line.

35. **Warehouse Employees' Salaries** -- Enter the salaries for all Warehouse Employees on this line.

36. **Courier/Driver's Salaries** -- Enter the salaries for all individuals employed as couriers and drivers on this line.

37. **Payroll Taxes** -- Enter the payroll tax figure associated with lines 30 through 32 on this line.

38. **Dist Vehicle/Equip Depreciation, Lease, or Rental Payment** -- Enter the figure on this line that represents the depreciation on any delivery equipment (vehicles, trailers, pallet trucks, dollies, blankets, etc.) you intend to purchase. If you intend to lease or rent this equipment, use the monthly lease or rental payment.

39. **Distribution Vehicles - Expenses** -- Enter an amount for day-to-day expendables used with the delivery equipment such as oil, tires, maintenance costs, rope, cleaning fees, etc.

40. **Depreciation, Lease Payment, or Rental of Warehouse Equipment** -- Enter the figure on this line that represents the depreciation on any warehouse equipment (fork lifts, pallet racks, pallet trucks, warehouse automation equipment, carts, etc.) you intend to purchase. If you intend to lease or rent this equipment, use the monthly lease or rental payment.

41. **Warehouse Equipment - Expenses** -- Enter an amount for day-to-day expendables used with the warehouse equipment such as oil, propane, etc.

42. **Dist/Whse Related Travel and Entertainment** -- Place all distribution or warehouse related mileage expense, business lunches, airfare and lodging expense, car rental, and promotional entertainment expense such as theatre or sports tickets on this line. Check with your accountant to determine the portion of these expenses that is deductible.

43. **Freight/Shipping Charges** -- This line is for outbound freight charges. If you pay freight and shipping charges and then invoice your customers for this charge, you must put the amount you are billed here and include the amount you bill your customers under Gross Sales in the Revenue section.

44. **Warehouse Supplies** -- Enter a cost for expendable items used in the warehouse such as tape, marking devices, pallet wrap, etc.

45. **Total Distribution Expense** -- Add lines 34 through 44 and enter the total on this line.

General and Administrative Expenses

46. **Officer's Salaries** -- Enter the amount you wish to pay yourself and any other officers or partners of the company on this line.

47. **Accounting Salaries** -- If you intend to hire a bookkeeper, place the monthly amount you will be paying this individual on this line.

48. **Administrative Salaries** -- Enter on this line the total amount paid to all administrative personnel. This would include general office workers, receptionists, associates, etc.

49. **Purchasing Salaries** -- If you intend to hire a purchasing agent, enter the monthly amount you will be paying this individual on this line.

50. **Payroll Taxes** -- Payroll taxes vary from area to area. It will be necessary for you to contact your accountant to determine the proper calculation for the amount to place on this line. Remember that unless your business is a corporation, your personal taxes will be calculated differently from your employees. You will have additional social security taxes to pay since you are not considered an employee of the company.

51. **Employee Benefits** -- Enter the total dollar amount of the employee benefits on this line. Employee benefits include such items as health, eye, and dental insurance, contributions to union or other pension funds, company paid uniform expenses, life insurance payments for employees (not yourself), etc.

52. **Franchise Fees** -- If you purchased a franchise and you must reimburse the home office on a monthly basis, enter this estimated amount here.

53. **G&A Vehicle Depreciation, Lease or Rental Payment** -- Enter the figure on this line that represents the depreciation on any general and administrative vehicles you intend to purchase. If you intend to lease or rent this vehicle, use the monthly lease or rental payment.

54. **G&A Vehicles - Expenses** -- Enter an amount for day-to-day expendables used with the vehicles such as gasoline, oil, maintenance costs, etc.

55. **G&A Travel and Entertainment** -- Place all general and administrative mileage expense, business lunches, airfare and hotel expense, car rental, and promotional entertainment expense such as theatre or sports tickets on this line. Check with your accountant to determine the portion of these expenses that is deductible.

56. **Office Equipment Depreciation, Lease or Rental Payment** -- Enter the figure on this line that represents the depreciation on any office equipment you intend to purchase. If you intend to lease or rent this equipment, use the monthly lease or rental payment.

57. **Office Equipment - Expenses** -- Enter an amount for day-to-day expendables used with the equipment such as toner, ribbons, paper, etc.

58. **Building Rent** -- Enter your monthly building rent or lease figure in this box. If you received special terms on your lease whereby you are not required to make any payments for the first few months, you must still enter a figure on this line. To calculate this figure, add up the total amount you will pay over the term of the lease and divide it by the total months you will be in the building. Example: You lease a building for 5 years and the landlord gives you 6 months of free rent and then the rent will be $1000 per month. Your actual monthly expense is (54 months X $1000 per month) / 60 months = $900 per month.

59. **Insurance** -- Enter your anticipated cost for all insurance except life and health related insurance on this line. This will include workman's compensation insurance, general liability insurance, and any special policies your business may require.

60. **Utilities** -- Enter estimated costs for gas, electricity, sewer, cable TV, etc. here. Don't forget the service activation fees on the first month and any possible deposits that may be required.

61. **Repairs and Maintenance** -- Include janitorial services and other anticipated repair and maintenance expenses on this line. This would include repair fees for store machines (copiers, faxes, phone system, etc.) as well as general building repairs. If you do not have a "full service" lease on your store, check with your landlord to determine how much

money you should allocate to repairs and maintenance on a monthly basis. (If your lease includes wording like "net/net/net" or "triple net", you are personally liable for repair costs even though you do not own the building.) If you have an alarm system on your building and pay a monthly fee, insert the amount on this line also.

62. **Dues and Subscriptions** -- Enter magazine and newspapers subscription fees, monthly dues for business clubs, etc. here.

63. **Legal and Accounting** -- Enter any fees paid to your accountant, financial advisor, or attorney on this line.

64. **Telephone** -- Monthly telephone fees. Don't forget that there will be a service installation charge your first month and possibly a deposit. Call the phone company for an estimate. If you are purchasing a phone system, include the monthly payment on this line also.

65. **Stationary and Printing** -- Enter the fees paid to your printer for letterhead, business cards, envelopes, shipping labels, invoices, statements, checks, special forms, etc.

66. **Taxes and License Fees** -- This line is for any special taxes you may be required to pay (not income taxes and not payroll taxes).

67. **Other** -- Any special item not falling into one of the above categories. Write the description on the dotted line and enter the amount.

68. **Other** -- Any special item not falling into one of the above categories. Write the description on the dotted line and enter the amount.

69. **Other** -- Any special item not falling into one of the above categories. Write the description on the dotted line and enter the amount.

70. **Total General and Administrative Expenses** -- Add lines 46 through 69 and enter the total on this line.

71. **Total Expenses** -- Add lines 23, 33, 45 and 70 and place the total on this line.

72. **Operating Profit/Loss** -- Subtract line 71 from line 8. If the answer is positive, congratulations, you made a profit — now go back and look for a mistake — make sure all your numbers are realistic and you have not overlooked something.

   If the answer is negative, you lost money this month. Keep a running total of your profit/loss year to date. This will tell you approximately how much money you will need to set aside to start this venture.

73. **Other Income or Expense** -- If you have any additional sources of income or expenses, enter the amount on this line. Usual items are additional funding by the owners, interest earned from the original investment amount, or interest expense on an amount borrowed to start the company. Income is entered as a positive number and expenses are entered as negative numbers.

74. **Net Income <Loss>** -- Add line 72 to line 73 and enter the total on this line. This is your net income (if the number is positive) or loss (if the number is negative) for the month.

Projected Income Statement

Month of _____ (Page 1 of 4)

Revenue

1. Projected Gross Sales .... _____

2. Less allowance for returns .... _____

   Less Cost of Goods Sold

   3. Purchased Products Cost .... _____

   4. Raw Material Cost .... _____

   5. Purchased Parts Cost .... _____

   6. Contract Labor .... _____

   7. Building Permits .... _____

8. **Gross Profit** .... _____
   (Line 1, minus line 2 through line 7)

Expense

Selling Expenses

9. Sales Manager's Salary .... _____

10. Inside Sales Salaries .... _____

11. Inside Sales Commissions .... _____

12. Telephone Sales Salaries .... _____

13. Telephone Sales Commissions .... _____

14. Field Sales Salaries .... _____

15. Field Sales Commissions .... _____

16. Payroll Taxes for Sales Employees .... _____

17. Sales Vehicles Depreciation, Lease or Rental Pmt _____

18. Sales Vehicles Expenses .... _____

19. Sales Related Travel and Entertainment .... _____

Projected Income Statement

Month of _____ (Page 2 of 4)

20. Depreciation - Store fixtures .... _____

21. Advertising and Promotion .... _____

22. Catalog Costs .... _____

23. Total Selling Expense .... _____
(Add lines 9 through 22)

Manufacturing/Construction Expenses

24. Mfg/Const Manager's Salary .... _____

25. Mfg/Const Employees Salaries .... _____

26. Mfg/Const Payroll Taxes .... _____

27. Mfg/Const Vehicle Deprec, Lease or Rental Pmt _____

28. Mfg/Const Vehicles Expenses .... _____

29. Mfg/Const Related Travel and Entertainment ... _____

30. Packaging Costs .... _____

31. Mfg/Const Supplies .... _____

32. Small Tools .... _____

33. Total Mfg/Const Expense .... _____
(Add lines 24 through 32)

Distribution/Warehouse Expenses

34. Distribution/Warehouse Manager's Salary .... _____

35. Warehouse Employee's Salaries .... _____

36. Courier/Driver's Salaries .... _____

37. Payroll Taxes .... _____

Projected Income Statement

Month of _____ (Page 3 of 4)

38. Dist Vehicle/Equip Deprec, Lease or Rental Pmt _____

39. Distribution Vehicles - Expenses .... _____

40. Whse Vehicle/Equip Deprec, Lease or Rental Pmt _____

41. Warehouse Vehicles - Expenses .... _____

42. Dist/Whse Related Travel and Entertainment .... _____

43. Freight/Shipping Charges .... _____

44. Warehouse Supplies .... _____

45. Total Distribution Expense .... _____
(Add lines 34 through 44)

General and Administrative Expenses

46. Officers Salaries .... _____

47. Accounting Salaries .... _____

48. Administrative Salaries .... _____

49. Purchasing Salaries .... _____

50. Payroll Taxes .... _____

51. Employee Benefits .... _____

52. Franchise Fees .... _____

53. G&A Vehicle Depreciation, Lease or Rental Pmt _____

54. G&A Vehicles - Expenses .... _____

55. G&A Travel and Entertainment .... _____

56. Office Equipment Deprec, Lease or Rental Pmt . _____

57. Office Equipment Expenses .... _____

58. Building Rent .... _____

Projected Income Statement

Month of _____ (Page 4 of 4)

59. Insurance .... _____

60. Utilities .... _____

61. Repairs and Maintenance .... _____

62. Dues and Subscriptions .... _____

63. Legal and Accounting... _____

64. Telephone .... _____

65. Stationary and Printing................................ _____

66. Taxes and License Fees .... _____

67. Other .... _____

68. Other .... _____

69. Other .... _____

70. Total General and Administrative .... _____
    (Add lines 46 through 69)

71. Total Expenses (Add lines 23, 33, 45, and 70) ... _____

72. Operating Profit or <Loss> .... _____
    (Line 8 minus line 71)

73. Other Income or Expense...................................... _____

74. Net Income <Loss> before Taxes .... _____
    (Line 72 plus line 73)

Projected Cash Flow Statement

This statement shows **Cash Receipts** (money *received*), **Cash Disbursements** (money *paid*) and **Monthly Cash Surplus or Deficit** (how much money you have left) at a specified point in time based on when you *receive* the cash and when you *pay* your bills.

By completing these worksheets, you will see the effect that each month's activity has on your cash supply. The Cash Flow Statement is subtly different from the Income statement—both appear to project profits; the Income Statement is based on sales and the Cash Flow Statement is based on cash receipts. As entrepreneurs we can get caught in "cash flow" — we can be profitable according to the income statement but never have any cash. Why? We have customers that pay 30, 60 or 90 days after we invoice them for the work—so instead of *cash* we have *accounts receivable*. Our vendors (the people from whom we buy our products) want to get paid right away—sometimes even COD when the business is new. Consequently, we see cash going out in both directions—early payments to vendors and credit terms to customers. Sometimes this spread can be several months from the time we pay for the product and when our customer pays us. This is known as cash flow.

It is important to produce 12 Projected Cash Flow Statements, one for each month of your first year in operation. This will help you to see the effect of this "float" on your cash supply. The Projected Cash Flow Statements will assist you in determining how much cash you will have to put into your venture, when you will start seeing a monthly cash return, and when you will actually recover your initial start-up costs.

I have attempted to make the "look" of the Cash Flow Statement very similar to the "look" of the Income Statement. This will make it easier for you to place the numbers from the Income Statement and more difficult for you to forget any of the figures. Remember that the Cash Flow Statement reflects when you *PAY* for the services, not when they were rendered. These worksheets begin on page 261.

Cash Receipts

Cash Sales -- If you have any cash sales, enter the dollar amount on this line.

Accounts Receivable Collections -- If you extend credit to your customers, this line represents the amount of the payments you expect to receive during this month. You will need to consider your total outstanding Accounts Receivable (A/R) amount, and what percentage of these customers will pay in 30 days, 60 days, 90 days, and 120 days. Unfortunately, not all customers pay as promptly as we would desire. If you do not have a "feel" for your customer's paying habits, check with your accountant, trade associations, or other merchants in your line of business.

Other Receipts -- Enter any other sources of cash on this line.

Total Cash Receipts -- Add lines 1 through 3 and place the total on this line.

Cash Disbursements

For a more complete description of what is included in each of the numbered categories below, please refer to the descriptions in the Projected Income Statement section of this appendix.

5. **Payments for Inventory or Material Purchases** -- Enter the amount you expect to *pay* this month for inventory and material purchases. Look at the purchases you made the prior month, the credit terms you have from your suppliers, any COD shipments you expect to receive this particular month, and any special discounts offered by your suppliers for prompt payment.

6. **Contract Labor** -- Enter the amount paid during this month.

7. **Building Permits** -- Enter the amount paid during this month.

9. **Sales Manager's Salary** -- Enter the amount paid during this month.

10. **Inside Sales Salaries** -- Enter the amount paid during this month.

11. **Inside Sales Commissions** -- Enter the amount paid during this month — commissions may be a little tricky to calculate depending on whether you pay the commission at the time the sale is made or when the customer pays.

12. **Telephone Sales Salaries** -- Enter the amount paid during this month.

13. **Telephone Sales Commissions** -- Enter the amount paid during this month.

14. **Field Sales Salaries** -- Enter the amount paid during this month.

15. **Field Sales Commissions** -- Enter the amount paid during this month — commissions may be a little tricky to calculate depending on whether you pay the commission at the time the sale is made or when the customer pays.

16. **Payroll Taxes for Sales Employees** -- Contact your accountant to determine when you must make your payroll tax deposits; it may be every pay period, monthly, or quarterly.

17. **Sales Vehicles Purchase, Lease or Rental Payment** -- Enter the amount of the *payments* paid — not the depreciation amount.

18. **Sales Vehicles - Expenses** -- Enter the amount paid for day-to-day expendables used with the sales vehicles such as gasoline and maintenance costs.

19. **Sales Related Travel and Entertainment** -- Enter the amount paid during this month.

20. **Loan Payments - Store Fixtures** -- Enter your monthly payment amount — not the depreciation amount.

21. **Advertising and Promotion** -- Enter the amount paid during this month.

22. **Catalog Costs** -- Enter the amount paid during this month.

24. **Mfg/Const Manager's Salary** -- Enter the amount paid during this month.

25. **Mfg/Const Employees' Salaries** -- Enter the amount paid during this month.

26. **Payroll Taxes** -- Contact your accountant to determine when you must make your payroll tax deposits; it may be every pay period, monthly, or quarterly.

27. **Mfg/Const Vehicles Purchase, Lease or Rental Payment** -- Enter the amount of the *payments* paid — not the depreciation amount.

28. **Mfg/Const Vehicles - Expenses** -- Enter the amount paid during this month.

29. **Mfg/Const Related Travel and Entertainment** -- Enter the amount paid during this month.

30. **Packaging Costs** -- Enter the amount paid during this month.

31. **Mfg/Const Supplies** -- Enter the amount paid during this month.

32. **Small Tools** -- Enter the amount paid during this month.

34. **Distribution/Warehouse Manager's Salary** -- Enter the amount paid during this month.

35. **Warehouse Employees' Salaries** -- Enter the amount paid during this month.

36. **Courier/Driver's Salaries** -- Enter the amount paid during this month.

37. **Payroll Taxes** -- Contact your accountant to determine when you must make your payroll tax deposits; it may be every pay period, monthly, or quarterly.

38. **Dist Vehicle/Equip Purchase, Lease or Rental Payment** -- Enter the amount of the *payments* paid — not the depreciation amount.

39. **Distribution Vehicles - Expenses** -- Enter the amount paid during this month.

40. **Depreciation, Purchase Pmt, or Rental of Warehouse Equipment** -- Enter the amount of the *payments* paid — not the depreciation amount.

41. **Warehouse Equipment - Expenses** -- Enter the amount paid during this month.

42. **Dist/Whse Related Travel and Entertainment** -- Enter the amount paid during this month.

43. **Freight/Shipping Charges** -- Enter the amount paid during this month.

44. **Warehouse Supplies** -- Enter the amount paid during this month.

46. **Officer's Salaries** -- Enter the amount paid during this month.

47. **Accounting Salaries** -- Enter the amount paid during this month.

48. **Administrative Salaries** -- Enter the amount paid during this month.

49. **Purchasing Salaries** -- Enter the amount paid during this month.

50. **Payroll Taxes** -- Contact your accountant to determine when you must make your payroll tax deposits, it may be every pay period, monthly, or quarterly.

51. **Employee Benefits** -- Enter the amount paid during this month.

52. **Franchise Fees** -- Enter the amount paid during this month.

53. **G&A Vehicle Purchase, Lease or Rental Payment** -- Enter the amount of the *payments* paid — not the depreciation amount.

54. **G&A Vehicles - Expenses** -- Enter the amount paid during this month.

55. **G & A Travel and Entertainment** -- Enter the amount paid during this month.

56. **Office Equipment Purchase, Lease or Rental Payment** -- Enter the amount of the *payments* paid — not the depreciation amount.

57. **Office Equipment - Expenses** -- Enter the amount paid during this month.

58. **Building Rent** -- This calculation is different from the one in the Projected Income Statement. Just enter the actual amount paid here.

59. **Insurance** -- Enter the amount paid during this month.

60. **Utilities** -- Enter the amount paid during this month.

61. **Repairs and Maintenance** -- Enter the amount paid during this month.

62. **Dues and Subscriptions** -- Enter the amount paid during this month.

63. **Legal and Accounting** -- Enter the amount paid during this month.

64. **Telephone** -- Enter the amount paid during this month.

65. **Stationary and Printing** -- Enter the amount paid during this month.

66. **Taxes and License Fees** -- Enter the amount paid during this month.

67. **Other** -- Enter the amount paid during this month.

68. **Other** -- Enter the amount paid during this month.

69. **Other** -- Enter the amount paid during this month.

70. **Total Cash Disbursements** -- Add lines 3 through 69 and enter the total on this line.

71. **Monthly Cash Surplus <Deficit>** -- Total Cash Receipts from the first page of the Cash Flow Statement minus line 70.

72. **Cash Balance at the Beginning of the Month** -- Enter the amount of cash you anticipate to have at the beginning of this month. This figure should be the same as line 73 (Ending Cash Balance) from the prior month's Cash Flow Statement.

73. **Ending Cash Balance** -- Add lines 71 and 72 and place the total on this line.

If the answer is negative, you are out of cash and will need additional funding in the form of an additional personal contribution, a personal loan, a bank loan, etc.

If all of this seems too overwhelming, contact your accountant who will be happy to assist you in preparing your projections.

Projected Cash Flow Statement

Month of _____ (Page 1 of 4)

Cash Receipts

Cash Sales .... _____

Accounts Receivable Collections........................... _____

Other Receipts .... _____

Total Cash Receipts...................................... _____
(Add lines 1 through 3)

Cash Disbursements

3. Purchased Products Invoices Paid .... _____

4. Raw Material Invoices Paid .... _____

5. Purchased Parts Invoices Paid .... _____

6. Contract Labor Invoices Paid .... _____

7. Building Permit Fees Paid.................................. _____

Selling Expenses

9. Sales Manager's Salary Paid............................... _____

10. Inside Sales Salaries Paid .... _____

11. Inside Sales Commissions Paid .... _____

12. Telephone Sales Salaries Paid .... _____

13. Telephone Sales Commissions Paid .... _____

14. Field Sales Salaries Paid .... _____

15. Field Sales Commissions Paid .... _____

16. Payroll Taxes for Sales Employees Paid .... _____

17. Sales Vehicles Purchase, Lease or Rental Pmt ... _____

18. Sales Vehicles Expenses Paid .... _____

Projected Cash Flow Statement

Month of _____ (Page 2 of 4)

19. Sales Related Travel and Entertainment Paid ... _____

20. Loan Payments - Store fixtures .... _____

21. Advertising and Promotion Fees Paid .... _____

22. Catalog Costs Invoices Paid .... _____

Manufacturing/Construction Expenses

24. Mfg/Const Manager's Salary Paid .... _____

25. Mfg/Const Employees Salaries Paid .... _____

26. Mfg/Const Payroll Taxes Paid .... _____

27. Mfg/Const Veh Purchase, Lease or Rental Pmt .. _____

28. Mfg/Const Vehicles Expenses Paid .... _____

29. Mfg/Const Related Travel and Entertainment Pd _____

30. Packaging Costs Paid .... _____

31. Mfg/Const Supplies Paid .... _____

32. Small Tools Cash Purchases or Invoices Paid ..... _____

Distribution/Warehouse Expenses

34. Distribution/Warehouse Manager's Salary Paid _____

35. Warehouse Employee's Salaries Paid .... _____

36. Courier/Driver's Salaries Paid .... _____

37. Payroll Taxes Paid .... _____

38. Dist Veh/Equip Purchase, Lease or Rental Pmt . _____

39. Distribution Vehicles - Expenses Paid .... _____

40. Whse Veh/Equip Purchase, Lease or Rental Pmt _____

Projected Cash Flow Statement

Month of _____ (Page 3 of 4)

41. Warehouse Vehicles - Expenses Paid .... _____

42. Dist/Whse Related Travel and Ent Paid .... _____

43. Freight/Shipping Charges Paid .... _____

44. Whse Supplies Purchased for Cash or Invoices Pd _____

General and Administrative Expenses

46. Officers Salaries Paid .... _____

47. Accounting Salaries Paid .... _____

48. Administrative Salaries Paid .... _____

49. Purchasing Salaries Paid .... _____

50. Payroll Taxes Paid .... _____

51. Employee Benefits Paid .... _____

52. Franchise Fees Paid .... _____

53. G&A Vehicle Purchase, Lease or Rental Payment _____

54. G&A Vehicles - Expenses Paid .... _____

55. G&A Travel and Entertainment Paid .... _____

56. Office Equip Purchase, Lease or Rental Payment _____

57. Office Equipment Expenses Paid .... _____

58. Building Rent Paid .... _____

59. Insurance Paid .... _____

60. Utilities Paid .... _____

61. Repairs and Maintenance Paid .... _____

62. Dues and Subscriptions Paid .... _____

Projected Cash Flow Statement

Month of _____ (Page 4 of 4)

63. Legal and Accounting Paid .... _____

64. Telephone Invoices Paid .... _____

65. Stationary and Printing Invoices Paid .... _____

66. Taxes and License Fees Paid .... _____

67. Other Invoices Paid .... _____

68. Other Invoices Paid .... _____

69. Other Invoices Paid .... _____

70. **Total Cash Disbursements** .... _____
    (Add lines 3 through 69)

71. **Monthly Cash Surplus <Deficit>** .... _____
    (Total Cash Receipts minus Line 70)

72. **Cash Balance at the Beginning of the Month** _____

73. **Ending Cash Balance (line 71 plus line 72)** _____

Break Even Analysis

A common question among new business owners is "How much do I have to sell to break even?" This question isn't as difficult to answer as you may think. You just need three pieces of information to do the calculation: the average price of whatever you sell, the average cost of whatever you sell, and the total fixed costs (those costs that remain constant regardless of how much you sell, such as rent, utilities, insurance, etc.)

Subtract the average *cost* per item from the average *price* per item and divide this number into your *total fixed costs*. For example, suppose your average item sells for $150 and costs you $100 to buy or make, and your total fixed costs run $100,000 per year. To calculate your break-even point subtract $100 from $150 giving you $50 gross profit per item. Now divide this $50 into your annual fixed overhead of $100,000 giving you 2000 units per year or 167 item per month. This tells you that you must sell 167 items per month to break even. Sell more than that and you will make money—sell less and you will lose money. It's that simple.

You cannot cross the sea merely by standing and staring at the water.

Rabindranath Tagore

Appendix B

Sample Company Policy Manual

INTRODUCTION

The purpose of this manual is to provide employees with general background information on ABC Company, the business function of the company, and the employees' role within that business function. This procedure has the purpose of enabling employees to see themselves as an integral, important part of the company; to know of, and be able to work together as a team for the company's goals; and to gain a sense of identification and importance in regard to those goals and the company's performance.

Please understand that this booklet only highlights company policies, practices, and benefits and is not intended as a legal document. In addition, circumstances may require that the policies, practices, and benefits described in the handbook change; consequently, ABC Company reserves the right to amend, supplement, or rescind any provisions at its sole and absolute discretion. The exception to this is the at-will employment relationship, which cannot be changed without a written notification signed by the President.

COMPANY OVERVIEW

ABC Company specializes in programming, training, and servicing computer systems for small businesses. It has grown and prospered because of its commitment to providing software expertise and user support services. ABC Company is generally recognized as a leader and innovator by its peers and clients.

LOCATION

The company's facilities are leased and located at 123 Main Street, Anytown, California. The company has resided at this location since

1978. Its premises are approximately 9000 square feet with additional space available for expansion.

OWNERSHIP

Originally founded in March of 1973 as a partnership between Sam Smith and Bill Jones, ABC Company incorporated in California in November of 1979. The original principals still retain full ownership and are active in the business. Mr. Smith's background includes technical, sales, and managerial experiences in the data processing industry. After graduating from Prestigious College with a degree in economics, he started working with the XYZ Corporation in 1968 as a programmer trainee. In 1971 he was promoted to Management Information Services Director for XYZ's Northern California and Nevada Computer center. Mr. Smith is currently the President of ABC Company. Mr. Jones's background is also in data processing technology and management. He received the Outstanding Computer Science Student award at Big School, and a scholarship to Bigger University. He began his career at XYZ's Northern California Division in 1969 and, in 1972, was promoted to management. He is currently Vice President of Systems and Programming at ABC Company, and is responsible for product development and maintenance.

PRODUCTS

ABC Company originated as a Service Bureau whose main applications were processing general accounting and inventory control systems. ABC Company soon realized the benefit of specializing in certain markets and, consequently, began developing vertical market applications. The company's first system was for the dairy industry and ABC Company soon became a recognized leader in this area. Representatives from Federal and State Regulatory Agencies frequently attended local user meetings. Through the strength of the user group, they were able to influence several new regulations.

etc., etc., etc.

BUSINESS FUNCTION

As a business, ABC Company's primary function and goal is to make a profit by providing dependable and on-going data processing services and the sale of related equipment to customers within specialized industries. For the immediate future, ABC Company has additional goals of expanding its service line for the industries already served and aggressively competing in the microcomputer market.

EMPLOYEE ROLE

Employees are the key to effectively developing and implementing company plans. As such, the role of each employee is to support other ABC employees in making the company function well and efficiently, to create customer satisfaction, to strive for both company and personal growth, and to take personal responsibility for the success of the company.

OPPORTUNITIES AT ABC COMPANY

ABC Company is a young company with young management in a state of change and growth. As a result, ABC Company offers its employees opportunities to create; to make a visible contribution to the company's success along with their own, and to work in a low-key, informal environment with easy access to management. ABC Company also offers its employees profit sharing and other benefits as described later in this Policy Manual.

EMPLOYEE POLICIES

PURPOSE

The purpose of this standard procedure is to introduce and explain company policy in regard to Employee Benefits, Personnel, and Operations. Policy is the position that the company takes with regard to recurring questions. The purpose of this policy is to standardize the company's response to situations requiring routine decisions.

Once management has decided upon the best way to handle a situation and has declared that decision as policy, all the analysis and weighing of alternatives that went into making that decision the first time need not be repeated. A repetitious personal explanation of policy decisions to each employee is also not necessary. A written policy, then, saves everybody's time.

In summary, a written company policy benefits the company and employees alike by...

- standardizing the company's response to various situations.
- saving time at decision-making levels.

RESPONSIBILITY AND AUTHORITY

The management committee is responsible for setting both company policy at all levels of the company and enforcing that policy through the department managers, who in turn are responsible for such enforcement in their departments.

The President may delegate authority to set policy to a department manager where that policy does not affect operations outside that department, except that under no circumstances will the President delegate authority to change the at-will basis of any employee's employment. Furthermore, any delegation of authority still requires that individual policies do not conflict, and are in keeping with applicable local, state, and federal laws.

POLICY ISSUANCE AND REVISIONS

ABC Company reserves the right to change, amend or rescind any provisions at its sole and absolute discretion.

EMPLOYMENT RELATIONSHIP

As indicated at the time of your employment, all employment relationships with ABC Company are on an at-will basis. This means that you or ABC Company may terminate your employment at any time, with or without cause, and with or without notice. Accordingly, there is no promise that your employment will continue for a set period of time nor that your employment will be terminated only under particular circumstances. No person other than the President of the company has authority to enter into any agreement for employment for any specified period of time or to make any agreements contrary to the foregoing policy.

This agreement supersedes any and all other agreements, either oral or in writing, between the parties hereto with respect to the employment of the undersigned employee by ABC Company and contains all of the covenants and agreements between the parties with respect to that employment in any manner whatsoever. Each party to this agreement acknowledges that no representation, inducements, promises, or agreements, orally or otherwise, have been made by any party, or anyone acting on behalf of any party, which are not embodied in this written agreement, and that no other agreement, statement, or promise not contained in this agreement shall be valid or binding on either party, whether it has been previously made or is made in the future. Any modification of or addition to this agreement will be effective only if it is in writing and signed by the President of ABC Company.

EMPLOYEE BENEFITS

HOLIDAYS:

The company will be closed for nine days per year, besides weekends, as follows:

New Year's Day	January
Martin Luther King Day	January
Presidents' Day	February
Memorial Day	May
Independence Day	July
Labor Day	September
Thanksgiving & day after	November
Christmas	December

In addition, you will be granted a day off in recognition of your birthday. A holiday schedule with the specific week, day, and dates for the above holidays will be posted each year on the employee bulletin board. Your birthday is a floating holiday. You must receive your manager's approval for taking off your birthday; this holiday may be rescheduled at the discretion of your manager.

HEALTH BENEFITS:

Employees are covered by the National Health Plan, which offers extensive coverage except for a nominal fee per visit. Under this plan subscribers must accept a National doctor. ABC Company pays all premiums. If employees are covered by another plan and do not wish to take advantage of the National plan, the employee may sign a waiver of National Insurance. In lieu of National coverage, the employee will receive a monthly cash payment to be paid through payroll with normal payroll taxes deducted.

Employees also have the option of having dental insurance. The employees are asked to contribute a portion of the monthly fee for the dental coverage.

Any questions regarding the medical or dental benefits should be directed to the accounting department.

INSURANCE:

Employees are covered by $5,000 of group life insurance from Really Big Insurance Company. The company pays the premium for such life insurance coverage. Questions regarding life insurance should be directed to the accounting department.

PROFIT SHARING:

Employees, after their first year with the company, and if they are over 21 years of age, and if they are not covered by a collective bargaining agreement, are eligible to participate in the company's profit sharing plan. This plan is managed by the management committee. For details regarding the profit sharing plan, please request a copy of the Summary Plan Description from the personnel department.

VACATIONS:

Paid vacation time, defined as paid time off earned from the previous year, is provided for employees by the company at the earned rate of:

Two (2) weeks per year after completion of one year's employment earned at the rate of one day per month up to a maximum of ten days per calendar year. New employees earn vacation also at the rate of one day per month/ten days maximum per calendar year, but cannot take vacation until after January 1, following the beginning date of employment with the company.

Three (3) weeks per year after completion of seven years employment, earned at the rate of 1.25 days per month.

Four (4) weeks per year after completion of twelve years employment, earned at the rate of 1.66 days per month.

Additional days of vacation time will be given to employees who do not exceed four days of sick leave during the year. This will be based on the following schedule:

0 sick days taken	5 additional vacation days
1 sick day taken	4 additional vacation days
2 sick days taken	3 additional vacation days
3 sick days taken	2 additional vacation days
4 sick days taken	1 additional vacation day

The scheduling of all vacation days are subject to your manager's approval. An employee's vacation time earned from the previous year is considered due and available as of each January 1. Employees leaving the company will be paid their vacation earned, but not yet taken.

Vacation time for each employee will be scheduled on a seniority basis within each department and must be approved by the general manager. Generally, not more than two employees within the same department will be allowed to take vacation at the same time for purpose of continuity of operations. Vacation is encouraged to be taken during the middle of a month rather than at the beginning or end because of the peaks in workloads at those times.

SICKNESS:

Paid sick leave is provided to employees by the company at the earned rate of ten (10) days per year or 0.83 days per month. Employees are required to call the office in a timely manner if they cannot report to work due to illness. The department manager retains the right to request a doctor's certification of illness for employees in their department before accepting absences as qualified sick leave.

If employees are sick for more than the allotted time, they will have the option of making up the excess time or having it deducted from their paycheck. The arrangements for this are to be made by the department manager with the employee.

PAY ADVANCE:

Pay advances to employees are discouraged and will be granted only on an exception basis.

LEAVE OF ABSENCE:

Leaves of absence will be granted employees upon request only on an exception basis. The general manager will approve/disapprove such requests when made in writing based upon the circumstance and justification.

DISABILITY:

Employees are covered by workman's compensation insurance. The provisions of this benefit are explained in a notice posted on the employee bulletin board. Further questions regarding this benefit should be addressed to the accounting department.

EDUCATION REIMBURSEMENT:

Employees continuing their education while employed with the company will qualify for reimbursement of 50% or 75% of their tuition expense (subject to $750.00 maximum per year) by the company upon completion of each quarter/semester if the following conditions are met:

- The course(s) must be approved by the President as either directly or indirectly related to the employee's job or future ability to contribute to ABC Company.

- The course(s) must successfully be completed at no less than a B (3.0) grade average.

- The course(s) must be taken outside of the employee's working hours at ABC Company.

The 50% reimbursement rate will apply for education courses evaluated by the department manager as generally related to the employee's job.

The 75% reimbursement rate will apply for education courses evaluated by the department manager as specifically related to the employee's job, such as accounting, computer, or sales courses.

SPECIAL EVENTS:

Special events are held at the sole discretion of the President and Vice President. Generally, a company Holiday function is held in December of each year for employees only, at company expense and at a location determined by the President.

A company activity for employees and their families is held each year on a weekend to be determined at the sole discretion of the President and Vice President.

LUNCH ROOM:

An employee lunch room is provided on company premises for the use and convenience of employees during breaks and meals. The lunch room facilities include a refrigerator, microwave, and coffee machine as well as appropriate furniture.

UNEMPLOYMENT INSURANCE:

The company pays a yearly contribution to the state unemployment fund for each employee. Administered by the state, the Unemployment fund benefits employees terminated from the company for non-disciplinary reasons beyond their control such as a reduction in the work force due to a drop in company sales. Questions regarding the eligibility and collection of unemployment insurance should be addressed to the California Unemployment Insurance Bureau.

PERSONAL POLICY

Working hours are from 8:30 a.m. to 5:00 p.m. Monday through Friday for most employees unless set otherwise by their supervisor. Work hours for service and support personnel will be scheduled by the supervisor according to the work load and department needs.

PAYING OF EMPLOYEES:

Employees will be paid once a month, on the 26th of the month unless otherwise specified by state law.

BREAKS:

Employees are entitled to two 10 minute breaks during each eight (8) hour day or shift and a separate half hour meal break. The breaks are to be taken as one break before the meal period and one sometime after the meal period, or as otherwise established by each employee's supervisor based upon the appropriateness and efficiency to the job being performed. Meal breaks are not counted as time worked. The 10 minute breaks are counted as time worked.

OVERTIME:

Overtime for other than salaried employees is authorized by the appropriate manager only as needed to maintain company performance levels. Overtime is considered as work performed over eight hours per day or forty hours per week, and will be paid at one and a half times the non-salaried employee's regular hourly rate. Salaried employees who are exempt from wage-hour laws are not eligible for overtime compensation.

PARKING:

Sufficient parking space for employees is provided in both the front and rear of the company building.

TARDINESS:

Employees are expected to report to work on time. If for any reason an employee is unable to be at work on time, the employee is expected to notify his/her direct supervisor or the company office as soon as possible, providing the reason for such tardiness. Should tardiness become excessive, as determined by the employee's department manager, forfeiture of pay for the lost time from work, and/or disciplinary action rests with that employee's department manager, depending upon circumstances involved.

SUBSTITUTION OF SHIFTS:

Hourly employees will work and be paid for only their scheduled hours unless a change is approved by the employee's department manager.

PERSONAL BUSINESS:

Absence from work for personal business will be left to the discretion of the employee's direct supervisor who will be accountable to the department manager or President.

PERSONAL TELEPHONE CALLS & VISITORS:

Personal telephone calls are not allowed during work hours except during breaks and meal time. Personal long distance telephone calls are not allowed at any time. Employees are discouraged from receiving visitors during work hours.

MOONLIGHTING:

Any ABC Company employee regularly working at least 35 hours per week is expected to work as an employee for ABC Company only except as approved on an exception basis by the President. It is understood that employees are expected to devote their full energies to their job at ABC Company as the activity of first priority. Unauthorized moonlighting will be considered a serious policy violation.

PAY RAISES:

Pay scales of all employees will be reviewed yearly according to the cost of living, employee merit, and company profits.

PROMOTIONS:

Promotions are based entirely on merit. Vacancies in the organization will be filled from within at the manager's discretion.

EMPLOYEE CHECK CASHING:

Employees may not cash either payroll or personal checks with the company.

GARNISHMENTS:

Garnishments of wages, such as the withholding by the company of employee payroll taxes, will be made in accordance with local, state, and federal regulations.

BUILDING KEYS AND ALARM PASS CARDS:

Keys and alarm pass cards to the building or portions of the building are issued on a "as-needed" basis. Decisions regarding the distribution of keys and pass cards shall be left solely to the discretion of the President.

EMPLOYMENT:

ABC Company is an equal opportunity employer. Each applicant for a position with the company will be accepted or rejected based solely on his/her qualifications and merits. Current employment of a relative in the organization will not influence the decision whether or not to accept an applicant for employment.

Please note that the employment relationship between you and ABC Company can be terminated by you or the company at any time.

SUGGESTIONS:

The President and individual department managers **welcome** employee suggestions.

ALCOHOL AND DRUGS:

Drinking of any alcoholic beverages, including beer, by an employee will not be allowed during that employee's working hours unless otherwise authorized by the general manager. The taking of, or being under the influence of illegal drugs, or being under the influence of alcohol is specifically forbidden by employees while on company premises.

DISCIPLINE AND DISCHARGE:

Employees are expected to observe certain standards of job performance and good conduct. In many cases where these standards are not being met, ABC Company believes counseling with an employee can correct the problem.

However, some violations are immediately unacceptable. They include but are not limited to:

- Abuse of customers.

- Theft or pilferage of company property.

- Intentional damage to company property.

- Intoxication from alcoholic beverages during work hours.

- Intoxication from or possession of illegal drugs on company premises.

- Unauthorized use of computer equipment.

- Conviction of a felony crime.

- Insubordination.

- Non-responsiveness to supervision.

In every case it should be remembered that employment is at the mutual consent of you and ABC Company. Therefore, either you or ABC Company can terminate the employment relationship for any reason, at any time, with or without cause.

TERMINATION OF EMPLOYMENT:

Employees leaving the company for their own reasons are expected to give the company a minimum of two weeks notice. Employees terminated by the company for reasons other than the specific serious violations listed above under the heading, "DISCIPLINE AND DISCHARGE" will receive two weeks in lieu of notice pay from the company, provided they have completed six months employment with the company.

VOTING:

All employees are expected to vote outside of business hours, unless an employee needs time off in accordance with Section 14350 of the State Election Code.

JURY DUTY:

The company makes no provision to compensate employees for time lost because of jury duty.

COMPANY-OWNED VEHICLES:

The President retains the authority to grant permission and guidelines for the use of company-owned vehicles. Company-owned vehicles are presently provided for purposes of management, company deliveries, and sales calls only.

OCCUPATIONAL SAFETY AND HEALTH ACT (OSHA):

Employees are expected to comply with the requirements of the Occupational Safety and Health Act as the act applies to this company. Managers will ensure that employees are familiar with applicable provisions of OSHA.

EMPLOYEE INJURY:

Any injury to an employee should be reported immediately to the general manager or to the department manager in the absence of the

President for his notification and assistance. In the President's absence, a report is to be written by the appropriate department manager for the President listing the injury, employee, time, place, circumstances, and action taken.

FUND RAISING:

The company will not be a collection agency for fund raisers. Management will neither demand nor accept employee contributions to any organized charity, except on an individual basis through employee motivation.

PEDDLING, SOLICITING, LOTTERIES, ETC.:

Office pools, solicitations, selling of tickets or merchandise, "passing the hat," and other such activities will not be permitted except with the prior approval of the President.

FUNERALS:

Employees will be allowed to attend funerals of members of their immediate family. Forfeiture of pay for periods of absence longer than one day will be determined on an individual basis by the employee's department manager.

MILITARY SERVICE:

Employees who are members of active reserve or National Guard units will be permitted unpaid leave to attend summer field training with their units. This unpaid leave will not count against regular vacation time.

OPERATING POLICY

CUSTOMER COMPLAINTS:

Any employee receiving a customer complaint or otherwise aware of a customer complaint from non-company sources is to bring the complaint to the attention of the general manager or, in the general manager's absence, to a responsible customer support employee.

COPY MACHINE:

Use of the company copy machine for personal use is conditional upon the specific approval of the general manager.

SUPPLY ROOM:

Access to company supplies and the supply room is available only through the secretary/receptionist. Employees are expected to take only those supplies from the supply room necessary to the performance of their jobs. Taking supplies for personal use outside the company is forbidden.

_____
President

_____
Date

Appendix C

I'll assume that you are back here because you have hit some rocky roads. Problems are just a normal part of the growth process. There is no need to panic. Chances are your employees know what the problems are and have suggestions on how to correct them. Confide in your employees to give you *honest* answers to the following questions. Assure them that your intentions are to use the information to improve the business. Tell them that after the survey you will go over the results with everyone in a company meeting.

After everyone has completed the survey and you have isolated the problems, brainstorm solutions in the company meeting. Don't lose control of the meeting and let it turn into a gripe session. The purpose is to find solutions, not rehash the problem. Remain the leader, but encourage everyone to suggest ideas. Once you've agreed on a strategy, ask for everyone's commitment in supporting the decisions and the steps to be taken. If you don't have wide-spread support, you don't stand a chance. •

You may find the following survey painful to administer. Chances are you will hear some things that are going to hurt you. It takes courage to open yourself up to this extent during times of crisis. However, this may be exactly what is needed to save your company. It is better to have a bruised ego and a successful company than no company. When all is said and done, your employees will respect you for having turned the situation around.

Let me warn you that administering the survey and not following up on the results by making changes will destroy your credibility and damage moral. Before you start, make sure you are willing to follow through, no matter how painful the process might be to you personally. (You may find that *you* are part or all of the problem.) You must be willing to listen and change. You will be a better person and your company will be stronger having done it.

Company Effectiveness Survey

GOALS AND EXPECTATIONS

1. How well do you understand the goals and objectives of the company?

   - ☐ 1. Very Little Understanding
   - ☐ 2. Some Understanding
   - ☐ 3. Average Understanding
   - ☐ 4. Good Understanding
   - ☐ 5. Excellent Understanding

   Briefly list the top three goals of the company.

   1. _____

   2. _____

   3. _____

2. How well do you understand your boss's goals and expectations of you in your job performance?

   - ☐ 1. Not well at all
   - ☐ 2. A Little
   - ☐ 3. Average Understanding
   - ☐ 4. Good Understanding
   - ☐ 5. Excellent Understanding

3. Do you experience any conflict between the company goals?

   - ☐ 1. A Great Deal of Conflict
   - ☐ 2. A Lot of Conflict
   - ☐ 3. Some Conflict
   - ☐ 4. A Little Conflict
   - ☐ 5. No Conflict

4. Do you think your co-workers have a clear understanding of the company goals?

☐ 1. Little or No Understanding
☐ 2. Some Understanding
☐ 3. Average Understanding
☐ 4. Good Understanding
☐ 5. Excellent Understanding

Additional Comments: _____

_____

_____

_____

_____

STRUCTURE

5. To what degree does the company function smoothly?

☐ 1. Not At All Smoothly
☐ 2. Rarely Functions Smoothly
☐ 3. Occasionally Functions Smoothly
☐ 4. Usually Functions Smoothly
☐ 5. Always Functions Smoothly

6. To what degree do you feel you are responsible for managing your own work?

☐ 1. Not At All Responsible
☐ 2. Somewhat Responsible
☐ 3. Average Responsibility
☐ 4. Mostly Responsible
☐ 5. Completely Responsible

7. To what extent are you negatively affected in your job by the way the company is structured?

    ☐ 1. To a Very Great Extent
    ☐ 2. Affected Quite A Lot
    ☐ 3. Somewhat Affected
    ☐ 4. A Little Affected
    ☐ 5. Not At All Affected

Additional Comments: _____

_____

_____

_____

_____

RELATIONSHIPS

8. How much support is provided to you by your boss?

    ☐ 1. Almost No Support
    ☐ 2. Very Little Support
    ☐ 3. Average Support
    ☐ 4. Good Support
    ☐ 5. Great Support

9. How much support is provided to you by your co-workers?

    ☐ 1. Almost No Support
    ☐ 2. Very Little Support
    ☐ 3. Average Support
    ☐ 4. Good Support
    ☐ 5. Great Support

10. To what extent is the emphasis in the company toward getting problems or conflicts out in the open to resolve them?

   ❑ 1. No Emphasis
   ❑ 2. A Little Emphasis
   ❑ 3. Average Emphasis
   ❑ 4. A Lot of Emphasis
   ❑ 5. Great Emphasis

11. How much is teamwork encouraged in the company?

   ❑ 1. No Encouragement
   ❑ 2. A Little Encouragement
   ❑ 3. Average Encouragement
   ❑ 4. A Lot of Encouragement
   ❑ 5. Great Encouragement

12. What level of conflict do you believe exists in the company?

   ❑ 1. Tremendous Conflict
   ❑ 2. A Lot of Conflict
   ❑ 3. Average Conflict
   ❑ 4. Very Little Conflict
   ❑ 5. No Conflict

13. To what extent do you believe good working relationships exist in the company?

   ❑ 1. Little or No Working Relationships
   ❑ 2. Some Working Relationships
   ❑ 3. Average Working Relationships
   ❑ 4. Good Working Relationships
   ❑ 5. Excellent Working Relationships

Additional Comments: _____

_____

_____

REWARDS

14. To what extent do you feel you are rewarded or recognized for a job well done?

   - ❏ 1. Little or No Reward or Recognition
   - ❏ 2. Some Reward or Recognition
   - ❏ 3. Average Reward or Recognition
   - ❏ 4. Good Reward or Recognition
   - ❏ 5. Excellent Reward or Recognition

15. To what extent are the rewards given motivating you?

   - ❏ 1. Little or No Motivation
   - ❏ 2. Some Motivation
   - ❏ 3. Average Motivation
   - ❏ 4. Good Motivation
   - ❏ 5. Excellent Motivation

Additional Comments: _____

_____

_____

_____

LEADERSHIP

16. Does your boss demonstrate good teamwork through his/her actions?

   - ❏ 1. Little or No Motivation
   - ❏ 2. Some Motivation
   - ❏ 3. Average Motivation
   - ❏ 4. Good Motivation
   - ❏ 5. Excellent Motivation

17. To what extent does your boss evaluate your effectiveness and keep things running smoothly?

    ☐ 1. Not At All
    ☐ 2. A Little
    ☐ 3. Some
    ☐ 4. A Lot
    ☐ 5. A Great Deal

18. To what extent does your boss work with you and your co-workers to bring out the best in each of you?

    ☐ 1. Not At All
    ☐ 2. A Little
    ☐ 3. Some
    ☐ 4. A Lot
    ☐ 5. A Great Deal

19. How do you view your boss's openness to employee suggestions for improving their performance or job task?

    ☐ 1. Very Closed to Suggestions
    ☐ 2. Somewhat Closed to Suggestions
    ☐ 3. Doesn't Respond One Way or The Other
    ☐ 4. Usually Open to Suggestions
    ☐ 5. Very Open to Suggestions

20. Make a check mark next to the words that most describe the feelings in the company.

    ☐ Involved   ☐ Formal
    ☐ Stimulated   ☐ Informal
    ☐ Tense   ☐ Relaxed
    ☐ Calm   ☐ Energetic
    ☐ Disorganized   ☐ Confident
    ☐ Orderly   ☐ Frustrated
    ☐ Competitive   ☐ Depressed
    ☐ Supportive   ☐ Open

Additional Comments: _____

_____

_____

_____

STRENGTHS AND WEAKNESSES

What are the major strengths and weaknesses of the company?

Strengths: _____

_____

_____

_____

_____

_____

Weaknesses: _____

_____

_____

_____

_____

_____

What suggestions would you make to improve the company?

_____

_____

_____

_____

_____

_____

_____

_____

What other comments do you have about the company?

_____

_____

_____

_____

_____

_____

_____

Once you have all the completed surveys, you will need to tally the results. Looking back at question number one, you will see that each response has a number associated with it — 1 for Very Little Understanding, 2 for Some Understanding, 3 for Average Understanding, etc. We will average all these responses to arrive at composite ratings for each question. To do this, you will need to analyze the questions one at a time.

The easiest way to do this is to get a tablet and number the pages 1 through 20, one page for each question. Write the numerical value associated with the chosen answer on the appropriate page in your tablet. For example, on the first survey the individual selected *Average Understanding* for the first question. This answer has a 3 next to it so write down 3 on page 1 of your tablet. For the second question, they chose *Excellent Understanding*, so place a 5 on page 2 (for question 2). Continue to do this for all twenty questions. Do the same for the second questionnaire. When you finish, you should have two numbers on each page; one for each person's response to that question. Now continue to do this for the remaining questionnaires.

Next add up all the numbers on page one and write the total somewhere on the page. Repeat this process for the remaining 19 pages. Return to page one and count the number of responses (individual numbers, not counting the total). Divide this number into the total to arrive at the average score. Write this number on the page and circle it.

Example:
> You have 15 employees. When you finished tallying the survey you had the following numbers on page one. (2, 4, 2, 3, 4, 2, 5, 5, 3, 4, 4, 5, 4, 2, 3.) Totaling these numbers gives us 52. Divide this number by 15 and we get 3.5 (rounded). So company-wide your employees feel that they have an average to good understanding (3 = Average Understanding and 4 = Good Understanding) of the company goals and objectives.

Take an extra blank copy of the survey and write this answer to the left of the answer boxes for question number one. Continue to do this for the remaining questions. When you finish, you will have your "master" sheet with all the average responses.

The next step involves analyzing everyone's understanding of the company goals. How closely do the answers come to your understanding of the company goals? If everyone does not understand the goals, then you need to communicate them more clearly.

Analyze all the "Additional Comments" and paraphrase the responses on your master sheet. Be honest. If the comments are mostly negative, then what you write on the master sheet should be mostly negative.

Do the same for Strengths, Weaknesses, Suggestions, and Comments.

Now pick a quiet place where you can analyze the answers. Spend some time thinking about what everyone said. You are now ready to have the meeting with all your employees and discuss the results. The meeting should be highly productive and several things will probably come out that weren't on the survey. Allow several hours for this meeting. It is best to have it after hours. Take everyone out to dinner and tell the restaurant that you would like a private room, or have pizza brought in. Choose the format that is most comfortable to you.

This will probably be one of the most rewarding evenings of your business career. Good Luck.

If you feel uneasy about this process or would like some professional guidance, contact Gary Ware, Ph.D., Director, OceanView Counseling and Consultation, 822 Deleware Street, Berkeley, CA 94710, or phone (510) 649-5845. Dr. Ware is an organizational development consultant.

Appendix D

$25,000 Idea

Did you ever hear of the single idea for which a man was paid twenty-five thousand dollars? Well, it was worth every penny of it!

The story goes that Charles M. Schwab, the great steel magnate, had granted an interview to an efficiency expert named Ivy Lee. Lee was telling his prospective client how Lee's firm could help him do a better job of managing the company, when Mr. Schwab broke in to say something to the effect that he wasn't at present managing as well as he knew how. He went on to tell Ivy Lee that what was needed wasn't more knowing—but a lot more doing. He said, "We know what we should be doing; now if you can show us a better way of getting it done, I'll listen to you—and pay you anything you ask, within reason."

Well, Lee then said that he could give him something in twenty minutes that would INCREASE HIS EFFICIENCY by at least 50%. He then handed the man a blank sheet of paper and said: "Write down on this paper the six most important things you have to do tomorrow."

Well, Mr. Schwab thought about it, and did as requested—it took about three minutes. Lee then said, "Now number them in the order of their importance to you and to the company." Well, that took about five minutes. And then Lee said, "Now put the paper in your pocket, and first thing tomorrow morning, take it out and look at item number one. Don't look at the others, just number one, and start working on it; and—if you can—stay with it until it's completed. Then take item number two the same way; then number three, and so on until you have to quit for the day. Don't worry if you have only finished one or two. You'll be working on the most important ones. The others can wait. If you can't finish them all by this method, you could not have finished them with any other method. And without some system, you'd probably take ten times as long to finish them—and might not even have them in the order of their importance."

"Do this every working day," Lee went on. "After you've convinced yourself of the value of this system, have all of your executives, managers, supervisors, and foremen try it. Try it as long as you like, and then send me your check for whatever you think the idea is worth."

The entire interview hadn't taken more than a half-hour. In a few weeks, the story has it that Mr. Schwab sent Ivy Lee a check for $25,000 with a letter saying the lesson was the most profitable, from a money spent standpoint, he had ever learned in his life.

Things I Gotta Do!

Date:_____

"A" PRIORITY

1 _____
  _____
2 _____
  _____
3 _____
  _____
4 _____
  _____
5 _____
  _____
6 _____
  _____
7 _____
  _____

"B" PRIORITY

1 _____
  _____
2 _____
  _____
3 _____
  _____
4 _____
  _____
5 _____
  _____
6 _____
  _____
7 _____
  _____

"C" PRIORITY

_____   _____
_____   _____
_____   _____
_____   _____
_____   _____
_____   _____

DON'T QUIT

When things go wrong, as they sometimes will,
When the road you're trudging seems all uphill,
When the funds are low and the debts are high,
And you want to smile, but you have to sigh,
When care is pressing you down a bit —
Rest if you must, but don't you quit.

Life is queer with its twists and turns,
As every one of us sometimes learns,
And many a fellow turns about
When he might have won had he stuck it out.
Don't give up though the pace seems slow —
You may succeed with another blow.

Often the goal is nearer than
It seems to a faint and faltering man;
Often the struggler has given up
When he might have captured the victor's cup;
And he learned too late when the night came down,
How close he was to the golden crown.

Success is failure turned inside out —
The silver tint of the clouds of doubt,
And you never can tell how close you are,
It may be near when it seems afar;
So stick to the fight when you're hardest hit, —
It's when things seem worst that you mustn't quit.

Author Unknown

Appendix E

Balance Sheet

As of February 1, 1993

Current Assets	
Cash	$ 222,212
Accounts Receivable	312,782
Deposits	2,720
Forms/Supplies Inventory	11,857
Product Inventory	43,313
Notes Receivable	67,003

Total Current Assets	659,887
Fixed Assets	
Computer Equipment	139,123
Computer Software	107,500
Office Furniture and Equipment	477,369
Company Vehicles	14,836
Accumulated Depreciation	(516,947)

Total Fixed Assets	221,881
TOTAL ASSETS	**881,768**
Current Liabilities	
Accounts Payable	43,396
Sales Tax	9,419

Total Current Liabilities	52,815
Long-Term Liabilities	
Notes Payable -- Less Current	146,222

Total Long-Term Liabilities	146,222
TOTAL LIABILITIES	**199,037**
Stockholders' Equity	
Capital Stock	15,000
Paid in Surplus	285
Retained Earnings	520,758
Profit or Loss	146,687

Total Stockholders' Equity (Net Worth)	**682,730**

Total Liabilities and Equity	**881,767**

Income Statement

For the period ended January 31, 1993

Sales	281,839
Cost of Goods Sold	45,973

Gross Profit	235,866
Expenses	
Salaries and Wages	146,562
Payroll Taxes	7,353
Employee Benefits	7,513
Advertising and Promotion	1,837
Travel and Entertainment	5,114
Auto and Delivery Expense	242
Rent	8,288
Utilities	3,518
Telephone	5,840
Office Supplies	1,285
Dues, Subscriptions, Books	420
Building Maintenance and Security	1,412
Office Equipment Maintenance	100
Postage and Shipping	603
Legal and Accounting	644
Computer Supplies	778
Depreciation	5,681
Interest Expense	276

Total Expenses	197,466
Net Profit or Loss	**38,400**

I'm Your Customer Who Never Comes Back

I'm a nice customer. All merchants know me. I'm the one who never complains no matter what kind of service I get.

When I go to a store to buy something, I don't throw my weight around. I try to be thoughtful of the other person. If I get a snooty clerk who gets nettled because I want to look at several things before I make up my mind, I'm as polite as can be; I don't believe rudeness in return is the answer.

I never kick, complain, or criticize, and I wouldn't dream of making a scene as I've seen people doing in public places. No, I'm the nice customer, but I'm also the nice customer who never comes back.

That's my little revenge for being abused and taking whatever you hand out, because I know I'm not coming back. This way doesn't immediately relieve my feelings but in the long run it's far more satisfying than blowing my top.

In fact, a nice customer like myself, multiplied by others of my kind, can ruin a business. And there are a lot of nice people just like me. When we get pushed far enough, we go to another store where they appreciate nice customers.

He laughs best, they say, who laughs last. I laugh when I see you frantically advertising to get me back, when you could have kept me in the first place with a few kind words and a smile.

Your business might be in a different town and your situation might be "different," but if your business is bad, chances are good that if you will change your attitude, the word will get around and I'll change from the nice customer who never comes back to the nice customer who always comes back — and brings friends.

ANONYMOUS

Appendix F

478 Business Ideas

Accounting Service
Adult Day Care Center
Advertising Agency
Aerial Photography
Aerobics Instructor
Air Ambulance Service
Air Conditioning Repair
Air Compressor & Pump Repair
Amusement Park
Animal Boarding
Animal Training
Antique Repair & Restoration
Antique Store
Apartment Locator Service
Aquarium Cleaning Service
Aquarium Supplies
Art Dealer
Art Instruction
Artist
Arts & Crafts Supplies
Asbestos Removal Service
Asphalt Paving
Astrologer
Athletic Club
Auctioneer and Liquidator
Auditor
Auto Broker
Auto Detailing
Auto Dismantler
Auto Inspection Center
Auto Painting
Auto Parts Store
Auto Repair
Auto Upholstery Shop
Autograph Dealer
Baby Shoe Bronzing
Baby Sitting Service
Baby Store

Back Hoe Services
Bail Bonds
Bakery
Balloon Delivery Service
Balloon Rides
Baseball Batting Range
Baseball Card Shop
Barber Shop
Beauty Salon
Beauty Supply Store
Bed and Breakfast Inn
Bee Keeper
Billiard and Pool Parlor
Billing Service
Biofeedback Therapy & Training
Blacksmith
Boat and Marine Supplies
Boat Rental Service
Boat Repairing
Boat Sales
Boating Instruction
Book Publisher
Book Store
Bookbinder
Bookkeeping Service
Bowling Alley
Bowling Instructor
Braille Supplies
Brake Shop
Breeder
Brick Mason
Bridge Lessons
Building Construction Consultant
Burglar Alarm Sales & Installation
Business Brokerage
Butcher Shop
Butler
Cabinet Maker

Cake Decorating Instruction
Camera and Photo Store
Camp Ground
Camping and Outdoor Supplies
Candle Shop
Candy Store
Car Wash
Carpet and Upholstery Cleaning
Carpet Layer
Card Shop
Catering Service
Ceiling Cleaning
Cellular Phone Service
Ceramic Shop
Chauffeur
Check Cashing Service
Child Care Service
Children's Store
Chimney Sweep
China and Glassware Store
Christmas Tree Farm
Clock Repair
Clock Shop
Clown
Coffee and Tea Store
Coffee Shop
Coin Dealer
Coin Operated Laundry
Collection Agency
Comic Book Shop
Commercial Fisherman
Compact Disk Store
Computer Network Wiring
Computer Portraits
Computer Programming
Computer Repair Service
Computer Store
Concrete Boring
Concrete Pumping Service
Concrete Sawing
Construction Cleanup

Consulting Business
Convenience Food Store
Cookie Shop
Cooking School
Copy Shop
Cosmetics Shop
Costume Shop
Courier
Cowboy
Craft Store
Cross Country Trucking
Dance Instructor
Data Entry Service
Data Processing Service
Dating Service
Day Care Center
Delicatessen
Detective and Protective Service
Demolition Service
Desktop Publishing
Diaper Service
Disc Jockey
Donut Shop
Drafting Services
Drapery Cleaner
Dressmaker
Driving Instructor
Drug and Alcohol Counselor
Dry Cleaners
Dry Wall Contractor
Educational Toy Store
Electronics Store
Embroidery and Engraving Service
Employment Agency
Energy Conservation Store
Envelope Stuffing Service
Equipment Rental Service
Escort Service
Executive Recruiting Service
Exterminator
Fabric Shop

Farmer	Gourmet Food Store
Fencing and Deck Contractor	Graffiti Removal Service
Fiber Glass Fabricator	Grant Proposal Writing
Film Developing	Graphic Artist
Financial Aid Services	Graphic Arts Supply Store
Financial Planner	Grocery Store
Fingernail Salon	Gymnastics Instructor
Fire Alarm Systems	Hair Salon
Firewood Broker	Ham Radio Store
First Aid Instruction	Handicapped & Disabled Services
Fish & Seafood Store	Hardware Store
Fish Pond Construction	Hazardous Material Consultant
Fishing Expeditions	Health Food Store
Fishing Instructor	Health / Fitness Center
Fix-It Service	Hearing Aid Store
Flower Arranging	Helicopter Rides
Flower Shop	Herb Farming
Fly Fishing Lessons	Hobby Shop
Fly Tying	Hockey Lessons
Flying Instruction	Home Health Care
Food Delivery Service	Home Inspection Service
Formal Wear Rental Service	Home Remodeling
Framing Shop	House Cleaning
Free-lance Writing	House Painting
Freight Brokerage	House Sitting
Frozen Food Locker	Hot Dog / Hamburger Stand
Frozen Yogurt Shop	Hunter Safety Training
Fruit and Vegetable Farming	Hydroseeding Service
Furniture Restoration	Ice Cream Parlor
Gardener	Ice Skating Rink
Gas Station	In-Home Care Service
General Contractor	Independent Insurance Agent
Gift Basket Service	Industrial Catering
Gift, Novelty & Souvenir Store	Insulation Contractor
Glazier	Interior Decorator
Golf Club Repair	International Trade Consultant
Golf Instructor	Import / Export Business
Golf Practice Range	Instant Sign Store
Golf Shop	Interior Decorator / Designer
Golf Tours	Janitorial Service

Jewelry Maker
Jewelry Store
Juggler
Kitchen Remodeling
Knife & Scissor Sharpening
Knitting Instruction
Knitting Shop
Lawn Care
Lawn Mower Sharpening & Repair
Landscaping
Language Instruction
Laundromat
Leasing Company
Leather Shop
Limousine Service
Lingerie Shop
Linoleum Layer
Liquidator
Locksmith
Loan Broker
Luggage Store
Lumber Yard
Machine Shop
Magazine Sales
Magic Shop
Maid Service
Mail Delivery Service
Mail Order Business
Martial Arts Instruction
Maternity Shop
Medical Alarms
Medical Billing Service
Medical Transcription Service
Messenger Service
Microfilming Service
Midwife
Miniature Golf Course
Mobile Automotive Window Service
Mobile Bookkeeping Service
Mobile Home Rentals

Mobile Home Sales
Mobile Home Park
Money Broker
Monogram Service
Monument Dealer
Motel
Motorcycle Repair
Muffler Shop
Music Box Store
Music Lessons
Music Store
Musical Instrument Repair
Musician
Nanny Placement Service
Newsletter Publishing
Newsstand
Night Watchman
Nursery & Garden Center
Off-Site Data / Record Storage
Office Supply Store
Ornamental Iron Work
Old Time Photos
Packaging and Shipping Service
Parasailing Rides
Painter
Paper Hanger
Parking Lot Striping Service
Party Goods Store
Pawn Shop
Personal Financial Planner
Personal Fitness Trainer
Pest Control
Pet Grooming
Pet Sitting / Walking Service
Pet Store
Photo Finishing
Photographer
Physical Fitness Center
Piano Mover
Piano Tuner

Pizza Parlor
Plumber
Pool Hall
Print and Poster Shop
Printing Shop
Printer Maintenance Services
Private Investigator
Private Mailbox Service
Property Management
Property Tax Auditing
Public Relations Agency
Quilt Making
Quilting Lessons
Radiator Shop
Radio, TV and VCR Repair
Racquet Restringing Service
Raft Trips
Railroad Tours
Rabbit Raising
Recording Studio
Recycling Center
Reducing Salon
Real Estate Appraiser
Real Estate Property Manager
Realtor
Refrigeration and A/C Repair
Religious Gift / Book Store
Removable Tattoo Parlor
Rental Yard
Restaurant
Resume Writing Service
Retirement Home
Riding Lessons
Rifle / Pistol Range
River Trip Organizer
Rock Shop
Roller Skating Rink
Rubber Stamps
RV Parts and Supplies
Saddle Shop

Safety Consultant
Sailmaker
Sandblasting
Sandwich Shop
Saw Sharpening & Repair
Scuba Instructor
Secretarial Service
Self-Storage Service
Seminar Promoting
Senior Day Care Center
Sewing and Needlework Shop
Shoe Repair
Shoe Store
Sight-Seeing Tours
Sign Language Lessons
Sign Painter
Silk Plant Store
Silk Screen Printing
Singing Lessons
Singing Telegrams
Skateboard Shop
Ski Tours
Skiing Instructor
Sky Diving Lessons
Sky Writing
Small Appliance Repair
Smog Inspection Station
Sod & Sodding Service
Soil Testing
Solar Energy Consultant
Sporting Goods Store
Sports Memorabilia Store
Square Dance Lessons
Stable
Stained Glass Shop
Stamp Dealer
Stationary Store
Street Vendor
Stenciling Service
Stenographic Service

Stereo Store
Sunglass Shop
Swimming Pool Care
Swimming Pool Contractor
Swimming Pool Repair
T-Shirt Shop
Tank Testing & Inspection
Tanning Salon
Tax Service
Taxidermist
Technical Writer
Temporary Help Service
Ten Minute Oil Change
Tennis Court Construction
Tennis Instructor
Telecommunications Consultant
Telephone Answering Service
Television Repair
Termite Inspector
Theater
Theatrical Agent
Thrift Shop
Tire Shop
Tour Guide
Towing Service
Toy Store
Transmission Shop
Travel Agent
Tree Service
Trophy Shop
Truck Driving School
Tutoring Service
Tool and Die Maker
Tool Store
Toy Store
Truck Detailing
Truck Painting
Truck Repair
Typing Service
Upholsterer

Used Book Store
Used Car Lot
Used Car Rental Agency
Used Clothing Store
Used Furniture Store
Used Merchandise Store
Utility Bill Auditing
Utility Consultant
Vacuum Cleaner Repair
Vacuum Cleaner Store
Valet Service
Vending Machine Repair
Van Conversions
Video Game Arcade
Video Store
Video Taping Service
Vinyl Repair Service
Voice Lessons
Wallpaper Hanging
Wallpaper Removing
Watch, Clock and Jewelry Repair
Waterproofing Contractor
Weed Control Service
Wedding Planning Service
Welding Shop
Western Apparel
Well Drilling
Wheel Chair Lifts and Ramps
Wig Shop
Window Cleaning
Window Tinting
Window Washing Service
Windshield Repair
Woman's Accessories Shop
Woman's Apparel Shop
Woodworking
Worm Farm
Yard Cleanup & Hauling
Yarn Shop
Yoga Instruction

Would you like me to give you a formula for ... success? It's quite simple, really. Double your rate of failure ... You're thinking of failure as the enemy of success. But it isn't at all ... You can be discouraged by failure — or you can learn from it. So go ahead and make mistakes. Make all you can. Because, remember that's where you'll find success. On the far side of failure.

Thomas J. Watson
(IBM)

Appendix G

Miscellaneous Suppliers

These companies are all mail order suppliers. Call them for a current catalog.

Audio Visual Equipment

Duplication Equipment Brokerage
1501 W. Tufts Ave # 102
Englewood, CO 80110-5538
(303) 781-1132

Educational Industrial Sales, Inc.
2225 Grant Road, Suite 3
Los Altos, CA 94022
(415) 969-5212
(800) 621-0854 ext. 777

Audio/Video

Crutchfield
1 Crutchfield Park
Charlottesville, VA 22906
(800) 955-9009

Business Forms

Deluxe Business Forms & Supplies
1275 Red Fox Road
P.O. Box 64046
St. Paul, MN 55164-0046
(800) 328-0304

Gold Coast Business Forms
P.O. Box 469
Arnold, CA 95223
(800) 553-0770

Calculators

EduCALC
27953 Cabot Road
Laguna Niguel, CA 92677
(800) 535-9650

Clearance Centers

Damark
7101 Winnetka Ave. N.
Minneapolis, MN 55429-0900
(800) 729-9000

Computer Furniture

Devoke
1500 Martin Ave.
Box 58051
Santa Clara, CA 95052-8051
(800)822-3132

Computer Supplies

Global Computer Supplies
9404 Hemlock Drive
Hempstead, NY 11550
(800) 472-0101

Inmac
2465 Augustine Drive
Santa Clara, CA 95052-8031
(800) 547-5444

Misco
One Misco Plaza
Holmdel, NJ 07733
(800) 876-4726

Visible
1750 Wallace Avenue
St. Charles, IL 60174
(800) 323-0628

Computers - Mailorder

CompuAdd
(800) 477-0328

Crutchfield
1 Crutchfield Park
Charlottesville, VA 22906
(800) 955-9009

Dell Computers
(800) 274-0696

PC Connection
6 Mill Street
Marlow, NH 03456
(800) 800-0026

Custom Binders

Crestline Company, Inc.
18 West 18th Street
New York, NY 10011
(800) 221-7797

Jack Nadel, Inc.
9950 West Jefferson Blvd.
Culver City, CA 90230
California (213) 870-8651

Myron Manufacturing Corp.
205 Maywood Avenue
Maywood, NJ 07607
(201) 843-6464

Data Communications

Black Box Corporation
P.O. Box 12800
Pittsburgh, PA 15241
(412) 746-5530

Patton Electronics Co.
7958 Cessna Ave.
Gaithersburg, MD 20879
(301) 975-1000

Electronics

Eagle Electronics
1233 E. Colorado Blvd.
Glendale, CA 91205
(818) 244-3191

MCM Electronics
650 Congress Park Drive
Centerville, OH 45459-4072
(513) 434-0031

Products International
8931 Brookville Road
Silaver Spring, MD 20910
(800) 638-2020

First Aid Kits

Masuen First Aid & Safety
490 Fillmore Avenue
Tonawanda, NY 14150
(800) 831-0894

Furniture

Global Business Furniture
9404 Hemlock Drive
Hempstead, NY 11550
(800) 472-0101

National Business Furniture
905 Mateo Street
Los Angeles, CA 90021
(800) 558-1010

Graphic Arts Supplies

Fidelity Products
5601 International Parkway
New Hope, MN 55428
(800) 842-2725

Identification Products

GM Nameplate, Inc.
2040 15th Ave. West
Seattle, WA 98119-2783
(206) 284-2200

Seton Name Plate Company
P.O. Box TC-1331
New Haven, CT 06505
(800) 243-6624

Tech Products, Inc.
105-A Willow Avenue
Staten Island, NY 10305
(800) 221-1311

Industrial Safety Supplies

Industrial Safety Co.
1390 Neubrecht Road
Lima, Ohio 45801
(800)537-9721

Conney
3202 Latham Drive
Madison, WI 53744-4190
(800) 356-9100

Industrial Supplies

Consolidated Plastics Co., Inc.
(Rubbermaid & Matting catalog)
1864 Enterprise Parkway
Twinsburg, OH 44087
(800) 362-1000

Mailing Lists

American Business Lists, Inc.
5707 South 86th Circle
P.O. Box 27347
Omaha, NE 68127
(402) 331-7169

Direct Media
200 Pemberwick Road
Greenwich, CT 068300
(203) 532-1000

Quality Lists
P.O. Box 6060
Miller Place, NY 11794
(516) 744-7289

Mailing List Software

Melissa Data Corp.
32122 Paseo Adelanto
San Juan Capistrano, CA 92672
(800) 443-8834

Mailroom Furn. & Equip.

W.A.Charnstrom Co.
10901 Hampshire Ave. So.
Minneapolis, MN 55438
(800) 328-2962

Office Supplies

Pennywise
4350 Kenilworth Avenue
Edmonston, MD 20781
(800) 942-3311

Reliable
1001 W. Van Buren St
Chicago, IL 60607
(800) 735-4000

Viking Office Products
13809 S. Figueroa Street
P.O. Box 61144
Los Angeles, CA 90061-0144
(800) 421-1222

Visible Office Supplies
1750 Wallace Ave
St. Charles, IL 60174
(800) 323-0628

Pens & Pencils

Atlas Pen & Pencil Corp.
3040 N. 29th Avenue
Hollywood, FL 33022
(800) 327-3232

Personal Organizers

Day-Timers, Inc. .
One Dat-Timer Plaza
Allentown, PA 18195-1551
(215) 266-9000

Promotional Products

Crestline Company, Inc.
18 West 18th Street
New York, NY 10011
(800) 221-7797

Nelson Marketing
210 Commerce Street
P.O. Box 320
Oshkosh, WI 54902-0320
(800) 722-5203

Siegel Display Products
P.O. Box 95
Minneapolis, MN 55440
(800) 328-6795

The Executive Gallery, Inc.
814 W. Third Avenue
Columbus, OH 43212
(614) 421-3400

Scheduling Boards

Caddylak Systems, Inc.
131 Heartland Blvd.
Brentwood, NY 11717-0698
(800) 523-8060

Magnatag Products
2031 O'Neill Road
Macadon, NY 14502
(315) 986-3033

Methods Research Corp.
Asbury Avenue
Farmingdale NJ 07727
(800) 631-2233

Scientific Items

Markson Science, Inc.
10201 S. 51st Street
Phoenix, AZ 85044
(800) 528-5114

Telephone / Fax

Crutchfield
1 Crutchfield Park, Dept HO
Charlottsville, VA 22906
(800) 521-4050

Hello Direct
140 Great Oaks Blvd.
San Jose, CA 95119-1347
(800) 444-3556

Tools & Tool Kits

Jensen Tools, Inc.
7815 S. 46th Street
Phoenix, AZ 85044-5399
(602) 968-6231

Specialized Products Company
3131 Premier Drive
Irving, TX 75063
(800) 866-5353

Techni-Tool
5 Apollo Road, Box 368
Plymouth Meeting, PA 19462
(215) 941-2400

Trophies / Plaques

Dinn Bros., Inc.
68 Winter Street
Holyoke, MA 01041-0111
(800) 628-9657

Trophyland, USA
7001 W. 20th Avenue
P.O. Box 4606
Hialeah, FL 33014
(305) 823-4830

Woodworking Supplies

McFeely's
712 12th Street
Lynchburg, VA 24505-0003
(800) 443-7937

Meisel Hardware Specialties
P.O. Box 70
Mound, MN 55364-0070
(800) 441-9870

Trend-Lines
375 Beacham Street
Chelsea, MA 02150
(800) 767-9999

Woodworker's Supply
1108 North Glenn Road
Casper, WY 82601
(800) 645-9292

Work Clothes / Uniforms

Wear-Guard Work Clothes
P.O. Box 400
Hingham, MA 02043
(800) 343-4406

Workman's Garment Company
15205 Wyoming Avenue
Detroit, M48238
(313) 834-7236

Bibliography

Advanced Development Technology Center. *The 1989 Survey of State Sponsored Seed Capital Funds*. Athens, OH: National Business Incubation Association, 1989

Alarid, William. *Money Sources for Small Businesses: How you can find private, state, federal, and corporate financing*. Santa Maria, California: Puma, 1991

Area Wage Surveys. Washington DC: U.S. Government Printing Office

Barry, John W. and Porter Henry. *Effective Sales Incentive Compensation*. New York: McGraw-Hill

Blanchard, Kenneth and Spencer Johnson. *The One-Minute Manager*. New York: Morrow, 1982

Bolles, Richard. *What Color Is Your Parachute?* Berkeley: Ten Speed Press, 1990

Breen, George E. and Albert B. Blankenship. *Do-It-Yourself Market Research*. New York: McGraw-Hill, 1989

Cohn, Theodore and Roy A. Lindberg, *Compensating Key Executives in the Smaller Company* . New York: American Management Accociation

Collins, Eliza G. C. and Mary Anne Devanna. *The Portable MBA*. New York: John Wiley & Sons, Inc., 1990

Covey, Stephen R. *Seven Habits of Highly Effective People*. New York: Simon & Schuster, 1989

Davidson, Jeffrey. *Marketing on a Shoestring*. New York: John Wiley & Sons, 1989

Directory of Occupational Wage Surveys. Washington DC: U.S. Government Printing Office

320

Ehrman, Kenneth A., *"Settling Disputes Through Mediation,"* Nation's *Business*, (November 1992), pp. 48-49

Fritz, Roger. *Nobody Gets Rich Working for Somebody Else, An Entrepreneur's Guide.* New York: Dodd, Mead & Company, 1987

Gaston, Robert. *Finding Private Venture Capital for Your Firm.* New York: John Wiley & Sons, Inc., 1989

Handy, Charles. *The Age of Unreason.* Harvard Business School Press, 1989

Hawkens, Paul. *Growing a Business.* New York: Simon and Schuster, 1987

Henrici, Stanley. *Salary Management for the Nonspecialist.* New York: American Management Association

Herzberg, Fredrick. "One more time: How do you motivate employees?", *Harvard Business Review*, Janaury-February 1968.

Hill, Napoleon. *Think and Grow Rich.* New York: Fawcett Crest, 1960

James, William. *The Varieties of Religious Experience.* New York: Random House, 1932

Kahn, Sharon & The Philip Lief Group. *101 Best Businesses to Start.* New York: Doubleday, 1988

Kirsch, M. M. *How to Get Off the Fast Track -- and Live a Life Money Can't Buy.* Los Angeles: Lowell House, 1991

Lasser, J. K. Tax Institute. *How to Run a Small Business.* New York: McGraw-Hill, 1989

LeBoeuf, Michael, Ph.D. *How to Win Customers and Keep Them for Life.* New York: Berkeley Books, 1988

Lesko, Matthew. *Government Givaways for Entrepreneurs.* Kensington, Maryland: Information USA, Inc., 1992

Levinson, Jay Conrad. *Guerrilla Marketing Attack.* New York: Houghton Mifflin, 1989

Meyer, Richard T. *The 1990 Survey of Seed Capital.* Atlanta: Emory University, 1990

National Survey of Professional, Administrative, Technical, and Clerical Pay. Washington DC: U.S. Government Printing Office

Ogilvy, David. *Ogilvy on Advertising.* New York: Random House/Vantage Books, 1985

Peters, Tom and Nancy Austin. *A Passion for Excellence.* New York: Random House, 1985

Peters, Thomas J. and Robert H. Waterman, Jr. *In Search of Excellence.* New York: Warner Books, 1982

Ramacitti, David. *Do-It-Yourself Marketing.* New York: AMACOM, 1990

Reichheld, Fredrick F. and W. Earl Sasser, Jr., *"Zero Defections: Quality Comes to Services," Harvard Business Review,* (September-October, 1990), pp.105-111

Ronstadt, Robert. *Entrepreneurial Finance: Taking Control of Your Financial Decision Making.* Natick, Mass: Lord Publishing, 1988

Ronstadt, Robert and Jeffrey Shuman. *Venture Feasibility Planning Guide.* Natick, Mass: Lord Publishing, 1988

Schwarts, Carol A. *Small Business Sourcebook.* New York: Gale Research, 1991

Sinetar, Marsha. *Do What You Love, The Money Will Follow.* New York: Dell Publishing, 1987

Swain, Madeleine and Robert. *Out the Organization*. New York: Donald Fine Inc., 1989

Teff, Donald R. "Which Business is Best for You?", *Home Office Computing*, (April 1991), pp. 42-45

Ward, John. *Creating Effective Boards for Private Enterprise*. Jossey-Bass, 1992

Yates, Martin John. *Hiring the Best*. Bob Adams, 1989

Your Business Plan. Eugene, Oregon: Oregon Small Business Development Center Network, 1992

Even when walking in a party of no more than three I can always be certain of learning from those I am with. There will be good qualities that I can select for imitation and bad ones that will teach me what requires correction in myself.

Confucius

Index

C

Capital Construction Fund Program   89
cash
  basis accounting   189
  disbursements   50, 253, 254
  flow   51, 209, 253
  flow statement   253
  receipts   50, 253, 254
  surplus or deficit   51
Certified Development Companies   89
collective bargaining agreements   36
College Placement Council   129
Commercial Fisheries Financial Assistance Program   87
commitment   18
communications   134
Community Development Block Grant Funds   86
company
  paid benefits   27
  policy manual   79
Compensating Key Executives in the Smaller Company   129
Computer Science Corporation Credit Services   197
computer site preparation   186
computers   181
Consultant and Consulting Organization Directory   142, 186
consultants
  computer   186
  general   141
contingency fees   145
contracts   214
corporation   26, 27, 28
cost of goods sold   204
credit
  cards   197
  check   196
  extending   196
criticism   170
current ratio   205
customer

F

factoring receivables   122
family businesses   30
Farmers Home Administration   87
financial planning   225
financial strategies   189
float   253
floor planning loan   85
fringe benefits   134
full-service lease   212

G

Gale
   Consultant and Consulting Organization Directory   142
   Directory   157
   Encyclopedia of Associations   198
   Research   142, 186
general and administrative expenses   244
general ledger   179
general liability insurance   217
goals   71
gross
   lease   212
   profit   204, 238
   sales   204, 237
growth   78

H

hardware   176
hiring employees   127, 136
Hiring the Best   147
hours   133

I

income statement   50, 204, 253
Independent Computer Consultants Association   186
industry remarketers   181, 182
Institute of Business Appraisers   52

Institute of Certified Financial Planners   226
insurance   131, 217
integrated software   178
interest subsidies   87
International Association of Financial Planners   226
International Business Broker's Association   52
International Franchise Association   47
interviewing potential employes   137
inventory
  loan   85
  options   22
invoicing   199
Israel-U.S. Binational Industrial Research and Dev   122

J

job satisfaction   135

L

lawsuits and alternatives   216
The Desktop Lawyer   147
leadership   164, 170
Lease vs. Buy vs. Rent   191
leases
  finance   193
  operating   193
leasing office space
  triple net   212
leasing options   25
Legal Aid Societies   146
Legal Services Corporation   146
leveraged buy out   123
liabilities   204
life cycle   6
lifestyle   18
limits to growth   78
line of credit   85
liquidity ratios   205

R

relatives   31
residual value   192
retail   19
return on equity   205
return on total assets   205
return on total investment   205
revenue   50, 236
revolving loan fund   85
rumors   167

S

S corporation   28
Salary Management for the Nonspecialist   129
salary surveys   128
Sales Incentive Compensation   129
sales promotion services   150
SBA phone number   86
security deposit   213
seed capital funds   90
selling
  expenses   238, 239
  options   22
Service Corps of Retired Executives   88
sick time   132
Small Business Administration   86
Small Business Development Center   52
Small Business Investment Companies   88
software   176, 181
sole proprietorship   26, 27, 28
soliciting advice   12
Sons of Bosses   31
source code   184
Standard Rate and Data Service   157
stockholders   27
structure   21
surety bond guarantees   124
Survey of Seed Capital   90

Receive two <u>free</u> issues of the *Entrepreneur Newsletter.*

See other side of this page for details!

Entrepreneur Newsletter updates and compliments *Secrets of a Successful Entrepreneur*. Feature articles and expanded source listings ensure that you are kept informed of the most up-to-date information and trends. Order your complimentary issues today!

Support your local bookstore.

If they don't have *Secrets of A Successful Entrepreneur* in stock, I'm sure they'll be happy to order if for you.

To receive two <u>free</u> issues of the ***Entrepreneur Newsletter***, make a copy of this page, fill out the Order Form with your name and address information, check the appropriate box and mail it to us. (Please include $2.50 help cover the cost of postage and handling.)

✻ It is <u>not</u> necessary to order a book to receive the free newsletters.

K&A
Publications

Order Form
ISBN 1-883635-01-2

K & A Publications
4847 Hopyard Road, Suite 3201B
Pleasanton, CA 94588

❑ Please rush me a copy of *Secrets of a Successful Entrepreneur.* Enclosed is my check or money order for $27.45 ($24.95 plus $2.50 postage and handling). Books shipped to California addresses require California sales tax for a total of $29.71.

❑ Please send me two free issues of *Entrepreneur Newsletter*. Enclosed is $2.50 to help cover the cost of postage and handling.

Name _____

Address _____

City _____

State_____ ZIP _____

Bulk purchase inquiries invited.
